MANAGEMENT AND LEADERSHIP IN EDUCATION SERIES

Series Editors: PETER RIBBINS AND JOHN SAYER

Understanding Primary Headteachers

TITLES IN THE MANAGEMENT AND LEADERSHIP IN EDUCATION SERIES

Understanding Primary Headteachers

Conversations on Characters, Careers and Characteristics

CHRISTINE PASCAL and PETER RIBBINS

CASSELL

Cassell
Wellington House
125 Strand
London WC2R 0BB

370 Lexington Avenue
New York
NY 10017-6550

British Library Cataloguing-in-Publication Data
A catalogue record for this book is available from the British Library.

ISBN   0-304-70268-4 (hardback)
        0-304-70269-2 (paperback)

Typeset by Janice Baiton Editorial Services
Printed and bound in Great Britain by Redwood Books Ltd, Trowbridge, Wilts

Contents

Notes on the authors

CHRISTINE PASCAL is Professor and Director of the Centre for Research in Early Childhood at Worcester College of Higher Education. She directs a national research project on 'Effective Early Learning: An Action Plan for Change'. She is a past national president of the British Association of Early Childhood Education and is currently vice-president. She taught in infant schools in Birmingham for ten years. Her research includes studies of admission policies, 4-year-olds in school, the training of early years teachers throughout Europe, quality evaluation and improvement in the early years, and the development of innovative nursery centres. Her work on the House of Commons Committee of Inquiry into the Quality of Provision for Under-Fives in 1990 established her reputation. She was a member of the Royal Society of Arts Start Right Inquiry into Early Learning and is a member of the Early Years Inquiry Team of the Labour Party. She is co-founder of the European Early Childhood Education Research Association.

PETER RIBBINS is Professor of Educational Management and Dean of the Faculty of Education and Continuing Studies, University of Birmingham. He has worked in a college of education, as an education officer, a school teacher and in industry. He has published over 20 books and more than 70 articles. His recent books include *Managing Education*; *Greenfield on Educational Administration*; *Improving Education*; *Developing Educational Leaders*; *Headship Matters*; *Delivering the National Curriculum*. He was founding editor of *Pastoral Care in Education* and is currently editor of *Educational Management and Administration*. He has co-edited two series: *Blackwell Studies in Personal and Social Education and Pastoral Care* and *Management and Leadership in Education* for Cassell. His interest in the study of headship dates back 20 years and he has published books and many articles on this theme.

CHAPTER 1

On heads and headship: views from the primary school

Introduction

We know even less about headteachers in primary schools than we do about their secondary counterparts. For whatever reasons, they have simply not attracted anything like the same attention from the research community (Ribbins and Marland, 1994) and have been much less prone to write about themselves and their lives and careers. Even so, headship in the primary school has been the subject of increasing, if by no means always flattering, interest in all kinds of public and professional circles. That this is so can be illustrated by examining the response to the third report of Her Majesty's Chief Inspector of Schools published on 4 February 1997. The next day *The Times* was moved to include no less than *three separate articles* in response. In the first, the Chief Inspector discussed aspects of his report in the context of a plea to 'Leave Ofsted alone' (Woodhead, 1997). In the second, the paper's leading editorial, entitled 'Labour's inspector', invited us to leave the Chief Inspector alone (*The Times*, 1997). In neither article was any reference made to the quality of leadership in schools. This was left to the third, an article located in the middle of the paper's *front page*. In this, in commenting upon the Chief Inspector's report, the author chose to restrict his observations to the claim 'that almost 3000 (head teachers) were failing to provide adequate leadership. Woodhead said in his annual report that about one in seven primary heads ... were failing to give clear direction' (O'Leary, 1997, p.1). The author's resolution to focus upon what the report had to say about headship and the editor's decision to place it on the front page is an apt indication of the kind of public concern which headship now attracts.

Even so, the essentially negative character of this article is disappointing given the Chief Inspector's acknowledgement that 'there are real strengths in our education service' and that some 'progress' had been made since his last report (p.16). On the other hand O'Leary's orientation is perhaps not so surprising since the greater part of what Woodhead (1997) has to say deals with 'stubborn weaknesses' and the need for 'substantial improvements in standards ... in about one in twelve primary schools in teaching 5 to 7 year-olds, in about one in six in teaching 7 to 11 year-olds ... In particular it needs to be emphasised (once again) that standards of literacy and numeracy remain too low' (p.16). In what may come to be regarded as a classic case of 'getting his retaliation in first' he confesses he did 'not expect today's headlines to do justice to this complexity' nor was he 'sanguine about the quality of the debate that will follow' (ibid.). If his predictions prove to be justified it may be that the Chief Inspector must himself share some of the responsibility. In the case of the observations quoted above which have to do specifically with 'leadership' and 'headship' in the primary school it is curious how these concepts have been conflated. This notwithstanding the fact that OFSTED, in its Handbook on *Guidance on the Inspection of Nursery and Primary Schools,* stresses that 'leadership and management should be judged as a whole, taking into account the contribution of the governing body and staff, as well as the headteacher. While the personal contribution of the headteacher is crucial, the focus of inspection should not be exclusively on what the headteacher does' (OFSTED, 1995, p.100). Even this statement contains at least one debatable assumption – that there is some equality in the partnership between heads and governing bodies in the management of schools, indeed that heads may legitimately be regarded as the senior partner. Whilst this may offer a description of practice which is often justifiable, a close reading of the 1988 Act suggests that it may be a reality built on remarkably shaky legislative foundations. As Ribbins (1989) has concluded 'the mandatory powers apportioned to heads as compared with those allocated to governing bodies by the Education Act, often seem slight. Furthermore, the language which is used to describe the powers of headteachers is, for the most part, of *enablement* rather than *entitlement*' (p.203). Is this view justified and, if so, does it matter?

We believe it does represent a truth and that it can matter a great deal. Reporting on a study of the available literature and personal research which was undertaken before 1992, Ribbins (1992) concluded that 'there is evidence ... that some governing bodies have begun to interpret their powers and responsibilities in a much more assertive manner than they commonly have in the past' (p.52). As a case in point, he quotes an example he had been given by one head of the situation of a colleague in a neighbouring secondary school in which:

> The chairman of the governing body, a very forceful man, is unemployed and can spend a great deal of time in the school. He has now insisted that he should have his own office and secretarial support. He is at the school for up to four days a week. The other governors have gone along with this. It has had very serious consequences for the management of the school. He keeps second guessing the head. Many important decisions need to be taken at least twice. Nobody knows who is supposed to be in charge anymore. All kinds of factions are developing. As you can imagine, the place is rapidly going to the dogs. It is an impossible situation for the head. (p.49)

This is not an isolated problem nor one restricted to secondary schools. Liz Paver has an excellent relationship with her own chairman of governors but, from her perspective as a member of the Council of the NAHT, is aware that:

> I am very fortunate in that many governing bodies have made head-teachers' lives a misery in wanting to be too much involved in detail and on a day to day basis. I don't think that is what governing bodies are for. The conflict you are beginning to get between chairman and heads all over the country is horrendous. It happens where people are told they have power and feel they have to use it. Some parents will say something bad about the school to the chairman of governors who will then burst in and say to the head you are suspended. Nearly 30 heads have been suspended nationally and over half of those because of a conflict between the governors and the head.

That this can happen is corroborated by Anat Arkin (1997) in a *Times Educational Supplement* article entitled 'heads on the block'. Arkin quotes, *inter alia*, the cases of two headteachers, Dugald Wylie of Kempsey Primary School and Maric Younic of Belfairs Community College, who faced dismissal proceedings instigated by their governing bodies. In resisting these attempts, these two heads relied upon a variety of bodies including their professional associations, Redress, the courts and the Secretary of State. Liz Paver, along with others, has tackled the Secretary of State on this and related issues. As she says:

> The NAHT, along with other teacher unions and associations, have produced a code of practice for governing bodies which, we hope, will be adopted nationally. It will attempt to clarify what the remit of the governors is and what the remit of the head is ... We have had this on an agenda with Gillian Shephard and she said go away and do it and we will support it, but we won't do it for you. The department doesn't see it as their remit to write the code of conduct but if there is one they will be happy to support it.

If all this demonstrates that people are interested in headship it does not necessarily establish that they are curious about headteachers. In thinking about this issue we found support in some unexpected places. David Lodge (1996), for example, in a discussion of the place of biography and autobiography in literature, claims that:

> it is somewhat disingenuous to suggest that the lives of novelists are of little interest; to their readers ... they are of intense interest. This seems to be a legacy of the Romantic poetic of literature as self-expression, which the critical counter-revolution of our time (the modernist cult of 'impersonality', the post-structuralist declaration of the Death of the Author) have hardly dislodged. The curiosity readers feel about the human source of the novel they hold in their hands is something that the media and the literary market-place

eagerly exploit – through interviews, profiles, meet-the-author events, and so on. (p.142)

We feel that much the same might be said of leaders of all kinds.

Certainly leadership has generated as much or even more attention and controversy than has authorship. How much of this is prurient or puffed is debatable. Some of the most distinguished of contemporary commentators are very critical. For Hodgkinson 'the swamp of literature on leadership ... goes on and on and ranges from the sublime to the ridiculous with little in between. If you could burn words at the stake in the same way as the Nazis burnt books, the first word I would suggest is leadership' (in Ribbins, 1993, p.21). Kets de Vries is less scathing but even he concludes that 'the current literature on leadership ... is overwhelming and often confusing' (Kets de Vries, 1995, p.197). Against this backdrop, in this introduction we seek to justify the existence of yet another study of leadership and leaders and to explain how we undertook it. In doing so we describe the kind of 'biography as life' and 'career history' approach we employed in our research and use this as a framework to present some preliminary analysis of key aspects of our conversations with selected head teachers, each of which is reported in full in the following chapters.

Why yet another study of headship?

There are several objections which might be raised against the publication of yet another study of leadership. These include the idea that the importance of headship is much overrated; that there are already far too many studies of headship; and that we already know what we need to of headship. There is an element of truth in each of these claims, but we believe they, and related objections to a focus on the study of headship, obscure more than they reveal.

To an extent the proposition that the importance of headship is overrated is a variant of the larger, and increasingly fashionable claim, that the significance of leadership, however this might be described, is much exaggerated. Whatever the merits of such a claim, on this issue we stand with Howard Gardner (1995). His view, he accepts, is 'conservative' in so far as 'it builds on the assumption that there are individuals called leaders' and that: 'This stance will perturb those of a more radical stripe, who question whether leaders actually influence events, whether leaders *should* actually be allowed to influence events, or whether the conception of leadership itself deserves to survive.' Drawing upon his studies of Robert Oppenheimer, Martin Luther King and Mahatma Gandhi, he argues that:

> while acknowledging the rhetorical appeal of such accounts, I find them unconvincing in the light of human biology and human history. I invite those who question this enterprise to offer their own 'leaderless' accounts of the success of the Manhattan Project, the early course of the civil rights movement, or the securing of independence for India. (p.18)

In this sense, we are also 'conservative'. Why then do we think further studies of headteachers and headship in the primary school are necessary? This is an issue which one of the authors has considered in the context of a companion study of head and headship in the secondary school (Ribbins and Marland, 1994). In this, two main reasons are advanced. First, because much of the available literature on heads and headship draws upon research undertaken in the 1970s and before, and because times, particularly since the 1988 Education Reform Act, have changed a great deal and much of the data are badly out of date. Second, because 'the methods used to study headship in the past have tended to lead to the depiction of heads in monochrome' (p.4). As Rae (1993) states, they 'do not tell you much about what it is really like to do the job' (p.11). Even studies that do this may not be enough since what is really interesting is 'not just how (headteachers) did the job but what the job did to (them)' (p.12).

Building upon this proposition, Ribbins and Marland (1994) have suggested that what may also be needed are many more accounts of 'the ways in which the personality of the headteacher shapes how he or she interprets and plays the role'. To tackle 'these and related issues about the role of the contemporary headteacher requires not just more research, but new [or, to some extent, rediscovered "old"] methods of research' (p.5) which share a commitment to 'context' and the need to 'contextualize'. What these methods might entail are summarized by Gronn and Ribbins (1996) in the context of a paper which advocates the use of two relatively neglected methodological approaches to researching leadership: ethnography and biography. Those who wish to pursue this discussion can do so by turning to the paper, at this point we will restrict our observations to a brief examination of the concept of biography.

Biography in the study of educational leadership

In the quotes which follow, Gronn and Ribbins (1996) identify some of the advantages and disadvantages of biography as an approach to understanding leadership:

> First, as detailed case histories, biographies may be inspected for evidence for the development and learning of leadership attributes. Second, they provide analytical balance sheets on the ends to which leaders have directed their attributes throughout their careers within the shifting demands on, and options available to, them. Third, a comparative analysis of leaders' career paths as revealed in biographies can answer broader institutional-level questions, such as whether sets of leaders, sanctioned by their societies and organizations as worthy to lead them, share common attributes and whether those same societies and organizations screen their leadership cohorts in any way to guarantee conformity to preferred cultural types or models. (p.464)

> Using biographies presents problems. Apart from the rash of popular ones pandering to the relentless public appetite for scandal, gossip, and sensation about the lives of the rich and famous, most scholarly biographical accounts ... are written as ... well-researched appraisals of noteworthy contributions and careers. But their most serious disadvantage as source material for a comparative understanding of leaders and leadership is, of course, that they are usually written towards or at the end of a public life. (ibid.)

At its most profound, engaging in biography can be enormously demanding. Those who believe otherwise should read of Norman Sherry, Graham Greene's official biographer. David Lodge (1996) describes his task as 'a curse or a cross':

> Setting himself the Herculean task of retracing his subject's every journey ... Sherry suffered many trials and tribulations, experiencing temporary blindness, succumbing to dysentery ... and nearly dying from some tropical disease that required removal of part of his intestines ... [He] also surrendered the security of his tenured university chair without compensating enrichment by way of royalties – he is £78,000 in debt to his publishers. (p.42)

No wonder Lodge describes Sherry's work as 'a remarkable and heroic achievement' (p.60). We would be pressed to identify any biographer of a headteacher who has suffered similar privations for her or his art. Perhaps the closest parallel is Peter Gronn and his monumental 13-year study of the life and career of Sir James Darling, who was, among other things, headmaster for 32 years of Geelong Grammar, a leading Australian fee paying school. Gronn has published many papers on this theme and the definitive manuscript of his book is nearing completion. It, too, represents a unique and heroic effort.

However, biographically orientated research can take forms which are less demanding. Fenwick English (1995), for example, classifies it, with autobiography and prosopography, as the most advanced form of 'life writing' along with such other less advanced categories as 'diaries and journals, memoirs, profiles, sketches, portraits and portrayals' (p.208). A growing number of portrait based accounts of head and headship have been published in recent times although very few of these have focused on primary education. One that does is by Mortimer and Mortimer (1991) who invited a small number of primary headteachers to respond *in writing* to a series of issues specified by the researchers. To the best of our knowledge our book is the first of its kind to report on a series of *face-to-face conversations* with named primary heads. In the following section we will describe why we took this approach, with whom, and how.

We have already mentioned why we adopted a portrait based approach to our study of primary heads and headship. In summarizing the need for this we would rehearse the continuing relevance of the claim made some years ago by the Mortimers that 'there are few books which enable heads to speak for themselves' (1991, p.vii). No amount of survey-style studies, however well conducted, will fill this gap. They may more or less accurately represent the views of a defined population of headteachers in general across a series of issues. They may even tell us a good deal about the ideas of one or more headteachers on particular topics. What they cannot do is offer a rich and comprehensive understanding of the views and perspectives which individual headteachers bring to their work. For this to be possible the reader must be offered a much fuller access to their views across a range of themes and issues.

Such an approach would present the reader with a series of individual portraits derived from the accounts which individual headteachers give of their individual and professional lives each of which is reported in some depth. In their book, the Mortimers report the views of seven primary head-teachers each of whom responded to issues which dealt with 'the back-ground of the headteacher and the school; the headteacher's personal philosophy of education; organization and management of the school; orga-nization and management of learning; and personal reflections on headship' (1991, p.viii). In our study we wished to use an approach which enabled a greater spontaneity and a more open and shared process of agenda negotia-tion than seemed possible using the methods employed by the Mortimers. With this in mind we decided to talk face-to-face with our headteachers rather than invite them to respond in writing to a set of issues which we had sent them. We undertook this as follows.

Conducting the study

The researchers met several times to determine how the study was to be conducted, what issues it would explore and with which particular head-teachers. Given that we were unlikely to be able to include more than ten conversations in the final text, it was never our intention to attempt to offer a representative sample. Instead we have tried to select people we expected to be interesting, who worked in a wide range of primary schools (nursery, infant, junior, etc.), who were at a variety of points in their careers as head-teachers, who had different life experiences and views, and who were drawn from different parts of the country. In the event, two were selected for more specific reasons: David Davies because Blaengwrach Primary was one of the 11 schools identified by the National Commission on Education as 'thriving in the face of insurmountable obstacles' (see O'Connor, 1995, p.2) and Joan McConnell because St Mary's RC School had been included by OFSTED in its list of excellent primary schools in 1996.

Once all this had been agreed, the next stage was to approach selected headteachers to explore whether they would be willing to be involved. This usually took the form of an initial telephone call followed by a letter from researchers which, *inter alia*, noted that those who agreed would be involved as follows:

(1)   There would be an initial conversation of about two hours with one of the researchers. The main themes of this discussion were listed in an interview schedule included with the letter.

The schedule was intended as a framework not a strait-jacket. It would be possible for either party to identify further issues or sub-issues as the conversation progressed. If there were particular issues which the headteacher did not wish to discuss, this would be honoured.

(2)   The conversation would be taped and transcribed. One of the researchers would undertake a preliminary edit to ensure that it read fluently whilst remaining faithful to what the head had said and the way in which this was expressed. The transcript would then be sent to the head for any additions, revisions, excisions, etc they may wish to make. As far as possible, these suggestions, subject only to their implications for such considerations as the word length of the reported conversation, the laws of libel, the well being of named individuals, would be honoured in the production of the final published conversation.

(3)   It would be possible for any particular headteacher to withdraw at any time.

(4)   That the headteachers involved would be named in the final text.

Few of those approached responded negatively. In the event one felt unable 'to participate because I have reservations about the lack of anonymity' and another skilfully practised the strategy of delaying a final decision until we were, at last, encouraged to go elsewhere. Of those who agreed to take part, some engaged in much preparation and came to the conversations with substantial notes whilst others relied upon a more spontaneous approach. None ruled out any particular topic from our schedule and almost all had important ideas for further themes which they usually introduced during the discussion. Nobody asked to pull out at any stage.

We sent a detailed interview schedule to each head before their meeting with one or other of us (see page 44). The schedule was built around a number of key themes including:

(1)   The influence of family, friends, early life, schooling, etc. on their views/values/lives.

(2)   The influences which shaped their views/values as educators/managers.

(3)   Their careers before headship. Their reasons for becoming headteachers.

(4)   How they went about becoming headteachers. How well prepared did they feel?

(5)   Their vision for their institution. How do they seek to implement this?

(6)   The part they play in enabling effective teaching and learning. With what effect?

(7)   To whom are they accountable? Who manages them?

(8)   Their views on headship and the influences which have shaped this.

(9)   Their key educational and managerial visions/values.
(10)   How they manage people and resources.
(11)   How they cope with stress. Where they find support.
(12)   Are they, as heads, necessary? Are they democratic?

These conversations took place during 1996 and the final version of the last script was agreed in February 1997. As the research progressed, we gave increasing attention to the issue of how the conversations might be analysed. In determining this, and in undertaking the research project as a whole, we were much influenced by a number of ideas for life and professional career history approaches being developed at the time by Gronn, and by Day and Bakioglu.

Life and professional career history approaches to the study of headship

Such approaches propose that teachers' professional lives can usefully be regarded as having a natural history and follow a developmental pattern (Day and Bakioglu, 1996; Gronn, 1993; Gronn and Ribbins, 1996). In a paper which summarizes some of these ideas, Gronn and Ribbins (1996) use the concept of 'leadership career' as a framework to describe and order the biographical pattern of headteachers' professional lives. This term describes 'a mobility pathway or status passage through time' (p.465).

There have been a number of attempts to describe the various stages or phases in a 'leadership career'. Earlier in this chapter, we commented upon Gronn's study of the life and career of Sir James Darling, a famous headteacher and educationalist in Australia. From this study he usefully identifies four broad phases through which leaders commonly pass during the course of their 'career' (Gronn, 1993, 1994): Formation, Accession, Incumbency and Divestiture. Each individual leader will have her or his own journey through these phases but these phases are viewed as linear, progressive and, to some extent, inevitable. Ribbins and Sherratt (1997) argue that an individual's response to the job (or headteacher 'style') during these phases will be determined in important ways by the context in which the leader is operating. This will include organizational factors, institutional constraints and opportunities, as well as social and psychological experiences. They also suggest that cultural diversity and cultural experience will have an impact in shaping individual career patterns.

Day and Bakioglu (1996) in a study of 'headteacher development in post' identify an alternative framework which also consists of four phases: Initiation, Development, Autonomy and Disenchantment. This framework is focused on a headteacher's career pattern once they are in post (incumbent) and so may be useful as a way to view development within one phase (Incumbency) of Gronn's (1993) more encompassing framework.

We found such conceptual frameworks very helpful in interpreting and analysing the development of headteachers' professional lives and will use them as a frame of reference for the discussion of the professional lives of the ten headteachers we talked to. However, we also feel that the frameworks described above need to be modified as our data seem to suggest an alternative progression to those suggested. This is so in so far as both Gronn's, and Day and Bakioglu's frameworks, although to a varying extent, appear to suggest an inevitable pattern of creeping negativism which will lead inevitably to exit from the career (Disenchantment and Divestiture). Whilst the evidence presented within this study does recognize this as one possible pattern of headteachers' professional lives, there was clear evidence of an alternative progression which was more positive and creative.

This alternative pattern may be linked to the fact that our study, unlike those of both Gronn, and Day and Bakioglu, focuses upon primary headship, and there is some evidence that those who take on the professional task of working with younger children seem to have a more emotional commitment to the children they work with, and a more social and child focused approach to the job (Bertram, 1996). This may provide them with a refuge and cushion from some of the more negative aspects of the current tasks facing primary headteachers. It also may give them a deeper personal and emotional connection to their work which keeps them motivated and more hooked into the joys of managing the education of the young. In Bertram's terms, the 'educative dispositions' of the headteachers, which are key in maintaining professional motivation in the long term, arise from the social and emotional dimensions of their work, and this in turn facilitates the maintenance of job satisfaction in the long term. It seems that despite the many changes in primary education, a number of the headteachers in this study have managed, as we shall see, to sustain these dimensions at the heart of their work. We could have drawn upon almost all our interviews to make this case but two quotations from the conversations must suffice:

> we have an obligation to children to look behind their behaviour, to look at patterns in their behaviour and to think about why ... teaching is about listening and about encouraging children to challenge and question and to have a disposition to learn ... I really don't believe there are a lot of facts that are worth teaching. (Margy Whalley)

> It requires a personal commitment that is not just doing the job ... You will sink or swim according to the amount of emotional commitment you make to the job. (David Winkley)

Given this we would suggest some modifications of the original frameworks to allow for the expression of this alternative career pattern. As such, four broad phases are recognized in the development of headteachers' careers which are close to Gronn's (1993) descriptions but in this analysis are described as: Formation, Accession, Incumbency, but with Moving On replacing Divestiture. We take this view because whilst we agree that this final phase is about progression to another state, our evidence has shown that while divestiture does occur in many cases, in others an alternative route is followed. This alternative route is seen to involve a phase of reinvention or rebirth, in which the incumbent moves on towards a newly created professional life, within a significantly different context and with newly created parameters.

In addition, within the analysis of the phase of Incumbency, we shall also use Day and Bakioglu's four-phase framework of Initiation, Development, Autonomy but will replace their final phase of Disenchantment with what we describe as Advancement. Again, this last phase may take two alternative patterns: one characterized by 'Enchantment' and the other by 'Disenchantment'.

The suggestion in this analysis is that headteachers may have two main alternative career routes through their professional lives. Whilst they seem to have similar beginnings to their career, the second half may follow a different pattern. One route progresses rather negatively and is ultimately destructive in terms of career progression. It may be viewed thus:

- Formation
- Accession
- Incumbency:
  - Initiation
  - Development
  - Autonomy
  - Advancement:
    - Disenchantment
- Moving On:
  - Divestiture

The other career route is more positive and creative and may be viewed thus:

- Formation
- Accession
- Incumbency:
  - Initiation
  - Development
  - Autonomy
  - Advancement:
    - Enchantment
- Moving On:
  - Reinvention

In the following examination of ten headteachers' careers the above modified framework will be used. Each section will be prefaced with a brief description of the phase being explored.

Formation

Gronn (1993) has argued that prior to the assumption of leadership roles, there is a preparatory stage in which possible candidates shape themselves and/or are shaped for prospective high office. This seems to be true of a wide range of different kinds of educational leaders. It has, for example, been used by Ribbins and Sherratt (1997) in an earlier book in this series to examine the lives and careers of Secretaries of State for Education. We would claim that it is equally relevant to the study of headteachers and headship. As part of this general process of formation such leaders are socialized into various society and institutional norms and values – into codes of taste, morality, values, belief and authority – by three key agencies: family, school and reference groups. Sometimes the individual experiences consistent influences and conditioning within and between these agencies; on other occasions there is inconsistency and even contradiction. Taken as a whole, these agencies shape a prospective leader's personality and/or character by generating a conception of self, and the rudiments of a work style and outlook. A comprehensive examination of the influence of these agencies on the people who are the subject of this book is beyond the scope of this chapter. Instead, we will focus upon aspects of family and schooling as influences in shaping their attitudes, values and careers as pupils and teachers.

The making of ten pupils

Before undertaking these conversations we knew relatively little about the lives of most of the headteachers who are the subject of this book. Even so, we were not surprised to find major differences as well as some common ground. Several had been born and/or had spent many of their formative years in other countries. Some had even begun their careers elsewhere. Sue Matthew, for example, was born and educated in the United States and worked in Africa. She also did her PGCE there, studying for it at Makerere University in Uganda. She came to the United Kingdom to be with her husband, whom she had met in East Africa. Usha Sahni also spent most of her formative years elsewhere. She was born and educated in India, receiving her Master's degree there at 18. After this 'my university sponsored me for a doctorate and they got me a scholarship for study in the United States ... My parents had other plans! They found a husband and arranged a marriage for me. So within four weeks I was married ... and came to Britain'. Joan McConnell was nearer; she was born and went to school in Eire. Like Usha Sahni and Sue Matthew, she came to England as a result of marriage; her husband had a teaching post in London. Finally, Sue Beeson spent her formative years in Canada and South Africa and came to England when her father was appointed to a post here. The others were all born, bred and educated in different parts of the UK.

The ten came from a wide variety of backgrounds, socially and economically. Some were well off. For the most part they stress the significance of their father's occupation or education in determining this. Sue Matthew's and Sue Beeson's fathers held executive posts within large companies. Usha Sahni, although her father was not 'terribly wealthy', he nevertheless 'had a very big farm'. Michael Ashford's father 'sold feedstuffs to farmers'. His 'drive and energy' led him 'to the EEC where he became one of the civil servants who handled grain subsidies and created grain mountains'. David

Winkley's father was 'public school educated and came from a very wealthy background but the family fell on hard times'. Margy Whalley's father was also educated privately but came to view 'private education with a real antipathy'. Michael Gasper's father on emigrating from India had 'to re-qualify' as a doctor. Joan McConnell's father 'was an electrician' in a small village but 'had a background in accountancy and did a lot of work for the local shop keepers'. Finally, Liz Paver's father was a driver for the Co-operative Society.

In describing their mothers, the terms most often used were 'house-keeper', 'housewife' or 'home maker'. Very few were engaged in paid occupation. There were only two exceptions. Margy Whalley's mother had been a nurse and Sue Matthew's mother was the only teacher amongst all the parents of our heads. As Liz Paver says 'To the best of my knowledge we've had no teachers in the family.' Joan McConnell, however, recalled 'On my mother's side there were many teachers, but way back.'

The part of immediate and extended family members in shaping the educational experience of each of the ten is fully acknowledged. On the whole, and unlike an earlier study of secondary headteachers (Ribbins and Marland, 1994, p.13), the influence of fathers is strongly emphasized:

> From my first year in school when I came home my father would supervise homework and if I got anything wrong it would be gone over and over and I would be taught the proper way. He had a great insight into children and learning. He wasn't involved in teaching in any way, but felt very strongly each of us should have a 'good' education. (Joan McConnell)

> My father had a big influence on my outlook. He spent a lot of time working with disadvantaged children. He always had time for children, and perhaps that influenced me to go into teaching. (David Davies)

Mothers were also mentioned, along with the beneficial influence of both parents working in tandem and in doing so supporting their children. The force of these, and related themes, can be seen from the following quotations:

> We had lots of things I wish more of the children at Intake could have including a mother who would read with you and a father who would do sums with you. In my home, education was held in high esteem. (Liz Paver)

> In India … it is very expensive to send children to good schools and that is all that my parents spent their money on … In the evenings it was a very structured situation, like an academy. Any child in our extended family who was not doing well, or was at risk of going astray, would be sent off to our home. It was seen as the place where children just flourished and did well … I think for my parents it was a full-time occupation just to make sure that all of us got the support

> we needed. My mother would sit with us in the evening to supervise our study, and my father would sit with us in the mornings. They spent a lot of time with us. My father would keep in touch with the school. (Usha Sahni)

As this last comment suggests, members of the extended family can also play an important part in shaping the views of children on education and in supporting them in making the most of the opportunities that it affords. In our conversations we heard a numerous accounts of the significance of grandparents, aunts, uncles and others as follows:

> We also had a fantastic maternal grandmother who was absolutely committed to education. She had had to stop school when she was 12, and to all her numerous grandchildren she would always say 'I never had the chance to go to school beyond twelve, but you do, mind you read these books.' (Sue Matthew)

In summary it seems that almost all our heads came from warm, hard working and supportive families characterized by a high regard for the importance of education and a considerable respect for teachers. From this, it followed that most of their parents and other family members strongly supported the kind of values often identified as facilitating effective schooling. In addition, many of our interviewees received a great deal of practical support from their families in enabling them to undertake their studies. Against this backdrop, it is not, perhaps, surprising that several of them recall their schools and teachers positively. But whether or not this was so, these memories have usually had a profound influenced upon their own views and values as teachers and headteachers. It is to these themes which we will now turn.

Some were very happy at school:

> My primary school was formal, prescriptive, kindly and pleasurable. I thoroughly enjoyed my school time ... I then went to boarding school ... I was very young and very small and it seemed fearsome, but I loved it ... It was a very formal and basic education but very thorough. I appreciated that very much. (Joan McConnell)

> I remember going to pre-nursery and there was a lovely new school to go to which had a nursery. I stood with my nose through the railings wanting to go ... I can never remember not enjoying primary school. (Liz Paver)

Others did not enjoy aspects of their school days. David Davies recalled little about his infant schools, 'only milk every day and having to sleep for so long in the afternoon'. He did remember, vividly, his junior school: 'I hated it ... It didn't stimulate me at all. The only thing I liked was maths ... I disliked every other aspect of school ... I found school a barren place. At home there was woodland, ponds and lakes within walking distance. I thoroughly enjoyed that.' Sue Beeson stresses that her primary schools were 'probably not as important to me as they might have been if I'd stayed in one place. My overriding memory is of continually struggling to make friendships with people who wanted to know you because you were the new girl, then they wanted to revert to their original groups'. Her later years of schooling were also not recalled with much affection: 'I was quite frightened in a lot of my secondary schooling in South Africa (and in the UK). I found the school, a grammar school, rather repressive ... I was there for two years, and couldn't wait to get out.' Michael Gasper's response is more difficult to interpret. His opening statement was positive, 'I have to say that overall I was very lucky because I enjoyed my education right from the beginning.' This seems clear enough but he continues, 'That's not to say that all those memories are positive ones. If I go back to my earliest times, I started pre-school in a private nursery ... and I hated that.' He also remembers that 'when I moved into infant education I took a long time to settle'. Happily, he recalls his days in secondary education with greater warmth and ended up as head prefect 'which was a great honour'.

Each of these three headteachers, and most of the others as well, were able to talk many years later, often with considerable passion, about particular events and decisions from their school days which they still recalled as damaging in some way. Examples of these include the traumas of the 11-plus (Davies and Whalley), the effects of streaming and setting (Gasper and Whalley), and of being accelerated for one, or more, years (Beeson, Sahni and Winkley). Almost all could also readily identify individual teachers, and even headteachers, still remembered with contempt.

Some teachers, perhaps the worst, were seen as brutal. Sue Beeson remembered 'some of my South African teachers for their cruelty almost, two in particular were vicious – they would go around slapping everybody hard on the back and would force people to stand up. There was a boy with a terrible stutter. He was forced to stand up and read in class like the rest of us. There was no sympathy'. Others were unkind or unfair. Michael Gasper remembers 'one or two teachers who had been quite sarcastic ... [and] very unkind. I remember distinctly when we were being selected to be put forward for O or A level, [one] said "I shan't be sorry to lose you"'. More seriously he also recalls experiencing racial prejudice: 'in primary school I had a teacher who hated me, and I think it was connected with the fact that my father was an immigrant. He would go out of his way to find ways of finding fault and ridiculing me, and of course there was physical punishment ... so I used to get the ruler regularly'.

If this was one form of unfairness, David Davies gave us an example of another. Of the head of his junior school he says his 'office was upstairs: he'd come down for Assembly or you saw him if you were naughty, and at no other time. He gave me a hard time once for something I never did. I would never accept the blame for something I wasn't guilty of. I told my father who spoke to the head, and he came and apologized. He said, "Why didn't you tell me who your father was? I wouldn't have given you a row." I thought that disgusting – you should treat people fairly whatever their background'.

If this distressed Davies, he was, if anything, even more scornful of those teachers whose primary interest was in their subject and not in children. Michael Ashford, when asked which teachers he did not like, makes a similar point: 'They tended to be blinkered in their approach and saw nothing other than their subject and had little time for you as a pupil. You got very little chance to give anything back to them. I remember a French teacher I was terrified of, and because I was terrified of him I hated the subject.' For some, even worse were the lazy and professionally incompetent. As David Davies says 'Most of the teachers ... had come into teaching after the war – they were only concerned about their subject, they had barren classrooms ... I remember one person who had travelled the world in the war and had his map of the British Empire. Everything he did was linked to the British Empire. Until he retired his classroom stayed the same. It's very sad that children were exposed to such education. It did little for me.' Margy Whalley also remembers teachers and teaching who did little for her. She gives a number of examples of this. In one she talks of 'being taught "facts" about Richard III in history. I passionately loved history ... the teacher told us that "Richard III was an evil man", and I happened to have read the novel *Daughter of Time*, and I wanted to enter a debate with her. I said 'I've just been reading this book' and she said "Well, this is what I'm teaching you, this is what you're learning for O level." It was that narrowness that I found so awful.' Unsurprisingly, and without qualification, she concludes 'I didn't think that positively of my own teachers.' Like all her colleagues, Margy Whalley acknowledges the importance of good teaching but alone amongst them does not testify to the merits of any particular teacher. It seems that in so far as her ideas on good practice were derived from her own experience of teachers during her years as their pupil, this was essentially on how not to do it.

The rest of our headteachers are more positive about one or more of their teachers, indeed some speak in glowing terms and in doing so attest to the significance which these exemplars have had in shaping their own views and values on teaching. David Davies identified two who had 'encouraged' him. What, in his view, made them special was that

> They cared about all children but not in a soft way. They were perhaps the strictest teachers in the school. That didn't matter – they cared. They cared about me as an individual, whether I was successful or not. As it happened because of their care, I put much more effort in and did very well in their subjects. They were the ones who went on residential visits with you, stayed behind after school to run clubs for you and gave up their time for you. You responded to what they were doing for you.

The idea that it was possible to be a good teacher and still be demanding was echoed by several others. Michael Ashford takes this view. In doing so he also stresses the importance of communicating to children a love of one's subject. His 'art master' was 'vibrant and had a great enthusiasm for his subject. I have always felt I wanted to operate in that way, I wanted to communicate to children that I loved my subject ... With teachers like the art master it was a two-way process in which you had the chance to give back a lot. Sometimes he'd shoot you down but you wouldn't mind because you respected him'. The best were encouraging yet capable, when necessary, of expressing their disappointment in a calm but compelling manner. Joan McConnell and Michael Gasper describe how similarly two otherwise very different headteachers went about this. They also acknowledge how much this has influenced their own practice:

> I was lucky enough through my primary and secondary schools to have key figures who encouraged personal growth ... At primary level my old headmaster was a key figure. He was a wonderful man, and I still have him in my mind ... He was very human. One day I took a cap gun into school and let it off in the lesson, and I got sent to his office, and I was just reduced to a blubbering mass. He didn't actually say anything to me. I think he said 'Oh Michael, oh dear, oh dear', walked past, leaving me outside his room. After I'd been stood there for half an hour he just said 'You won't do that again', and he was right. (Michael Gasper)

> The head teacher was very ladylike ... She was a highly principled women – just and fair in all her dealings. If she was cross with you she would say to you 'I'm bitterly disappointed in you Siobhan. Now go away and don't disgrace your family'. Those words had tremendous impact on me because it brought home to me that how you behaved was crucially important in determining how other people viewed you. In my own dealings with children I find myself trying to act as she did. (Joan McConnell)

Furthermore, the impact of such encounters, along with the influence of key teachers at critical points in their school lives, led many of our headteachers to consider teaching as a career.

The making of ten teachers

Some discovered their teaching vocation very early on. Those who did tended to have unusually positive memories of their schools and teachers. Liz Paver, for example, recalls 'having an old air raid shelter in our garden which I turned into a classroom and having my desk out there ... I remember (my headteacher) taking me to read stories to the reception class when I was only seven. My mother says, "Miss Shearstone said to me 'she'll teach'." That was where the rest of my life was formed as far as work was concerned. I suppose the gene was always there'. Joan McConnell tells a similar story. Teaching 'was something I had always wanted to do – from my fifth birthday. I remember lining up on a tiny wall around my grandma's garden patch all my dolls and calling the register. That was my earliest memory of what school was about. It was always something I wanted to do'.

Margy Whalley also told us that 'the more I look back I think that I was very committed to teaching. I know I always wanted to be a teacher'. However, unlike Joan McConnell and Liz Paver, she 'didn't think positively of my own school teachers'. Even so, as with Michael Ashford and David Davies, it was a former teacher, if not one of her own, who had an early and decisive influence on her view of education and, perhaps, her decision to teach. As she puts it 'My father's godmother was one of the first women HMIs, and she used to come and stay with us. She was working in Liverpool and places like that, and she would talk about what classrooms were like in the 1950s. She was an enormous influence on me.'

For others, teaching became a career option during the latter years of their schooling. In some cases, the decisive suggestion actually came from a teacher or headteacher. Michael Ashford, for example, 'at seventeen ... began to realize I could give to others. From that moment, although I didn't realize it fully for a year or so, I was destined to become a teacher ... Everything was leading me into, although I didn't know it, becoming a teacher. This only dawned on me when a teacher sat me down and said "You've thought of teaching haven't you?" ... I respected him and thought he was a good teacher ... It was as simple as that'. Ashford's memories of schools, as we have seen, contained a mixture of the good and the bad. David Davies recalls much of his schooling, if by no means all his teachers, in more negative terms. As he says, 'I didn't want to be a teacher. I was keen on horticulture ... but ... my headteacher suggested a teaching course with horticulture as a subject. That is how I came to choose teaching. I had given it no other thought at all. If that hadn't happened, it wouldn't have come about in any other way ... If I am honest, initially, the holidays appealed, so I went in through the back door.' Even so, for this and other reasons, he remembers this headteacher 'with the greatest affection. He helped me to make one of the most important professional decisions in my life. If he hadn't suggested teaching I would not have done it. It would not have crossed my mind'.

Yet others came to the decision to teach after they had left school and after they had given serious consideration to, or even spent some time in, other occupations. David Winkley acknowledges that as he approached the end of his three-year degree course at Cambridge he began 'looking around for careers'. Initially, he had 'no thoughts whatever of teaching. I intended to go into journalism ... I came into teaching on a part-time basis ... during the university vacations I used to teach in different Birmingham schools ... They used to pay me a reasonable rate ... so I sort of edged my way into teaching, almost by default ... [But] I found I rather enjoyed it and got on well with children and felt it was a job with an awful lot of opportunity'. Even so, once started he 'had no intention of continuing in teaching'. As with David Davies, an inspirational headteacher made the difference. He 'kept me in the job and I think without him I would not be teaching now'. Usha Sahni, like David Winkley, became interested in children's learning during her university years. Majoring in educational psychology, her research 'was on learning patterns among young children. For my field work, I went into two schools quite regularly ... That is how I became interested in young children'. However, this better explains why she decided to work in primary schools rather than why she became a teacher. Given her choice she would have taken up an offer to study for a doctorate in the United States. Her parents, however, had other plans and so 'they found a husband and arranged a marriage for me ... So I married and came to Britain. I thought I would work, but I didn't know ... what to do. I thought I would continue my work with young children ... I started making applications for a teaching job'. For Michael Gasper teaching was not a first choice. At school he 'always talked about being a doctor. It was the one thing I wanted to be'. However, on leaving school he 'did two and a half years as an articled clerk before I left the law and went into training college to be a teacher'. Even so, looking back, he realized that although 'I had always talked about the law but I had always hankered after teaching. I looked at teachers and the life they led and the nature of what they had to do and it had its attractions. I always thought that I would end up as a priest, an actor or a teacher and in a sense teaching combines all of those.'

Like David Winkley, Sue Beeson also 'sort of went into' teaching. Before this she 'went through the vet thing and was told women did not become farm vets ... if I knew about myself what I know now, I would have gone down the fine art route. I had the chance to go to the Slade but lost my nerve ... Teaching was a "safe" option, something that girls did anyway. It fitted in with a family. It wasn't too terrifying, until I did my first teaching practice anyway'. Finally, Sue Matthew's route to a career in teaching also included an element of serendipity. During her degree course at Duke University in North Carolina she:

> became involved with various groups. One ... provided the key to my future teaching career, as it turned out. I went on a Summer Programme to East Africa called 'Operation Crossroads Africa' ... Our project was to build a school for the Wa-Arush people. I loved East Africa! So when it came to the time that I started thinking of what I would do after graduation I had no qualms at all in going to my adviser and saying 'I don't care what I do, but I must go back to East Africa'. I remember him taking out a book, flicking through the pages and saying 'Here is something called Teachers for East Africa, would you like to be a teacher?' and I said 'I will do anything to get to Africa, even being a teacher!'.

However, like all of those portrayed in this book, both those who decided early that they would be teachers and those who 'sort of fell into it', she soon found that 'the great thing about being a teacher is that when you do it, it is one of those professions that you know is right ... I think part of me was thinking that because my mother had been a teacher and my sister at that time was a teacher, maybe I should try something new, but I loved it'. How relevant these and related considerations are to how and why these ten teachers became headteachers is discussed in the next section of this chapter.

Accession

Following an initial period of preparation, candidates for headship, as for other forms of leadership, during this phase of their career life cycle develop, rehearse and test their capacity and readiness by comparison with existing office holders and prospective rivals. Accession is, as such, a developmental period geared to the accomplishment of two crucial tasks: the preparation and construction of oneself as a credible candidate for office and acquisition of a marketable performance routine to convince prospective talent-spotters and appointment panel members and selectors. This is the case with leadership positions at all levels within a school. As such positions become available, candidates learn to present and position themselves, to 'jockey' or compete with others for preferment and come to rely to a more or less significant extent on networks of peers, patrons and sponsors whilst awaiting the call to office. Furthermore, the lessons learnt and the contacts made in unsuccessful and successful attempts to achieve promotion at any one level may be relevant to the search for further preferment. In applying these ideas to an analysis of this aspects of our research we shall focus specifically upon the making of ten headteachers. In doing so we shall draw upon those aspects of our discussions with our contributors which focus on the history of their careers as teachers and managers and the extent to which this was a preparation, planned or otherwise, for the achievement of their first headship. In examining what they had to say on this we have focused upon four main themes: decision, preparation, support and process.

The making of ten headteachers

As with the decision to teach, the idea that they might wish to be heads dawned much more quickly on some of the ten than on others. However, those who came earliest to the decision were by no means always the quickest to act to satisfy their ambitions. Joan McConnell's career is a case in point. Asked when she first knew she replied 'From the beginning. When I graduated (as a mature student) a lecturer said to me, "You'll be a head within five years".' However, she spent 13 years in the first school to which she was appointed, recalling it as 'a happy experience if a tough one. I loved teaching and with things always changing at (the school) I felt no urgency to move out or up but always knew that headship was what I wanted'.

Others also quickly realized they wanted to be heads. Liz Paver had been in teaching less than three years before she was encouraged to apply for a deputy headship. Up to that point she was not especially ambitious but three years into her deputyship she 'became pregnant and was devastated. That I might have my own children had not entered into my thinking at all. I was going to be a head when I was 30 and that was it'. Within five years she had begun applying for headships but circumstances at the school meant that she 'couldn't leave'. Seeing 'people getting headships who didn't have my experience' meant that she became 'increasingly frustrated' and when she 'eventually got my first headship after seven and a half years', as deputy, she 'didn't feel it any too soon. I had missed my deadline, I was 31'. Michael Ashford was another who quickly discovered that 'within a year of teaching, I wanted my own school; I wanted to be a head'. Like Paver he wasted no time, 'after four years teaching and at 26 I applied for a deputy headship ... and got it'. Again, like Paver, he was 'committed to having my own school by the time I was 30 – that gave me four years. In fact I failed – I was 31'.

Others also climbed the promotion ladder but without any idea that this could, or should, lead to headship. As Michael Gasper put it 'I have never been content to stand still and when I joined the profession we were still in the age when the logical thing was, if you were any good, you looked for promotion. So that was an in-built expectation [....] As I went up the ladder I became a deputy. I worked for somebody who viewed her role as head as being to train me for headship. I don't think I had that in my mind and certainly, at the start, I wasn't necessarily imagining I would be a head-teacher. I think that when I was a deputy, the job was absolutely thankless, it was the worst job on earth. Once I realised that, it was inevitable that I would go for headship.' David Davies also came slowly to the idea that head-ship was for him. Initially, he was glad to be a classroom teacher. He made the decision to become a deputy because 'I increasingly found I didn't agree with some of the practices I saw going on in some classrooms. I wanted more of a say in how children should be taught. For that I needed a power base ... Before becoming a deputy I had been involved with *my children*. That was fine when I was with them in my class but what of other classes and what happened if my class went to a poorer teacher?' The advantage of being a deputy, as Davies saw it at the time, was that he could have an influence on all classes without, unlike headship, having 'to leave the classroom'.

Davies is committed to an active and experiential approach to learning. As such, it is not surprising to find that this approach, rather than any kind of formal training, characterized his preparation for headship. During his years as a deputy, his head 'was released two days a week because he worked for the authority. I was responsible but couldn't make any changes'. He then had a six month spell in an 'acting capacity' and for the first time 'began to realize the vast array of problems that face a headteacher which I had not been aware of as a class teacher or even as a deputy ... I began to become aware of what headship was about'.

Few of the ten had attended much targeted training for headship and several expressed doubts about this as an effective method of preparation. Usha Sahni, for example, neither sought nor received formal training for headship. She believes that those, such as deputies, who aspire to headship 'need to have structured opportunities for a lot of preparatory experience and work before they take on a headship ... You don't get [this] on courses ... there needs to be something like a period of acting headship, or some sort of hands-on experience before people can with confidence take over'. David Winkley takes a similar line. His scepticism concerning the merits of current developments in headship training anticipated the views of the

Chief Inspector of School. Referring to the proposed national qualification for headteachers, Woodhead is said to have 'questioned whether it is possible to teach leadership at all' (Gardiner, 1997, p.3). The report of this lecture notes that these 'comments came the day before the NPQH launch by the Teacher Training Agency'. Unsurprisingly, a spokesman from the TTA responded that 'Chris Woodhead is wrong. Leadership can be taught through practical training. This is done in other professions, why should teaching be so different?' This may be but as Winkley remarks:

> The TTA is currently looking at the kind of training programme that covers every conceivable possibility ... The problem I have with this is that it's possible to go through this kind of process and still not be terribly good as a head ... The danger is of creating the conception of school leadership as a managerial enterprise, as a tick list – you do all these things and then you're going to be a very competent head – that does not follow.

In developing his ideas on the skills and competencies which headteachers need, Winkley stresses the kind of philosophical dimensions which have been advocated by Greenfield (see Greenfield and Ribbins, 1993) and Hodgkinson (1997). Like them, he emphasizes that 'it doesn't matter how many courses you've been on, and how much you know intellectually about the processes of being a head' if you don't develop an appreciation of 'yourself as a person ... and [of] your own emotional understanding ... you will never make a good head'.

Sue Beeson, while she 'did not consciously prepare for headship', like Winkley, emphasized the importance of knowing yourself and others and, in this regard, identified a course on counselling as 'the most significant piece of professional development I ever did'. It was highly relevant to her work as a head because so much of this involves interacting on a one to one basis 'with individual parents or members of staff and certainly with individual children. There are tricks of the trade, key phrases, aspects of body language that enable people to feel more comfortable and to talk. I find it very useful because it helps to open up the real issues which may be getting in the way of somebody teaching or working with their child as well as they might'.

One of the very few who stressed the importance of further formal study was Sue Matthew. She was 'put on a senior management course when I shouldn't have really but the deputy head argued that "every teacher in small schools is senior management, so go on it" ... It was very good'. Shortly before applying for her first headship, she 'decided to take another course ... It was an excellent, six week, GEST-funded course. I found great satisfaction in reading about educational issues ... I was then looking for other opportunities to continue and my tutor said, "Why don't you think about a part-time MEd?" ... That was all set and then I got this headship. I remember saying to my tutor, "I can't be a new head and a student at the same time" and he said, "of course you can, it would be good for you" ... It was fascinating and I learned a lot. All teachers should have the chance to be teacher researchers!' Much more typical was Michael Ashford's attitude and approach. Asked how he prepared himself for headship he answered:

> At the time many of us, aspiring teachers, mixed twilight and residential courses. A lot talked about doing the Open University because they wanted to get on and felt it was important to have a degree ... I was too busy, I was heavily involved in school. My friends would come home and work but on their degrees. I considered this but came to the decision that I would try and do things another way. I would work hard in school and get as much practical knowledge as I could. I pursued that policy throughout.

If he did not seek to prepare himself through course-based training, Ashford, like most of those whose experience is reported in this book, did find support important in achieving headship. In this, the role played by one or more of the headteachers with whom they had worked, particularly as a deputy, was widely, if by no means universally, acknowledged. In addition Ashford, and several others, also recognized others who had played a role as key agents in enabling their development and supporting their promotion to headship. In Ashford's case, the two he identified for particular mention had been both his headteacher and an adviser in authorities in which he has worked over time. One was his first headteacher, 'a superb educationalist' who 'became the Senior Primary Adviser for Leicestershire'. The second was the headteacher who appointed him to his first deputy headship. Each had been 'a major influence on my professional life' with the second one being 'destined to be an adviser in Cheshire before finally coming to Buckinghamshire to be Senior Primary Adviser'. In the latter role, she played an important part in enabling Ashford to achieve his present headship. As well as advisers, some chief education officers also received an honourable mention. For Ashford, the great merit of Leicestershire, as a supportive and stimulating education authority during his early days within it, were in part due to the influence of its innovating chief officer. He describes Stewart Mason as 'the first real educationalist I met' and remembers him as having a real 'Primary philosophy'. Sue Matthew talks in similarly glowing terms. In explaining why she eventually decided to seek a headship she says 'I think back to Tim Brighouse, who was our Chief Education Officer. We were so lucky to have him for ten years in Oxfordshire. His vision was inspirational and he was so supportive of us all. I remember chatting to him once about headship becoming very administrative ... and how I felt people must come first. He said, "It's got to be people first" and I said, "If you promise me it is going to be about people, I can do that."'

In neither of these two cases, however, did the Chief Education Officer, unlike members of the local advisory service, play a direct role in encouraging either Michael Ashford or Sue Matthew to apply for a particular post in headship or in appointing them to one. In one or two cases the influence was more direct. We shall discuss this issue as a brief examination of aspects of the process of appointment as seen by some of our ten colleagues.

The reported conversations contain several quite full accounts of the process of application and appointment to headship. At a formal level, the process in most of the areas in which our ten headteachers worked seems very similar. Posts are advertised, applications received and long listed, those long listed are usually invited to the school where, subsequently, they are interviewed by professional officers. From this a short list is drawn up and those who remain in contention are invited for an interview which usually takes place in the offices of the authority and conducted by an appointments panel containing councillors, school governors and local officers. After these interviews either one of the candidates is offered the post or the panel decides to set the process in motion again. Against this background, we will focus on two aspects of the process in practice. First, the extent to which local officials, chief education officers and advisers have played a role in encouraging or enabling local candidates to put themselves forward for and to be appointed to specific headship posts. Second, the accounts which candidates give of their experience of the appointments process.

In our conversation, Michael Gasper offered a particularly full and clear description of the process of selection and appointment. In a sense he was unusually well placed to do this since, although he was still a young man when appointed to his first headship, this had followed a period where he had been acting head for a term in a different school to where he was deputy and, in addition, had 'had 13 interviews for headship within a matter of months'. Talking about the role of the authority he says 'I suppose there was still a lot of influence from the LEA inspectors who did know you and they certainly had seen me in action and knew what I had done in the acting headship.' Finally, 'the patch inspector in my acting headship came ... He was a fearsome man with a terribly severe reputation within the authority for being an absolute tartar ... He spent the whole of the day with me and watched me work. Once I had settled the children down he started asking me questions and he tutored me. Now at that stage I had one more interview ... Without his help I wouldn't have got that job'.

Unlike Michael Gasper, Liz Paver was offered the first post for which she was interviewed. Before that she had 'applied for two other schools' within the authority but had not been interviewed for either. She became:

> disillusioned. As is my wont I telephoned the Chief. He said 'I'll send somebody to talk to you.' He sent an inspector who said 'You will be a head' but I said 'Yes but I want to choose where I am to be a head. Why couldn't I be interviewed?' He answered 'You will be.' I was arrogant enough to think that if I had been interviewed for one of the others I might have got it. It wasn't in their great plan.

David Davies was appointed to the third school for which he applied and was interviewed. As with Liz Paver and Michael Gasper, the local authority and its advisory service played a determining role in his failures and success. As he puts it:

> The first [was] a teaching headship in a small school and the adviser said to me 'Don't apply for that, there's something better for you coming along.' I don't like to be told where my career should go, so I applied anyway ... I wasn't successful. I felt disappointed but the next day the adviser said 'Don't worry, that wasn't for you.' I said 'I should be choosing what is for me, not you.' He said 'No, no, there are better schools than that for you.' Shortly after I applied for another, a very good school. Again I was told 'Don't apply for that, it is someone else's job you have no chance of getting it.' I thought 'I'll give it a go.' ... I wasn't successful. The very next month the Adviser came to see me in my classroom, and said 'Have you applied for Blaengwrach?' 'No, I haven't ... I am not applying for it.' 'Apply for it.' ... So I applied, got on the short list ... I was successful.

He was not, however, successful without alarms:

> I found it soul destroying when I walked through the door for interview to hear a Governor speaking to another candidate ... say 'Don't you worry, the job is yours.' I then heard another Governor say to a second candidate 'I know you are in the Chapel, the choir, the opera, you will have this job.' I thought I may as well go home.

In seeking to move to a second headship, Liz Paver might just as well have gone home:

> I [had] applied for a headship in another mining community ... I was short listed with the current deputy of 22 years in that school, and the deputy head of the middle school attached to it. We went to be interviewed, and as we were sitting waiting to go in the adviser came out and said 'You haven't met Councillor X have you?' I said 'No', he said 'Be careful' ... I went in and sat at the end of a long table surrounded by people with the Councillor at its head. He said 'Is it Elizabeth, is it Caroline or is it Liz?' and I said 'It is Mrs Paver to you Councillor.' End of interview! ... So when I came out ... I thought fine, I haven't got it ... When I got back one of my nursery nurses came and said 'Sorry about the interview Mrs Paver.' I asked 'How did you know I didn't get it?' She said 'I went to the party last Saturday in the local working men's club for Mrs X, it was a celebration for her headship.' That was the day before the interview. It was a salutary experience.

As we shall see, the early days of headship as remembered by several of the ten headteachers could also be a salutary experience. We will now turn to this and to their years of incumbency in headship.

Incumbency

Incumbency marks the period of actual headship and runs from the time a head is first appointed to the time when a head leaves the headship behind and looks to a new personal and professional life. Incumbency is characterized by the taking on of the responsibilities of office and the exercise of leadership. Heads will have their own particular 'style' or outlook in the way they respond to these challenges and their style will shift and change over the natural life of any headship. Style will be shaped and modified, in particular, by the dialectical interplay between a leader's own sense of agency and the social structure within which the head is working (Ribbins and Sherratt, 1997). It should be noted that differing cultural perspectives will influence both a leader's sense of agency and the social structure within which they work. Margy Whalley was able to show this very explicitly in her cross-cultural experience.

> I was very culturally arrogant initially, and I think probably most of us are, as new heads. I did have a philosophy which was very child centred and was all about learning from observation. But I was very mono-cultural. I thought you could give a piece of paper and paints to any child and they would love it, but in the barrio they were actually frightened of blank paper. These children were very intimidated by what we were offering them and that's probably true of children in this country too.

The cultural dimensions of headship, stemming from the head's own cultural identity and that of the community in which they are working, are an important factor in the evolution of a role and individual style. Also, as Gronn and Ribbins (1996) point out, a head's performance in the role will require an expression of their potency, ambition and vision. This performance will not be static over a head's career, but will evolve and develop as the period of incumbency progresses.

Incumbency may be viewed as having four developmental sub-phases. Building on Day and Bakioglu's (1996) phases, our modified scheme comprises Initiation, Development, Autonomy and Advancement. We shall examine each of these sub-phases in turn and explore the contextual factors which effect an individual's response to the particular tasks of headship which characterize these periods. It should also be pointed out that these four sub-phases will come into play each time a head moves on to a new headship post.

Initiation

Following an appointment to headship there is an immediate process of 'induction' (Gronn and Ribbins, 1996) or 'initiation' (Day and Bakioglu, 1996). During this period the head is familiarized with the organizational and workplace norms, and the new roles they are expected to fulfil. This initiation process occurs every time a head switches role within a particular post (within post initiation) and when a head progresses through promotion to another headship post (new post initiation). This early period of headship can be seen to be evolutionary within itself, and the evidence indicates that it takes up to three years before a head is fully initiated into the post (Day and Bakioglu, 1996). During this phase heads often experience a range of feelings, beginning with a feeling of initial elation and enthusiasm, moving through a growing sense of realism and adjustment to what the real parameters of the job will be. As Sue Beeson commented, in the early days of her first headship 'I felt very optimistic. I suppose when you don't know what can go wrong you feel you can do anything.'

Some heads have a relatively smooth transition into post, others face greater difficulties. The quality of the 'beginning' experience can be seen to have been influenced, at least in part, by:

(1)   Their belief in themselves as a leader:

There was a sort of natural leadership there, and I recognized that within myself ... I felt 'Yes, I can work within this situation. I don't feel threatened, I don't feel undermined. I know that I can go out and do things.' (Michael Gasper)

(2)   The preparation they have had for taking on the post:

I was very fortunate because Pat Lewis, who was my head then, groomed me for headship. She was very inclusive in terms of problems that occurred within the organization or the culture of the school. (Michael Gasper)

(3)   The breadth of previous experiences:

A breadth of experience is important ... I did some work over the last two years with some outstanding women heads. They have all had that same broad career pattern, they've not gone step by step, they just haven't, and they haven't wanted to. It's not that they've been passed over or neglected, they've been hungry for different kinds of experience, and I think that's much richer. (Margy Whalley)

getting yourself wider perspectives in whatever field is so important because it gives you more space to understand where you are at. (Sue Matthew)

I think the central problem is one of people being locked into worlds that are necessarily limited ... If you have been at a school that's not terribly enterprising, or isn't terribly exciting, or even is just a good school of its kind, inevitably the pattern of experience limits your understanding of what schools can be. (David Winkley)

(4)   The relevance of their previous experiences:

As an acting head ... it was definitely a beneficial experience. It made me aware of the changes that were taking place with regard to Local Management of Schools, it made me aware of the problems a head might face, it gave me an insight into what was going on in headteachers' meetings etc. ... So from my point of view, acting headship was a definite bonus. (David Davies)

(5)   The transference of previous learning:

I just carried all those concepts of teamwork with me from working with Geoff, that I must let people go at their own pace, and I must respect people's differences, and I must build on their strengths. (Margy Whalley)

(6)   Having strong role models:

For a head it's invaluable to have had the experience of being managed well. If ... you have never been managed well, it's jolly difficult to do it yourself. (Margy Whalley)

(7)   Their ability to be reactive and to learn 'on the job':

I've always felt I can manage these sorts of conditions but once you're in there you realize there's a lot to learn and I don't think anyone could teach it to you ... Almost every single thing I've learnt of any use at all, I've learnt from being on the job, or watching other people on the job ... So it was very much about learning how to construct something creative out of disarray. (David Winkley)

(8)   The support structures in place:

after the first year I looked at a lot of other centres and the heads were cracking up. So I wrote a paper for the department saying it would be a lot cheaper if they bought me in a consultant, from a university, to take on this support role. (Margy Whalley)

One of the heads in the AESOP partnership was also on my initial new heads' training and has been a real support ever since. He's been a critical friend throughout the seven years and I have relied a lot on him. (Sue Matthew)

One of the first challenges for a new head is to modify their self concept to include a perception of themselves as a headteacher. This can take a little time to assimilate, and is evident in all kinds of minor aspects of behaviour which signal ownership of the role. Typically Sue Beeson describes how during her first days of headship, 'I knocked on my own door for a long time. It was a long time before I just walked into my office without hesitating to knock.'

During this early period, the head has to establish relationships with colleagues, learn to cope with the stresses and strains of the job, and begin to communicate a vision for the school. This is a time of steep learning and competency building, and although this often generates feelings of uncertainty and anxiety, it also provides feelings of great excitement, energy and the sense of fulfilment of ambitions. Michael Gasper commented 'I was delighted, speechless and elated. It was a definite achievement and I felt that now I had really done myself justice ... There was an acknowledgement there that lifted me.'

But he went on to talk of feeling very uncertain during the first few days in post, 'The first day I remember distinctly because I sat in my office thinking, well this is very nice. At that stage you could see the table, so I pretended to play about with a bit of paperwork, but there wasn't much because I was new to the job. Then I thought this is no good, I can't just sit here, this is ridiculous ... I honestly did not know what to do. I hadn't expected to be sitting behind a desk doing nothing. I think there was a bit of guilt maybe. Over the first three days that rapidly disappeared and as I got a feel of the organization, strategies suggested themselves to me.'

On reflection, a number of heads viewed this first phase of headship as extremely tiring and demanding, and remember existing on a wave of initial euphoria and energy which derived from a feeling of significant career progression and acknowledgement. Sue Beeson recalls 'I can remember after about the first six months saying, "I will never do this again" – it's a bit like childbirth! I can remember being totally exhausted after the first year of my first headship and thinking I could never do this again, just like when you have your first baby but then you forget. It wasn't until I was doing it again that I remembered!'

These feelings of huge demands, coupled with uncertainty generally make way after a few months to a more measured and realistic view of possibilities and constraints, and a developing ability to manage the job.

A number of the heads stressed how they had to tread carefully during the early days of headship. They pointed out how important it was to get the measure of the culture of the organization and the social networks and customs which operated before they started any attempt at more radical change. It was interesting to note that a number of the heads began with very practical aspects of the school such as the buildings, the physical environment and the displays. These matters seemed to provide an uncontroversial starting place for change, through which a number of significant ground rules could be worked out. Sue Beeson describes how she began on relatively uncontroversial elements of development initially in order to take the staff with her. She had a clear longer term strategy for more wide ranging improvement but she was prepared to take her time in order to pre-empt resistance and opposition:

> A lot needed doing to the fabric of the building, to the resources ...
> That gave me a good start because I could make changes that were
> visible without upsetting any real applecarts. But I had also been
> told by the advisers that the school was only 80 per cent effective as
> it could be ... there didn't seem to be a lot I could just go in and start

blasting away at, which I wouldn't have wanted to do anyway. I knew I would have to be cautious. There were people there who had been at the school for 16, 18 years. I think you must be very careful that you don't just go in and challenge or ignore people's history and culture.

David Davies also had a very practical, hands-on approach: 'I spent the first few months as a general handyman. If at all possible, if they asked me for something on Thursday evening, I would go and get what was needed that night, come in at six o'clock the next morning and have it up by the time they came in. When I was asked could we have that, my answer was yes, yes, yes, yes, yes, yes: I tried never to say no ... in return they began to sort of break down barriers, relax, to accept change.'

It is during this initial phase that the head's own style of headship emerges. This may be modified as the head's career and experience progresses but most of the heads in this study claimed that their view of themselves as a leader was consistent from these early days. Heads were also able to articulate a view of themselves as a leader. Liz Paver provides a personal perspective on her style, 'I have seen *Les Miserables* five times and I see myself on that cart with the big flag, and out in front. I like making decisions. I sometimes get things wrong, but I can't do it any other way. It is either come on follow me or it's nothing.'

A head's individual style also reflected their cultural background and the way they adapted this to the new contexts in which they were operating as a head. Usha Sahni exemplified this in her stance over her dress, which she has stuck to throughout her time in the profession. On her appointment she debated her ability to deal with disruptive pupils while continuing to wearing a sari with an LEA representative. As she says 'I remember having a long discussion with him as to why I would have to dress differently. He said, "They would not really respect you if you go in wearing a sari like you are." We had a long chat about why that would be so ... I have never worn Western clothes. It is not that I have anything against them, it's just that it's not me.'

Development

The second sub-phase constitutes a period of 'development' and takes approximately four to eight years (Day and Bakioglu, 1996). This phase is generally characterized by enthusiasm and growth. The head is in control, has the measure of the job and is developing the wide range of competencies required to carry it out effectively. The enormous range of roles and responsibilities required of headship has been taken on board and accepted positively as in the nature of the job. This is summed up well by Michael Gasper, 'You have to appreciate the totally ludicrous range of things you will be asked to do, from considering a budget, deciding on teachers' futures, working out whether children are going to be scrunched together in a large group or spread out, to being out in the pouring rain with your hand up a drainpipe. You have got to have the sense of humour that can cope with that. I know continental colleagues ... who come over and are mind blown at the range of what we have to do.'

They have developed a strong sense of confidence in their ability to manage the school and this allows them to face the many pressures they are put under which otherwise might shake this self belief. In fact, it was argued that without it heads would not survive. As Michael Gasper explains:

> It has to be the supreme arrogance to believe you can be a good head ... You have got to have a belief in yourself, you won't last without it. Once you are in that position, all the circumstances conspire to shoot bullets at your own belief in yourself and your ability to do the job. The world around and circumstances are constantly trying to undermine you and if you have the slightest lack of self-belief, you shouldn't even consider it.

Working relationships with colleagues are established, strategies for coping with the pressures of the job have been worked out and work is underway to realise the vision which has been articulated and understood by colleagues. This period of incumbency is usually viewed as very enjoyable and rewarding. The head, and those involved in the enterprise, have a realistic and clear vision of what they are working to achieve, improvement is seen as possible, and there are fewer difficulties because of a developing confidence and competence.

Each head will have his or her own vision of what they are trying to achieve and how to achieve it. The strategies employed to achieve this will be shaped by personal psychological style, but will also be influenced by professional experiences throughout each head's career. They will also vary over the period of incumbency. For example, David Winkley describes three phases in his headship of Grove School, 'I would say that I've really run three schools not one, each with a major turn over of staff. The periods are roughly five-year durations and they've each led to a recreation of the school, with a new deputy, new young staff and a constant rethinking and developing of ideas.'

Some primary heads do adopt a very calculated, systems-oriented approach but the majority of primary heads seem to acknowledge the central importance of the social and emotional dimensions of their work. Indeed, a number of heads cite this as being the reason for coming to work in this age phase of education. As Michael Gasper puts it, 'while systems and results are important, it's how you encourage that without losing the first element – the social dimension ... I am a people person first and foremost, rather than a systems and results person'.

Usha Sahni echoed the need for systems and structures to be brought to life through a consideration of the people and relationships within the organization, 'I think in primary schools you can create structures and systems but a lot of it is face to face work. It really comes down to talking to people.

You can't run a school on the basis of relationships of course, but you can't run it on the basis of systems and structures either.'

In accordance with this emphasis on people and social development, one of the recurring themes in the vision of the heads in this study is the raising of expectations for the children and families they were working with. They argue that this must be a key part of any improvement strategy. In addition, it reflected their deeper personal values and beliefs, which focused on providing opportunities for all children, whatever the social context:

> the school is located in a mining community ... a village community in the valleys with very little going for it. What we tried to do was to show the parents that there is a big wide world out there, that there are alternatives, that the expectations they have adopted are often just not realistic. (David Davies)

> part of my vision was a fairly political one ... I have qualms about American education but class is not an issue in American society. When I came here I couldn't believe how some families had no expectation of Higher Education for their children and I couldn't understand why ... it made me think I wanted to raise expectations. (Sue Matthew)

By this stage in their headship, the head has also often been able to make strategic staff and organizational changes which will facilitate the achievement of goals. Most of the heads in this study had done this over time, and saw it as a critical element in the achievement of their vision for the school. David Davies began this process of staff replacement early in his headship, he was fortunate, others had to wait longer, 'I was lucky to be able to appoint two teachers within a fortnight of being appointed. I've got a superb staff now, the best staff I've ever worked with. Out of the six here now, I have appointed three, plus one other who moved away from the area.'

Heads also have to develop strategies for working with staff they have inherited and who are sometimes reluctant to respond to change and improvement. This can provide major difficulties for heads and there may be no easy solution. David Davies took a long-term view of the issue:

> As a teacher I always thought that if I became a head I would simply say to weak teachers, 'You are not doing the job, change, do it.' But that doesn't work ... I realized very quickly that unless they are appalling, where you may have to go for dismissal, you have to make the best of every member of staff, and the best way you can do that is to take them on board with you. This may mean losing many battles before winning the war ... You may need to get to know them and what their problems are. There are times when you have to give up hope to be given back. You've got to win them round by giving them what they need before demanding what your school needs.

Other heads had a clear strategy of staff development which permeated the school and was central to addressing the issue of taking reluctant staff with them. The feeling was that all staff had to be taken along and that a school was only as strong as its weakest link. Staff development was a major and ongoing task for heads and there could be no excuse for giving up on any member of staff. As Margy Whalley pointed out:

> the organization is only as high quality as the weakest link in the chain, isn't it? So if I know there's somebody who isn't committed … then I feel we have a long way to go with that person. I feel everybody's got to come on board, the dinner ladies, the kitchen staff, everybody. Your school is only as effective as how loving your dinner ladies are with the children and how creative they are at lunch time … from the very beginning we spend a lot of time discussing issues with staff … How can I convince a member of staff that the way they are working is not an appropriate way of working? I mean a lot of it would be by modelling, some of it would be by introducing them to better practice. So we set up a system at the beginning where every member of staff has supervision … I think it's through this that we transmit a way of thinking and looking at children's learning … Unless you have that reflective, iterative, ongoing discussion they can have quite the wrong idea.

The head's developing confidence in this phase may be exemplified through a willingness to delegate responsibility and create new management structures within the school to take on certain management tasks. This is seen as the period of maximum effectiveness and when the greatest progress and velocity is apparent. Ongoing personal development is viewed as important and is achieved in a number of ways:

(1)   Moving to another headship:

With the first job everything was inspirational and not planned in the sense of me standing back from things a lot, but now it is much more conscious and I am much more strategic. (Michael Gasper)

(2)   Developing new roles within the same school:

the other bit of my life that I build in … has been the National Primary Centre … What we are trying to do professionally is find out where exiting things are happening, identify, celebrate and network, and publish them. (David Winkley)

(3)   Secondment:

I've been able to pursue a pattern whereby I've appointed an outstanding deputy, and then gone off and left the deputy to run the school. I've done that three times now and each time it's been successful, very good for the deputy, who promptly got a headship … In those years I've been involved in academia, largely in Oxford, I was a Fellow at Nuffield College. (David Winkley)

I got secondment to the regional headship Unit at Wooley Hall ... I went there to study Nursery Education because that's what we were going to develop next. For the first time I took time out and started thinking and looking towards the future. (Michael Ashford)

(4)　Further training:

The best help I have had was through the College management courses I have taken since I was appointed. These forced me to take a step back and to think much more carefully than I had ever done before about what I was doing, what the issues were and how to address them. (Michael Gasper)

Autonomy

This period comes after eight or more years into the job. The head at this point is generally very confident and competent. Experience and survival have given them a sense of control and the knowledge that they have mastered the job of headship. They have learnt strategies to cope with the personal stresses and strains of the job and are able to take a more open and longer term perspective on the problems they face. Intriguingly, this can make them even stronger in their leadership. Usha Sahni provides a good resume of this process:

There are a number of ways [I manage stress]. One is attitudinal and that has got better as time has gone on ... Whereas I used to get terribly upset and hurt, I don't. I take things much more as they come. I am able to see things in perspective and that only comes with experience and age. I am able to distance myself, I don't take things personally ... I am able to remove things from myself and not see them as personal insults ... I believe I am more resolute than ever, I persist and I pursue things, I don't let go easily. I am able to give it longer and I think my own repertoire of skills and my own approach to understanding what motivates the staff has developed. You learn that as you go along.

By this stage in their career they have come to terms with what the job of headship is about and how they are able to realistically respond to its demands. Michael Ashford describes how his role gradually developed over his incumbency to that of 'Chief Executive' of the school, 'As a young head I knew everything, or rather pretended I knew everything. I would answer any and all questions. I don't pretend now ... They know I am not the fountainhead of all knowledge but that I am in control. If I don't know the answer to a question I have somebody who does within the school. They appreciate my skills as a manager and that's where my strengths are ... I have learnt to step back ... I now get my satisfaction out of seeing others function effectively.'

Day to day professional life is generally much easier and at this stage in their career heads view themselves as 'management experts'. They have often managed to put in place their plan and vision for the school, at least in part, and because of this the phase is characterized as one of stability, with much less growth, development and innovation. In addition, by this stage they are often a step away from the immediate demands of educating the children and managing this process. By putting management teams in place and delegating responsibilities to them, the organization may have the appearance of running smoothly without a hands on approach. Overwhelmingly in this study the heads advocated a collegial or teamwork approach to managing the school, and claimed that this was not just desirable, but also very necessary if all the management tasks required in a school were to be achieved. They believed that a small organization, like a school, required this kind of collaborative partnership in order to function effectively, and that all members of the organization had an important part to play. Many viewed their own role very much as just one element of a mutually interdependent team. As David Davies puts it: 'A headship is just one aspect of providing for the children. In a way, my cook's job is as important as mine. If anybody does not contribute what they should the children suffer: and my children are not going to suffer ... Within the school every member of the staff is of equal importance: they don't work for me, they work with me. We work as a team. It is my intention that they have a major say in what goes on ... as a head you have got to be prepared to be flexible, to let them work alongside you.' But, they were also clear that this collegial style, relying on team work was not always easy or effective.

During this phase in their career, heads appear to see their role much more in terms of running a senior management team to whom they delegate many of the day to day responsibilities of running the school. As Liz Paver commented on her second headship, 'It made me look at headship in a different way really, much more as senior management team building and making sure that lots of delegation went on, and valuing other people as leaders.'

This change of emphasis may have negative and positive repercussions. Negatively, the head may feel a sense of loss of role and his or her critical importance to the educational enterprise, spending time on administrative and technical matters only. Day and Bakioglu (1996) begin to identify the seeds of disillusion and loss of commitment to the job during this period when, objectively, a head is at the height of their power. Stagnation may begin to set in, and with it a loss of enthusiasm for the job and a lack of energy to tackle new challenges and increasing external pressures. Characteristically, heads have also at this point reached the stage in their personal lives when they are beginning to reassess their life goals and think more deeply about the nature of life and what they want out of it. Some may be experiencing a sense of career frustration, if they have not achieved all they had envisaged and have a sense of feeling trapped in the post with nowhere to go. This sub-phase has been identified as one in which morale is often low and a feeling of disenchantment may begin to set in.

Alternatively, and positively, the head may feel a sense of liberation and the feeling that he or she has been released from the immediate demands of the job, and so have more time to tackle broader issues and look to wider horizons. As Sue Matthew commented, 'I have a feeling now after seven years that I have a bit more time and space now than I did as a very new head because I was just trying to come to terms with so many things ... I have been able to take on extra responsibilities ... maybe I feel that I can share a bit more of my time and energies now.'

Their increasing sense of competence and confidence may provide them with the strength to begin to tackle the broader educational issues faced both within the school, and beyond it. They may find time for involvement in other professional organizations and begin to view their experience as a base from which to tackle bigger and more fundamental issues facing the profession. In contrast to the analysis offered above, this can be an empowering time for a head and one in which their feelings of enchantment with the job may be more fully realized.

Advancement

This final period of incumbency is a transitional time for heads. It seems to be a period which is critical in dividing the profession into two directions. One characterized by 'disenchantment' (Day and Bakioglu, 1996), the other by perhaps even greater 'enchantment' with the profession. Many of the heads talked about the stresses and pressures of the job and their difficulty with coping with these at times. Michael Gasper described his struggle to cope with this:

> We have to face the fact that there are strains undermining what we are doing. You sometimes get the feeling that the world is conspiring to undermine everything you believe in or think you should be doing. The day to day, week to week activity is very much reactive, rather than proactive, unfortunately. Again, we are trying desperately to lift ourselves out of this. In my depressive moments I think it is all hopeless, but when you start looking carefully at what is going on I would say there are a lot of positive things happening and I can see that we are gradually lifting ourselves out of the morass.

Recent studies seem to paint a rather depressing picture of an inevitable progress towards disenchantment and subsequent exit from the position of headship (Day and Bakioglu, 1996; *TES*, 1997). Day and Bakioglu (1996) chart a chronological and downwardly spiralling process towards divestiture of the post. They argue for an urgent review of support for the significant proportion of heads who are currently in this state. While not wishing to dispute their findings and diagnosis of the problem, we would like to suggest that this may provide only a partial view of the situation and that a perhaps more optimistic prognosis may be found in our study of primary headship.

Hubermann (1993) identifies four necessary conditions for continued professional satisfaction, or in our terms professional 'enchantment':

(1)   Enduring commitment to the profession:

I wouldn't do anything else. I thoroughly enjoy my job. We are very privileged to work with children. I know I could earn far more doing something else but there is nothing more rewarding than working with children ... headship is a very special job, I wouldn't change it for the world. (David Davies)

To work with young children is an absolute joy. Talk about the 'gift of each day'. I think the children are giving to you as much as you give out. In fact, they give you three times back ... I can't believe there is a more important job. (Sue Matthew)

I suppose the choice has been strengthened by an increasing view that running a school is the engine room of the entire education system. The moment you cease running a school, you move to some degree into the periphery. If you really want to try and change the system and demonstrate that something can be done, you're in a much more powerful position as head of a school, simply because you can decide things that rapidly impact on children. (David Winkley)

(2)   Manageable job expectations:

When the National Curriculum came in we looked at the whole thing and said 'OK, what is new that we are not doing now that we must do?' We did the musts, we did not say we must do everything new. We have not chased bandwagons. (Liz Paver)

(3)   Good relationships with colleagues:

I always see the potential in other people. I get a lot of my energy from seeing people grow and change, and I do love working with adults. (Margy Whalley)

You've seen the people in this school. We have a caretaker in a million, we've got a secretary that would work until midnight, people that care so much about looking after children. They are a dedicated and excellent teaching staff. (Sue Matthew)

(4)   Balanced home and school life:

I try to go home from school and switch off from school completely. I have to. I could not keep up that level of commitment 24 hours a day. Lots of my colleagues take their problems home with them and they worry about them all night. I will not. I solve school problems in school. After I have left. I have left. (David Davies)

A number of the heads also emphasized the importance of making the effort to maintain leisure time activities. They believed these were great stress releasers and provided a complete alternative to the demands of work. They ensured that some time in a busy life was kept for feeding other dimensions of the individual's personality and meant that the pressures of work were put aside for at least a few hours in the week, 'I umpire badminton internationally, I travel all over the world with this; I keep a large collection of reptiles, I travel all over the world with that; I'm very involved with sub-aqua. So when I am in school, my mind is on school, I'm refreshed and I am full of enthusiasm for school. When I leave school I switch off from school and my batteries are recharged' (David Davies).

This ability to put in place a balanced home and school life appears to be a central factor in the maintenance of long term commitment, motivation and energy levels. Some of the heads in this study found this balance very difficult to achieve and this clearly had an impact on the sustenance of their enchantment with the job. Sue Beeson is 'very rarely ... conscious of being without a thought of school for any length of time ... I go to sleep thinking about school and I wake up thinking about school. I suppose I am obsessed with it really. I find it very difficult to be in a position where I haven't got to think about work, I feel guilty if I'm not thinking about work'.

It seems that these factors may be critical in our analysis of those heads who had managed to maintain their commitment, efficacy and motivation over the long term and those who had not.

Disenchantment

Certain heads in this study did appear to follow a pattern of disenchantment with the job. They exhibited declining confidence, a lack of enthusiasm and a feeling of increasing fatigue with the pressure of the job. The pressure of increasing levels of accountability and the very public exposure of their performance was inflicting an intolerable strain. Joan McConnell paints a graphic picture of the stress caused by her school's recent OFSTED inspection:

> It was harrowing; it was interesting but it didn't teach me anything about the school that I didn't already know. The children were desperately tired and stressed at the end of it. The teachers were totally demoralized even though we were well prepared and confident in what we were doing. It didn't feel good while it was happening. It was an horrendous process, horrifically stressful.

Yet, despite this experience she has managed to retain her commitment and enthusiasm for the job. Others were not able to do so. Complaints about the string of changes and innovations were common and feelings of efficacy to shape the direction of things had clearly declined. Michael Ashford's description of his feelings at the time of the introduction of the National Curriculum reveals how deeply some heads were affected by the scope of the changes, 'I just couldn't believe what happened. I thought there's no way I can take all this on board ... And so I asked myself if I really wanted to be part of this. I had done headship. Did I really want to stay in teaching? It was linked also with the break up of my marriage ... I began to ask myself was it time to make a break. To do something else.'

Heads have also been affected by the prolonged public attack on the value and esteem of the profession, and appear to view this rather cynically. Sue Beeson touched on this nerve in her comments. She tries 'not to get too embroiled in thinking about the politics of all this but I cannot help but feel there has been a systematic undermining of the profession and what it stands for so that certain things could be achieved ... Political parties can call the shots more easily if they have a weak profession which cannot stand up for itself. We've allowed ourselves to be pushed around for so long'.

Heads going along this route tend to be introspective in their reflections on what they are doing. Disillusionment and a level of cynicism and pessimism are evident. Their solution to resolving the anxiety caused by these feelings is to look to ways of 'getting out' and divesting themselves of what is increasingly viewed as an intolerable burden. Sue Beeson summed up how this process occurred very succinctly, 'I wouldn't like to be a teacher at the beginning of my career now. That may be a sign of old age and cynicism. I have a theory about Winnie the Pooh. I feel that heads probably all started out their careers as Tiggers, and they are on a continuum towards Eeyore. I'm fairly close to Eeyore now. When you get to Eeyore it's time to hang up your boots and call it a day.'

Enchantment

Other heads do not follow this pattern. Despite many years in the job they have retained a feeling of enchantment with it. If anything, they are even more confident, enthusiastic and visionary about what the possibilities are. They express a feeling of having lots left to do, new challenges to face and being able to commit more time and energy to doing so. Michael Ashford talked enthusiastically about future plans for his school, 'But there is still so much to do – take the buildings, we've still got outdoor toilets. Curriculum wise, it's really exciting. We are beginning to get to where we want to be.' David Winkley also expressed this optimism for the future, 'If we could get primary education right we'd transform the learning opportunities for all our children. That has got to be on the agenda for major public debate over the next 10 to 20 years and we will get there, but we're not there yet. The quality of the debate has got to become a lot more sophisticated and tougher minded.'

They are also able to see the job of educating the young in its widest sense and to look with experience at the range of factors which affect this – and to try and tackle some of these. They are searching for solutions to the real difficulties they face, and are often radical in their views of what is possible. Their professional wisdom is being used to the full and employed to generate ways in which they might reinvent themselves and their schools creatively towards a new vision.

A major characteristic of those who remain enchanted with the job relates paradoxically to the concept of accountability. The enchanted saw those to whom they were formally accountable as providing a matching level of support for them in the tasks they were facing. Sue Matthew expressed this balance between accountability and support, 'there's this mutual sort of interrelationship between all the people involved in the school. Every strand of accountability has an exact strand of support to match it, and thank goodness for that'.

Heads felt they were working in a partnership with these bodies and this gave them a sense of tremendous support and a feeling that the burden was shared. They also saw the children as the first, and sometimes only real, line of accountability. Other bodies were seen as much less significant in terms of their professional responsibility, and the level of significance diminished as the body moved further away from the immediate context of the child, family and school. Michael Gasper claimed, 'I am accountable to those little children that I stand in front of every Monday morning and at intervals during the week and that's my bottom line. If I feel I have done them justice, my conscience is clear, I can sleep with that.'

The children also gave them a continued sense of purpose and an enormous personal and emotional satisfaction in their work. Liz Paver was able to state, 'I still feel privileged to be a head. People and my work for the NAHT tell me headship is a very stressful occupation. Heads are answerable on so many fronts – financially, pupil performance, all the rest of it. Despite this, I say to my deputies and my staff, "we still have children to educate, we still have teachers to develop, we still have a curriculum to deliver"'.

Despite the enormous pressures, changes and demands of the job, heads in this study were still able to speak with a deep conviction about their work and the real rewards they received from being engaged in primary education. They worried about the negative tone of much of the debate surrounding primary education and the impact this was having on incumbents currently in post, as well as recruits to the profession. They spoke of the need to change the current climate of negativism to one of a positive celebration of the work. Liz Paver spoke powerfully on this:

> I think the worst thing happening to our profession is we are becoming too cynical. We take students from three institutions and when they come I always say 'Thank you for considering becoming a teacher. We need new enthusiastic teachers. Thirty years ago I was where you are now and I don't regret one single day of it. If you want to do it and can keep positive about it, it is a great profession to join.' I would say exactly the same to heads. We need heads to be young, enthusiastic, positive. You will get things wrong but you will be a leader and you will be very autonomous. It is good to be a head.

Moving On

The final phase of a head's professional life we describe as Moving On. This phase marks a progression from one state (incumbency) to another, but we offer an additional route to that of Gronn's (1993) Divestiture. This we call Reinvention. During this final phase heads' careers go through a gear change. For some the change is down, as they wind down professionally and finally exit the profession. This may be termed Divestiture. For others the change is a gearing up, as they add velocity to their professional activity and move to create a new vision of themselves, their profession and the work they do. This may be termed Reinvention.

Divestiture

This route sees heads anticipating and then divesting themselves of office, letting go and handing over the leadership role to a successor. The impetus for divestiture may be a move out to an alternative career or it may be perminent retirement from paid work. The cause of this may be just natural ageing, it may be illness, incapacity or, as is increasingly common, disillusionment and burnout (*TES*, 1997). Sue Beeson was looking ahead anticipating an early retirement, 'I'm in my fourth year as head of this school. I see it as being another one or two years and then I would like to retire. Whether I will I don't know. I would be 52. I think I'll be burnt out by then and probably the school will be ready for somebody new ... a third headship would probably finish me off. The more you know the harder it gets.' Michael Ashford was also anticipating a move in the not too distant future, 'Then, when I am 55, I will say, "Right, thank you, I have got 30-odd years in, I've got a reasonable pension, a nice home, things are OK." I'll go into some form of management training, if anybody wants me. If they don't I'll become a gardener. Can you think of a better second occupation for an educator?'

Divestiture may be many things: planned or unplanned, voluntary or involuntary, smooth or traumatic. Again, this will be affected by both the individuals sense of agency and the social structure within which they are operating. In the anticipation of divestiture we find heads looking back nostalgically to a previous time which they feel has been lost for good. Michael Gasper looks back 'with a certain amount of nostalgia to the times when things were just beginning to change as a sort of "golden age", where you still had the freedom to choose what to do, when being professional meant that you gave careful thought to what you provided and how you provided it, and when you worked together as a staff to plan your work'.

Heads who were looking to leave the profession had no view of moving forward and improvement on what has gone before. In contrast, those who remained committed and were looking to the rebirth of a new vision managed to draw some positive succour from a situation which they were having difficulty in coping with. Michael Gasper goes on to say, 'All this may sound rather gloomy but it isn't. It's realistic and serves to remind me how important it is to hold on to the principles which I believe in and to keep a balance within my school, rather than be forced into following one pathway.'

Reinvention

This route sees heads anticipating new beginnings, looking to an alternative vision and reinventing themselves in order to achieve it. Its impetus may come from within, whereby long-standing ambitions and visions are to be realized at last. Or it may come from external stimulation, new courses, new colleagues, new experiences and new knowledge which has opened up possibilities and provided a climate of innovation. Heads committed to reinvention tended to have a clear view that the nature of primary education had radically changed over recent years. The were often deeply angry about the nature of the changes and the manner by which these had been brought about:

> I think that while I have been involved in primary teaching the nature of it has changed out of all recognition ... I think the really sad part of all of this is that there are elements in some of these changes which were necessary and which could have been so much more positive if there had been proper consultation. The denial of the value of teachers' professional judgement has been an insidious ˙ and poisonous pressure which has directly contributed to the early retirement of many capable and valuable teachers. If the process of change had been proactive rather than imposed, and if there had been a willingness to listen, particularly to those closest to the children, teachers would have felt valued, trust could have been strengthened, and the profession encouraged to be positive about their development towards the millennium. An important opportunity was squandered. (Michael Gasper)

However, rather than being overwhelmed by this they saw the climate of innovation and change as providing an opportunity for further transformation towards a vision, which they perceived as providing an improvement on what was currently on offer within the existing system. They were also identifying the aspects of the process which could be improved upon in their diagnosis of what had gone wrong. This diagnosis provides a way forward and reveals an openness to be included in change even during this later stage of their career.

A variety of visions for primary education were put forward by the heads in this study. Some of these focused:

(1)   On a specific and narrow view of their own primary school:

ideally I would like to see our school become a 'centre of excellence'. (Michael Gasper)

(2)   On developing a new vision for headship:

headteachers need a career track ... We need to have patterns of support, clear secondments, with headteachers quite frequently having a day a week to do something else. (David Winkley)

I think increasingly heads are going to have to be more political ... one of their key roles in the future will be to remind everybody that we are dealing with young children who are growing and developing as people in their own right, and who have the right to be treated as individuals, not as empty vessels to be filled up with any current politically popular theory. I believe it is going to be up to primary heads to fight for recognition in the minds of people that the early stages of education are just as important as the later stages and require the same level of funding and resourcing. (Michael Gasper)

(3)   On the profession of primary teaching:

I'd like to see a restoration of the balance in our work, and an acknowledgement of teachers' professional ability to make judgements, rather than being limited to what has become an increasingly narrow curriculum ... And above all else I'd like to see a system which allows children to be children and not be seen somehow as having to be old before their time or to have undue pressures put upon them. (Michael Gasper)

(4)   On a broader and more radical view of what primary education in the future should be about:

I would like to see education as about lifelong learning, and I would like us to see school buildings as the community's buildings ... I think you could have a package where you've got a community building which is accessible for adult education, community education and young children's learning, where there is continuity through the system. I would certainly like to see early years services being for children from 0–6 years, and I would like to see the agencies working together, without those rigid divisions between education and care, and support for youth and support for families ... the vision is of a flexible and responsive service to children and families ... and I actually think I'd want my school, any school, to be just the same ... In one of Schiller's essays he talks about schools being that place on the street corner where everybody wants to come, and where everybody feels at home. (Margy Whalley)

The current failure in primary education seems to be its ad-hocery, its unpredictability, its dependence upon the variety of teaching skills and ability ... I want something very different. When we've identified a set of experiences of high quality, we then need to ask how best to deliver them. If you cannot find anybody in the school to do it, you ask other questions – do we buy in people from outside, or create much more targeted in-service training so somebody in the school will be trained to do it? ... This conception of what a school is about does have considerable organizational implications. (David Winkley)

Conclusion

In this introduction to our study, we have sought to examine aspects of our conversations with ten primary headteachers using an approach which identifies leadership careers in terms of a number of phases. However, since one of our own key claims is that if contemporary headship is to be fully appreciated, such a survey-based approach needs to be supplemented with portraits of the views and perceptions of individual headteachers across a comprehensive range of issues. The ten chapters that follow seek to achieve this.

Interview schedule

(1) **Could we begin by you telling me about your personal background – your home, family, local community, school, higher education and the people who have shaped the kind of person you are and have had a significant influence on your life?**
How would you describe your life from your earliest years to the end of your full time education? What influence did your parents and other members of your family, your friends and other members of your peer group, your teachers/lecturers and class and school/college/university contemporaries, and any other significant individuals or groups have in shaping your views on life, your values, your aspirations and ambitions and your actions? On reflection, how important and how compatible and consistent were these various influences?

(2) **Describe your career to date. Why did you decide to teach?**
How and why did you become a teacher? Why did you choose to work with younger children?

(3) **How did your career develop to take you towards headship? What influences affected your decision to become a head and your early view of headship?**
How would you describe your career in the years before headship? Why and when did you decide you wanted to be a head? What was your view of headship during these years and who or what shaped that view? How influential were the heads you worked for or have known in other ways been in shaping your view and practice of headship?

(4) **How did you prepare for headship and for getting your first headship? How difficult was this?**
How did you prepare yourself for headship? Did you have a career plan? How did you go about trying to achieve your first headship? How difficult was this? What are your feelings about the processes of selection and appointment you experienced?

(5) **What was your early experience of headship like? And after this? To what extent do you think recent government-led initiatives will lead to better prepared heads? What would you do to improve things?**
What were your feelings when you were offered your first headship? How well prepared did you feel? What do you remember of your first day, week, and year of headship? How confident do you feel now? What advice would you offer others who might be considering headship?

(6) **Describe your career as a head. How well have your developmental needs been met? What have been the high and low points?**
How would you describe your career as a head? How do you approach the task of managing your school? What are your expectations for yourself and those who work with you? How do you measure your success?

(7) **Describe the school(s) in which you have been head. What particular vision for the school(s) did you have and what part did this play in your headship?**
How would you describe the school or schools of which you have been the head? What was your vision for it/them and how have you gone about trying to implement this? How successful have you been? What are your professional values and what is your vision for primary education? How have these influenced your work as a headteacher? What is the effect of your vision and values for the school(s) of which you have been head? What has been their effect beyond the school?

(8) **Describe the kind of head you are – as a leader – as a manager.**
What kind of a headteacher and leader are you? Has this changed over time and if so in what way and why? Has headship become less difficult as you have grown more experienced? How does a second headship differ from a first? Is it any easier and if so why and how? How do you enable others to lead?

(9) **How do you enable effective teaching and learning to take place in your school? How do you know this is happening? Do you see any changes in the way in which you do this over time?**
What part do you play in enabling effective teaching and learning in your school? Are you satisfied with your contribution? How do you manage people and resources?

(10) **To whom is a head accountable? Who do you answer to and how do you manage this accountability?**
To whom are you accountable? Who manages you? What do you see

as the role of governors (especially the Chair of the governing body), parents, pupils, the local community, the LEA, the DFEE in all this? How do you manage external relations?

(11) **How do you manage to maintain your own professional well-being and development? Where do you look to for support?**
How do you keep up to date? How do you cope with stress and manage when things go wrong? Which aspects of the role do you most and least like? Where do you find support for you?

(12) **Ted Wragg suggests 'You don't have to be a "nutter" to want to join the "barmy" army [of heads] but ...'. Do you think headship has become much more difficult in recent years and, if so, with what consequences? Do you enjoy it? More or less than you used to?**
Wragg's thesis is that 'demands on heads have escalated in the last few years' and the government 'by drowning [heads] under brain corroding bureaucracy has side-tracked them'. Has headship changed radically and for the worse in recent times? Can you still be an educational leader? Do you still enjoy headship? Are you barmy to do so? Would you give up headship if you could? If so, why? What would or will you do? Would schools be better off without heads anyway?

(13) **What changes do you think have taken place in primary education? How fundamental are these? Are they making things better or worse? What do these changes mean for your headship in the primary school?**
What changes have you seen in primary education in your time as a head? Do these changes represent an improvement on past practice?

(14) **How do you wish to see your own school develop? How would you like primary education to develop? What will all this mean for heads and headship?**
What do you think and what do you hope the primary school will look like in ten years time? What will this mean for headship? How will your school change?

References

Arkin, A. (1997) Heads on the block. *Times Educational Supplement* 14 February.

Bertram, A.D. (1996) *Effective Early Childhood Educators*. Unpublished PhD thesis, Coventry University.

Day, C. and Bakioglu, A. (1996) Development and disenchantment in the professional lives of headteachers. In Goodson, I.F. and Hargreaves, A. (1996) *Teachers' Professional Lives*. London: Falmer Press.

Editorial (1997) Labour's inspector. *Times Educational Supplement* 5 February.

English, F. (1995) Towards a reconsideration of biography and other forms of life writing as a focus for teaching educational administration. *Educational Administration Quarterly* **31** (2) 203–224.

Gardiner, J. (1997) Woodhead blasts leadership exam. *Times Educational Supplement* 28 February.

Gardner, H. (1995) *Leading Minds: An Anatomy of Leadership*. New York: Basic Books.

Greenfield, T. and Ribbins, P. (1993) Educational administration as a humane science: conversations between Thomas Greenfield and Peter Ribbins. In Greenfield, T. and Ribbins, P. (eds) *Greenfield on Educational Administration*. London: Routledge.

Gronn, P.C. (1993) Psychobiography on the couch: character, biography and the comparative study of leaders. *Journal of Applied Behavioural Science* **29** (3) 343–358.

Gronn, P.C. (1994) Educational administration's Weber. *Educational Management and Administration* **22** (4).

Gronn, P.C. and Ribbins, P. (1996) Leaders in context: postpositivist approaches to understanding educational leadership. *Educational Administration Quarterly* **32** (3) 452–473.

Hodgkinson, C. (1997) *Administrative Philosophy: Values and Motivations in Administrative Life*. London: Pergamon.

Hubermann, M. (1993) *The Lives of Teachers*. London: Cassell.

Kets de Vries, M. (1995) The leadership mystique. *Leading and Managing* **1** (3), 193–221.

Lodge, D. (1996) *The Practice of Writing*. London: Secker & Warburg.

Mortimer, P. and Mortimer, J. (eds) (1991) *The Primary School Head: Roles, Responsibilities and Reflections*. London: Paul Chapman.

O'Connor, M. (1995) Triumphs over adversity. *Times Educational Supplement* 10 November.

Office for Standards in Education (1995) *Guidance on the Inspection of Nursery and Primary Schools*. London: HMSO.

O'Leary, J. (1997) Heads face compulsory training. *The Times* 5 February.

Rae, J. (1993) *Delusions of Grandeur: A Head Master's Life*. London: HarperCollins.

Ribbins, P. (1989) Managing secondary schools after the act: participation and partnership. In Lowe, R. (ed.) *The Changing Secondary School*. Lewes: Falmer.

Ribbins, P. (1993) Conversations with a condottiere of administrative value: some reflections on the life and work of Christopher Hodgkinson. *Journal of Educational Administration and Foundations* **8** (1).

Ribbins, P. and Marland, M. (1994) *Headship Matters: Conversations with Seven Secondary School Headteachers*. London: Longman.

Ribbins, P. and Sherratt, B. (1997) *Radical Educational Reform and Conservative Secretaries of State*. London: Cassell.

The Times (1997) Editorial. *The Times* 5 February

Times Educational Supplement (1997) Editorial. Staff dissatisfaction peaks. *Times Educational Supplement* 17 January.

Woodhead, C. (1997) Leave Ofsted alone. *The Times* 5 February.

CHAPTER 2

Enabling 'true' primary education

MICHAEL ASHFORD WITH PETER RIBBINS

Michael Ashford is Head of Hamilton Combined GM School, High Wycombe, Buckinghamshire. He was born in Bridlington in East Yorkshire in 1948 and attended Pocklington School in York. He then went to Bede College Durham where he became college president and obtained a First Class Teaching Certificate and distinction in teaching practice. His first teaching post was at Battling Brook Primary in Leicestershire. After a spell at Wigston Waterleys Junior, also in Leicestershire, he became deputy headteacher at Robert Blackwell in Loughborough. He was appointed to his first headship in 1979 at New Pasture Lane in Bridlington before moving to his present post in 1990.

PR: Can you tell me about your background and how this has shaped you as a person?

MA: I grew up in a market town called Driffield in the centre of East Yorkshire – capital of the Wolds. It was a gentle place at a time when families were still families. My grandma and grandad lived across the road. One didn't stray far from the path of righteousness, not because of being anxious about being disciplined by one's father, but because one feared the discipline of one's grandfather. Mine was well known and respected in the town as policeman Ted. He was 21 stone, a fairly big fellow. Driffield was a delightful place to grow up in as a young child, but it suffered from the problems of growth so the schools weren't big enough to take all the local pupils. When I was 7 they told the families of my class they were very sorry but they were short of space in the primary school so we would have to be housed in the secondary school for the next year. This was traumatic. Our teachers went with us, but imagine what it was like for us 8-year-olds to go to a school where the other pupils were between 11 and 15.

My parents were hardworking. Mum was very much the East Yorkshire housewife, the maintainer – she kept the home. Dad sold feedstuffs to farmers in what has been described as the graveyard for salesmen – the East Riding. You couldn't sell anything to anybody, but he did. He worked on commission for Lever Feeds, so the more he sold the more he made. At night he played the double bass in a dance band. He worked every hour under the sun to give us a reasonable life.

To get me out of the schooling arrangement described earlier, my parents applied for me to go to Lyndhurst, the prep school of Pocklington Grammar. Pocklington was an independent school which relied on Forces families, local farmers and landlords sending their children there as well as a percentage of scholarship children going in on the old 11-plus. That decision changed my life. It meant that at 7.30 every morning I had to catch the train from Driffield – 30 miles – to Pocklington. Every evening the reverse. I was rarely home before six. It helped that there were about 30 of us doing this. You grow up quickly when you are doing that sort of thing at 8 years of age.

But the real trauma of it was not in the travelling. It was in the change in relationships back at home. There you were suddenly rubbing shoulders with all sorts of people who you didn't realize existed and talking about all sorts of different things which at first seemed alien. You were meeting people from very different backgrounds and having all sorts of new experiences. It really struck me the first time I was invited to the home of a new friend for tea and returning to my own home wondering why we hadn't got a swimming pool. I enjoyed the experience. I was very academic, I read a tremendous amount. When I got home instead of going and playing in the street I started to stay in and work. The kids in the street didn't like me any more. I didn't go to their school. That was the saddest part for me. I couldn't understand why this should happen.

At the prep school we were coached to pass the entrance exam. I had to pass the 11-plus. I remember coming home waving the brown envelope to my parents. I then embarked on seven years of secondary education at the grammar school on a scholarship. I'm a big man – six foot six. I had an enormous growth spurt between 13 and 15 and my life fell apart. I remember it very vividly. Until then I'd been into everything: I was very involved in school sport, I was academic. They decided to put me into an accelerated stream. I was getting very tired, my eyes went and I had to wear glasses. I remember vividly the trauma of this adolescent phase. I began to hate the school. I was still spending a large part of each day travelling, this seemed to get harder and harder. Around 15 I took my O-levels, a year early, and blew them. I took seven and got three. So instead of transferring into sixth form, I was caught up by the year group below me and ended up once again with what should have been my peer group.

That was the second major disruption in my school life and it seriously affected my development as a young person. I became disenchanted and started playing hooky. I did that once or twice a week over a period of about five or six weeks before anybody cottoned on. It is not that I was doing anything dramatic. I would just go off to Bridlington and wander on the beach. I hadn't really got any friends because of all the things that had happened to me. There came a point at which the school and my parents got together. Obviously my parents were working very hard and paying a lot to keep me there, the scholarship didn't cover everything. Through all of this I didn't see anything of my father because he was working so hard. It is only in later life that he began to bear any real influence on me. I have always respected him and understood what he was doing, but I resented being cheated of his companionship when I really needed him.

The decision was that I would board. It was felt I needed to be under the influence of the school more directly and not be given the degree of flexibility I had enjoyed. It was from this that my decision to teach ultimately came. What happened was that having bucked the system for two or three years I suddenly became part of the establishment. I was in a dormitory with 40 others. Within a week, having assessed the situation, I realized that the people who had the best life were the people who played the game and appeared to respect authority. They were often, in fact, people who led. I began to realize I had leadership qualities. I was put in charge of a dormitory of young children, forty 11-year-olds who'd just transferred into secondary education and whose parents were in the Forces all over the world. Some were very unhappy. They were lonely and needed friendship.

At 17 I began to realize I could give to others. From that moment, although I didn't realize it fully for a year or so, I was destined to become a teacher. I took more and more responsibility. Whenever I went anywhere, whenever I sat in a room people would look at me and say, 'Well, you can chair this' or 'You can lead us through that'. I became head of house and captain of rugby. Everything was leading me into, although I didn't know it, becoming a teacher. This only dawned on me when a teacher, Terry Hardacre, sat me down and said 'You've thought of teaching haven't you?' I said 'I don't know really whether I have?' He said 'My college is damn good. You ought to go there.' I said 'That sounds good' and because I respected him and thought he was a good teacher, I toddled off to Durham. It was as simple as that. The decision had little to do with the academic; it was being involved with people that made me want to do it.

PR: How influential was your mother? Also your grandfather?

MA: She was the carer – she was always there whenever I needed feeding. Women at that time in the East Riding traditionally played that role. She serviced my father so he could do the things he had to do. We didn't see a great deal of him. I hope I have inherited some of my mother's qualities of patience and tolerance. I learnt from her, and from my grandfather. He was a village policeman and was liked by people. I used to watch the way he worked and how he talked to people. When I was very little I used to ride on his bicycle – he had a little seat between himself and the handle bars. He couldn't get a hundred yards without somebody stopping him and talking to him about a problem they had. He was such a sensible man. His wife was also a strong influence on my life because the only holidays we got were at Bridlington. She managed a café on the sea front. I stayed there for my summer holidays and dug big holes in the sand and tried to beat the sea back. She was very placid. It was a gentle life. These are the people who have most influenced me in the way I try to deal with problems and life generally.

PR: How well educated were they? It sounds like they valued education?

MA: Now that I think of it none of them had a particularly good education. They were all village school educated and all left school at the normal leaving age of 14. My father who was by far the most intelligent also left school at that age. He was forced to leave because his father was very ill. He had to earn money to keep the family together. His mom used to drink a lot, I never knew her and have only heard the stories. Dad was an only child who had a very hard upbringing. His father insisted he be a chorister. Two or three times on every Sunday he would have to go to church and sing. He had to wear a starched collar and walk through the streets of Hull wearing it. Other boys would make fun of him. It did help to make him a very good musician and eventually he had his own dance band. During the war he ran RAF entertainments. But he never insisted that I did anything musically. I think this was because he had been forced by his father. I am sure that if he had had the chance my father would have gone on to Higher Education. As things turned out he put his energies into work and did extremely well. He worked for Lever Feeds for 20 years and built up his own business. He then moved to the Ministry of Agriculture, and went on to the EEC where he became one of the civil servants who handled grain subsidies and created grain mountains. He made his way because of his drive and his energy and I suppose I have inherited those qualities from him. Although he did not have the education he so obviously merited, he struggled hard to give my brother and I opportunities he felt he didn't have.

PR: What of your primary schools – you went to two kinds. Were they very different?

MA: In the first there was very much a community feel to it. It was very gentle. We would take a trip out into the garden, do some country dancing and come back and colour in a map and do a few numbers, there was no real rigour. The prep school was very different. We were being coached for the entrance exam. There was also a heavy religious influence there. I remember the head mistress suddenly announcing her father had died and we all must pray for this man we didn't know. I remember wondering why. There was a teacher at the prep school, Tim Curtis, who had a great deal of influence on me. He was young and lively. It has always been those sort of teachers that have attracted me. In the grammar school it was the art master, a very extrovert teacher, who appealed to me. He was vibrant and had a great enthusiasm for his subject. I have always felt I wanted to operate in that way, I wanted to communicate to children that I loved my subject.

PR: Which teachers didn't you like?

MA: They tended to be blinkered in their approach and saw nothing other than their subject and had little time for you as a pupil. You got very little chance to give anything back to them. They tended to be autocratic. I remember a French teacher I was terrified of, and because I was terrified of him I hated the subject. I spent my life in his lessons being afraid he was going to ask me something. With teachers like the art master it was a two-way process in which you had the chance to give back a lot. Sometimes he'd shoot you down but you wouldn't mind because you respected him. On the whole I enjoyed most of the people I have worked with. Early on I discovered that what you have got to do when you are working with people is look for the best in them. That's what I try to do.

PR: Can you say something about your Higher Education?

MA: I studied for a Teacher's Certificate at Bede College. It was a male training college. The one big drawback of Pocklington was the male-only thing. Ironically I chose a male-only college. We were next door to a female college and there was a close link, but it probably took me two years at college to get rid of the feeling you could talk to a girl without her believing you were trying to seduce her. It was not just that I had gone to an all-boys grammar school but also since it was 30 miles away from where I lived the social side at home didn't develop effectively. This meant it was hard to develop relationships, particularly with members of the opposite sex. So my first year at Durham was spent very much in sport – I had come out of school as captain of rugby and signed on at college as a rugby player. I then began to realize a lot of my friends actually had female acquaintances and that seemed quite pleasant. But it took me time to work my way into that – I was into my second year before I felt that I could develop a relationship with a girl. The college course we followed was appalling – I had three very good social years and did very little to extend myself academically or prepare myself for teaching other than during the school experiences which were magnificent. I loved to be in school, but much of teaching was a rejigging of the stuff I had been taught myself. We were offered little else. I tried to remember how my own best teachers had done things.

PR: You had made your mind up to be a teacher by the time you left school?

MA: Desperately. But I wanted to be in a classroom. I got very frustrated at college.

PR: Why younger children?

MA: I did History at A-level. I saw it as fairly easy to pass. I had no particular enthusiasm for any one subject, but an enjoyment in people generally and their development. I saw primary as a way of doing that. If I had gone into secondary I would have been heavily committed to a subject and not had the chance to do what I wanted to do. Also, in my teaching practices the primary schools were the places I really enjoyed. I remember going to a secondary in South Shields and it looked and felt like a public toilet. I remember the interview with the head, a nice man, who welcomed me to the school. He said 'Now lad, what have you got to offer us? What can you offer us other than just your teaching while you are here?' I said 'I am into sport, I am a qualified tennis coach.' It was the summer term, and he said 'I think we've got some tennis courts.' He leant out of the window and we looked and there was a tangled mass of barbed wire and nettles growing up it – it was horrendous. The school was the kind of place in which the staff left the staffroom in pairs. It seemed to me that when anybody got into trouble in that school they'd be sent to the head and he'd give them a football and they'd go and play on the field just to get them out of the way. I was given the O-level stream, which had five girls capable of doing English to O-level. I had to teach them précis. I was 19 and they were 15. I looked at them and they were beautiful. I thought there's no way I can work with children of this age and so I opted to be a primary teacher.

PR: Can you describe your teaching career?

MA: In my second year in college I formed a relationship with a girl in her third year. She left to live in London. We wanted to continue the relationship so I agreed to settle for between London and Durham. We stuck a pin in the map and it was Leicestershire. That decision turned out to be another landmark in my life. I got a distinction for practical teaching and had a Class One Certificate of Education. I applied to Leicestershire. At that time we presumed we would get a job – not like today when these poor kids wonder if they will. I only applied to Leicestershire. I came down for a 'pool' interview. Three LEA Officers interviewed me. I had to apologize for not wearing a tie, I'd hurt myself playing rugby the day before and my neck was swollen. The officer interviewing me had a sling on because he'd broken his arm playing rugby. There was an immediate rapport. They didn't interview me, just said 'We've got a recommendation from college, we'd like to appoint you to our teaching pool, what sort of school would you like to work in?' I couldn't believe it. They then said 'We've got a number of possible posts here, we'll describe them to you – this one's got a swimming pool, so if you are a swimmer you can go and teach swimming; this one's on the edge of a council estate – a brand new school with a vibrant head.' This appealed to me. I felt I would have an empathy with the type of child there. 'Right,' they said, 'Catch a bus out to the school and meet the head.'

This was another major landmark. At Battling Brook County Primary I met the head, Roy Illsley. Roy eventually became the senior Primary Adviser for Leicestershire. As soon as I got there I realized it was an exciting place – he was a superb educationalist. He had opened the school two years previously and appointed the staff. They had come from all over because of his reputation – but had moved on. Six of us were coming in on that September, all young teachers. He and his deputy were starting again. It was a fabulous working environment. The deputy, Byron Thomas, was a 'lunatic' but a fabulous teacher with a great classroom. We lived our lives in the school, working through the weekends.

What was great about it was that we were in the centre of what was the roughest council estate in Hinkley – a hosiery town in decline. So we came to a brand new school in a beautiful environment, carpeted and curtained, which was in total contrast to what these children were coming out of. For them, it was a haven. It was next door to the Working Men's Club. Regularly at three o'clock the door would burst open and some woman would come in and say 'Where is the little bastard?' and a child would dive out of the back of the room with its mother in hot pursuit. I remember one horrendous Christmas, my first one there, the parents said they would have a disco in the Working Men's Club to raise money for the school. The disco didn't turn up and so with the teachers sitting there, a fight started and we just quietly left – it was that sort of environment. The great thing was that the children who came from very disadvantaged homes really appreciated what we were doing for them – the parents didn't, the children did. Then local firms started to build, at the side of the school, a private housing estate. Over the 18 months I was there I saw a gradual change take place. The pressures changed from the deprived to those created by the aspiring/pushy parents coming in. In formative terms, that whole experience was fabulous. It didn't matter I was straight from college; it didn't matter I was only young. When I wanted to do something I was listened to. The Authority was incredibly supportive and the in-service we went on was relevant and stimulating.

PR: Was Mason Chief then?

MA: It was based on the Mason plan – he was the first real educationalist I met. Sadly he retired whilst I was there. He had a primary philosophy and this big thing that the true middle school was for 10–14-year-olds. It was based on the idea of taking the primary philosophy into secondary education with primary heads running the schools. Of course secondary colleagues didn't like the thinking and it was very expensive. In the end they had to drop the scheme. It was a great shame because Mason really did want to create a true middle school with a primary base. I was very keen. I enjoyed education so much. I lived it, every single minute of it, but even at that stage, within a year of teaching, I wanted my own school: I wanted to be a head.

PR: I know of someone who decided she wanted to be a head before she became a teacher.

MA: I could not claim that. I did not think of having my own school until I saw what Roy was doing. I liked it and I wanted to do it. I wanted to support and facilitate the work of other teachers as well as run my own classroom. What happened was that during our first 12 months of working together we six young teachers got to know each other very well. So well that I married one. We quickly decided it probably wasn't a good thing to be spending all our time together and one ought to move. It was easier for me because I was doing games and related activities and got to know of another school looking for a PE specialist. As it happened the head of that school was a good friend of Roy so the word went out that if I would like to apply to this other school I'd be welcome there.

I discussed the move with Roy who said, 'As a contrast this is a good move for you. If you want to move on quickly and are interested in management go and look at it. Unlike ours, it is a very traditional school.' It was a very big junior school. I went there, after four terms teaching, on an incentive point for boys' games. The school had a traditional classroom environment, unlike my first school which was open plan. It turned out to be an amazing experience. Its headteacher was the worst I ever worked for. I learnt more about headship from her than I did from anyone else.

Take the case of her version of a staff meeting. We used to have one a term. We would all be there and the door to the staffroom would open. We would have been asked to meet after school but didn't know why. The caretaker would carry a table in and put it at the end of the staffroom and she'd come in and sit behind it, talk at us for 40 minutes and go out again. We had a school hall at one side of which there were steps which went up into the office block and her office. We were supposed to do PE in this area, but if children were heard she would walk out and stand with her arms folded and disappear again – nothing was actually said.

PR: School wasn't for enjoyment?

MA: Certainly not. But the children were pleasant. The school was strong in sport. It had a four form intake and the best football team in the area – I inherited it, maintained it and we won all the sporting events. It was a very different teaching environment to the one I had come from, but I learnt a lot, very quickly, from others. I spent two and a half years there and so was able to evaluate it against the 18 months I had had in my first school. All this made me think about what I would do in a school where I had a strong management influence.

After four years teaching and at 26 I applied for the deputy headship of a brand new open plan primary school in Loughborough and got it. It was situated on the edge of an area of growth and was planned to serve a owner–occupier estate being built. But the bottom fell out of the housing market and the building stopped but not before a school with 240 places had been built and staffed with a head and five teachers. We opened with 69 children. I was appointed by Nancy Kilburn who, like Roy Illsley, has been a major influence in my professional life. She had been a deputy in the County and was destined to be an Adviser in Cheshire before finally coming to Buckinghamshire to be a Senior Primary Adviser. Our school was her first headship, but her husband was head of an open plan primary school similar to the first school that I had worked in. It served a very rough, run down council estate area. He ran a very free school – sixties style.

PR: Informal, progressive ...

MA: Very informal, very progressive – if you talk to John Kilburn he would tell you 'It is our task to motivate children, to set up lots of things to stimulate them, but it is up to them to opt into what they want.' You would find very little class teaching going on. Nancy was less radical than John but what, for me, was glorious was the fact that having interviewed me she felt that, even though I'd only taught for four years, I had the sort of drive and energy she wanted. We worked together to make a success of the school. It was genuinely open plan – a rectangle with a little studio in the middle. A full three years later there were times when it was like a perpetual wet playtime. There were times when I had to stand up and raise my voice to get the rectangle quiet. No easy task with 240 children. Being a big fellow I had a big voice and they got used to me doing that.

Initially Nancy and I decided we had enough money to appoint two Scale 2 teachers and two other teachers because we were projecting a full school. This was before LMS, of course, and the Authority told you how many teachers you could have. So the LEA, not us, were in a mess when the children didn't come in. God alone knows what would have happened under LMS. We advertised the posts and we said to enquirers, 'The building's almost ready, if you are interested in coming here to teach, we are going to have a day when you can come to meet us.' Fifty turned up. Nancy and I talked to them all, and they inspected us and the building. As they left we said, 'If you are still interested, then apply.' We interviewed eight people in the morning for the Scale 2 posts and appointed two, then we asked those two to stay with us and the four of us appointed two more in the afternoon. It was like recreating my first school – we were a team. It was the most glorious teaching experience I have ever had. We team taught. As the school grew we had a three-teacher team working with the older children with very small numbers in the initial stages. I had two years when there were three of us working together – myself, Wal White and Ken Tyler. Ken had just walked back from India. I remember him well – long hair, gold glasses, looked like John Lennon, and a brilliant mathematician. He later went off to do research work with Shell – he was doing a lot of work in the 1970s on calculators and their influence in school. It was a unique teaching experience. I was committed to having my own school by the time I was 30 – that gave me four years. In fact I failed – I was 31. But it was a place to stay. As the community grew, we developed a community centre, raised money – built a swimming pool, did lots for this developing area and a lot of curriculum development work. What encouraged me to leave in the end was that Nancy Kilburn, who I worshipped for giving me such a wonderful opportunity, decided to become an Adviser and left. I found I could not work with her successor. He was a former County Advisory teacher for Science. He saw himself as the man from the LEA called in to put the school to rights. As far as he was concerned it didn't have a good reputation. He believed the children couldn't possibly be learning because of the high degree of informality that existed between teacher and child. Children and staff called each other by first names! In fact it was the most delightful teaching environment I've ever been involved in. He decided he was going to come in and do certain things. It was time to move, and the opportunity came to apply for a post 'back home'. I applied for two headships in Humberside, both new schools.

PR: You've got lots of experience of new schools?

MA: I've opened two now – one as a deputy and one as a headteacher in Humberside. I was interviewed in the morning – didn't get it. I went back in the afternoon, and it was the same damn panel – they had just brought three new governors in – but I was appointed to New Pasture Lane County Primary School in Bridlington. It was an almost identical situation to the place I had been in as a deputy. There was one big difference, the estate was a council estate. I was back with the type of child I thought I understood best. Many single parent families and very much a community school.

PR: What did you see as the role of the head and how did you prepare yourself for it?

MA: At the time many of us, aspiring teachers, mixed on twilight and residential courses. A lot talked about doing the Open University because they wanted to get on and felt it was important to have a degree. They'd gone through training colleges as I had, and were beavering away doing extra qualifications. I was too busy, I was heavily involved in school. My friends would come home and work but on their own degrees. I considered this but came to the decision that I would try and do things another way. I would work hard in school and get as much practical-based knowledge as I could. I pursued that philosophy throughout. I still remain without a degree.

I saw headship as a way of leading a group of people along the right path in terms of the way a school should operate. I saw it as facilitating, enabling and providing the best possible environment for teachers to work in. My views haven't changed much. What has changed from one headship to another is the distance I've moved away from the classroom. As a young head I was determined I would work alongside my teachers and pass on what expertise I had. I would also give people the opportunities to stand back from the classroom to evaluate what they're doing and to evaluate what I'm doing. At New Pasture Lane I was able to do that; I taught every class. This gave the teachers time to do whatever they needed to do.

PR: How did you prepare for headship?

MA: I was an effective deputy. I operated in what I thought was an exemplary manner. I worked incredibly hard, had a good classroom and good relationship with children, and tried to manage things in a way which made sure everybody else could operate effectively. I attended the professional development courses I thought relevant to the curriculum I was working in but was never schooled for headship in formal courses.

PR: Did you have a career plan, plotting your way to headship?

MA: Yes, I felt that the way to get there was by proving myself a good teacher and a good deputy so whoever was writing a reference for me would say this man is good and deserves his own school. I didn't do anything formal whatsoever. We had a deputies' group in which met and discussed management. But it was very informal. Leicestershire operated that way.

Within the County I used to run things. I ran a summer camp for disadvantaged children which would mean managing 30 or 40 teachers and volunteers. In my first term in teaching I ran a residential and took 45 children away for a week. I presumed these were the sort of things that you should do.

PR: Did you feel prepared when you began your first headship? Many of the heads I have talked to say they thought they knew what headship was like from being a deputy, but in fact the two are very different in important ways. Do you share this view?

MA: No, I don't. As a deputy I used to do a lot of work in the community and parents would come and talk to me. I found during my first headship I was doing exactly the same things – the only difference was I didn't have to report that back to anybody. The big difference was in my relationship with the governing body. As a deputy I didn't relate to the governing body, as a head and the head of a new school, I spent lots of time talking to governors about what we were doing. That was the biggest change.

PR: As a deputy you may have important responsibilities but do not 'carry the ultimate can'.

MA: That is true, but it never bothered me. When I took on my first headship, it seemed the natural thing to do. Coming back to your plotting a career question, I would say that although I knew I wanted to be a head I never tried to identify a series of steps designed to get me to a headship. I tried to be the most effective deputy I could be. There was no checklist. I did not spend my time ticking things off.

PR: Can you describe your career as a head?

MA: I was a young man in a brand new school in a brand new community. I was given a teacher by the Authority who I discovered they wanted to shift. She was of great use to me. She had tremendous links in the area and she knew the systems. I could ask 'What is the normal practice?' and she would know. I was impressed with Humberside as an LEA. It was a young Authority, anxious to support with many who wanted to help. There was some professional resentment in the area that a young man from another Authority had taken up a prime headship. It lessened when it emerged that I was a Yorkshireman coming home. There was suspicion from colleagues who saw my approach as non-traditional. I was interviewed in the local press and quoted on 'community education' – a radical concept! When I was appointed, I home-visited in the summer holidays all the parents of children coming to my school. So when I opened the doors in September, it mattered not that I couldn't remember the faces of all the parents, they all thought they knew me. The school got off to a very smooth start. In achieving this I drew on my experience as a deputy involved in opening a new school. There, all six of us, had worked hard together throughout the summer holidays to get ready for September, but when we opened there was a lot of anger and resentment because the parents were very anxious about the fact that this was a new, open plan primary school and they didn't know anybody on the teaching staff. The community were anxious about giving their children over to a group of young teachers with whom they felt no bond. I learnt from that. In my first headship I made it my business to give parents the opportunity to get to know me before their children moved in. There was a degree of trust from the beginning.

PR: What, at that time, was your vision of good primary school education? Has it changed?

MA: It hasn't changed. I firmly believe a good primary school is a place that a child very much wants to come to: a place they see as a haven, sometimes even an escape from the home, comparable to the home. A place which concentrates on their social development. I think that this is more important than anything else. The academic, of course, is also important and basic numeracy and literacy have always been dear to my heart and I want to encourage children in any way possible to develop those skills. These are things I tried to achieve in my first headship. The children came from backgrounds which found it difficult to give them as much support as they wanted and needed. It was a council estate: on it there were homes specifically built for single parent families. Most were young girls who'd had unfortunate experiences early in their lives. Either they'd been married and it had gone wrong or they'd never had a marriage. Many of the children hadn't got a father figure about, or if they had he flitted in and flitted out again.

I felt as a man I could provide the sort of role model that many of those children needed and we worked very hard to create a bond of trust between home and school. I did a lot of counselling and went on courses to learn how to counsel adults. I spent a lot of time on the estate counselling the parents. I suppose years ago people used to go to the vicar but now they tend to come into school and talk to their teacher or headteacher because he or she is the closest they can get to someone they can trust. It was an exciting time because we were coming into the LMS era, just beginning to understand more about the curriculum and its development and then all of a sudden along came the National Curriculum. That probably was the biggest change that hit me as a head. It was the first time I began to feel overloaded. There was so much to take on board.

PR: How successful were you in achieving the things you wanted to do? Why did you move?

MA: I wanted to create a school which offered true primary education. I also wanted a nursery. As I left the nursery building started. It was the right time to leave. Whilst I was there we went through a number of phases and at the end of each I would think it was time to move on. I had no sooner thought this when something exciting would come up.

PR: How long did this go on for?

MA: Ten years in which I became fully involved in the area as well as within my school. As a very young headteacher I played a full part in the area and a leading part professionally with colleagues. I became President of the National Association for Primary Education for Humberside and so ran conferences, got colleagues together to discuss primary education, encouraged visits and links between schools and all sorts of other things. I ran district Arts Festivals and I became a JP. I moved from being the young headteacher to becoming one of the bastions of local society.

PR: From young Turk to establishment figure?

MA: I'm afraid so. At the time I was living five miles from the school in a small rural community where of course the same thing was happening. I was Vice Chairman of the Parish Council and Secretary of the local Playing Field Association. Having built up this huge plethora of responsible posts I could well have stayed – it was tempting, I was very comfortable. I was beginning to feel overloaded but I could have coped with that.

However, then I got a secondment to the regional Headship Unit at Wooley Hall. The Unit was funded by a number of the Yorkshire Metropolitan Authorities, I think there were 15 of them. Various Authorities each term would send two heads to Wooley for half a term. I went there to study nursery education because that's what we were going to develop next. For the first time I took time out and started thinking and looking towards the future. This made me realize I ought to move from New Pasture Lane. It appeared to survive very well without me when my deputy took over. At the same time my marriage broke up. My wife was a teacher in the same town. If I had stayed we would have been meeting all the time. I contacted the Director of Education and said, 'Look, my marriage is in a mess, I need time to sort it out, I want to leave.' I did the secondment and they released me, they didn't even make me work my notice which was good of them. They gave me leave without pay and I left without any job to go to. That was in Easter 1989. At that point I had all sorts of anxieties about the National Curriculum. I believed what the Government was trying to do was sensible, but the way it was being done was appalling.

PR: Can we talk about the reforms more generally? What did you feel about them? You made use of one of their controversial aspects by going for grant-maintained status.

MA: I'd always believed there should be a national lead in terms of what we were trying to deliver in the curriculum, but never felt it should come about as it did. The government produced an incredible overload. It's always the same, isn't it, to leave these things in the hands of experts. You may have been one of them?

PR: I have criticized the process by which the National Curriculum was produced.

MA: During my years as a head and deputy head in new schools I had worked hard trying to formulate a reasonable curriculum. That's what I and my colleagues were doing all the time in our spare moments. At first, I was relieved. I thought to myself, they're going to give me a structure to work to and it's going to make my job much easier. I just couldn't believe what happened, I thought there's no way I can take all this on board.

PR: And all the assessment as well?

MA: Absolutely. And so I asked myself if I really wanted to be part of this. I had done headship. Did I really want to stay in teaching? It was linked also with the break up of my marriage. We were very keen, very involved in teaching and made a decision we weren't going to have children. We were going to work with other people's children. We had gone through the trauma of people thinking that we couldn't have children, and how sad this was. But as time passed we both grew apart – it was as simple as that. I began to ask myself was it time to make a break, to do something else. So I left the community I lived in and went to live with my parents for a term. They were great. They suggested I come back and think things through. I started looking at one or two other areas I might work in. I asked myself what other skills I had and discovered I was one of many thousands who were doing the same thing. Some interesting jobs came up like working for the Prince's Trust. I applied for this and 30 other posts. I didn't get one interview.

One of the joys of going back home was that I found I was able to enjoy the company of my father. He had stopped working and we did a lot of talking. My parents didn't put any pressure on me at all. But dad did say 'Why don't you go and do some supply teaching while you decide what to do?' So I did some work in local North Riding Schools. I was accepted once the heads understood that I hadn't just resigned because I'd abused some child or something like that. I am not sure they were all that happy about the fact that I had left because I had become rather disenchanted. But once I started working in their schools and they found I could teach I found myself solidly employed as a supply teacher. In doing so, I rediscovered my enthusiasm ...

PR: Within the classroom ...

MA: I loved it, I absolutely loved it. So I decided I must go back into schools. But could I go back in as class teacher? No, I had to go back in as a head. Being aware of the fact that there was a dearth of applicants in the south I thought I'd make an open application down here. My contact was Nancy Kilburn, who'd given me my first deputy headship. She had moved to Buckinghamshire as an Adviser. I rang her up and said 'What are things like down there? Have you got any schools you can't get heads for?' She said 'Yes, we've got three or four at the moment.' So I said 'Do you need somebody to do a head's job for a term?' She said 'Yes, make an application to the Authority.' That was the extent of her help – she didn't get involved in any interviewing. I came down and had an interview with the Area Education Manager here who said 'I've got a school I could put you into for a term if you'd like to do it?' So I went as head of a small first school while the deputy who'd got the headship completed their previous contract. It was the same size as the school I'd had before, it was a first school, they were totally disen-chanted as a staff because they were going through National Curriculum and hadn't had a permanent head for two years. I had a magnificent term with them and during that term the headship at Hamilton became avail-able. I applied and was successful.

PR: How long have you been at Hamilton?

MA: Since Easter 1990. Hamilton is the oldest primary in the area. It was founded in 1873 as an original board school. I took it over from a lady who had been here for 39 years and headteacher for the last 16. She started here as a teacher, became the deputy and then the head. It was *her* school. Eileen Dyer was a wonderful lady, and had built the school a tremendous reputation. They were wetting themselves about somebody else coming in and taking over. They had advertised the post in the previous September and had not appointed. It was then re-advertised in the January which is when I saw it. I knew nothing about Buckinghamshire just as I had known nothing about Leicestershire. I'd never even heard of Buckinghamshire because they didn't have a cricket team! I certainly didn't realize the county was selective and once I discovered it I was really interested. This was an aspect of primary education I had not looked at and so I was really fired up when I came. My philosophy has been changed by what I've experienced here and what I've seen this school achieve with children. When I assess what we are doing here now compared to what I did in that school where I thought I was the 'bees' knees' in Leicestershire in the 1970s, it makes me shudder.

PR: Can you describe the difference?

MA: I still think that the social development of children is of paramount importance. I have not changed on that. But the quality and rigour of what we offer now here in the curriculum compared to what I was offering to chil-dren in the 1970s in Leicestershire is of a different order. These children here receive a true entitlement. I don't think I was being altogether fair to the children that I worked with in my early years in teaching.

PR: Does that mean that you are clear about what you expect them to learn and the standards at which they should learn?

MA: I'm not clear about what they should learn. But I am clearer in so far as I know they need to be directed more than I ever used to do. We used to set up opportunities for children to learn, but at Hamilton there is much more direction and we are much more concerned with teaching skills. For example, the standard of music we have here is unparalleled in any primary school that I've been in, and it's all been achieved through teaching. The standard of singing, for example, is far beyond anything that I used to achieve with children when we just used to encourage them to enjoy making a noise – Hamilton's children are taught to sing and will have a quality of singing that will stay with them for the rest of their lives. I could say the same for almost every subject.

PR: In the past you believed it was enough to make a range of opportunities available but leave it to the child to determine what use they made of this. Now you feel you and your staff should make sure that children had opportunities and made use of them?

MA: Yes. And to some extent, even if they squawked and squealed a bit. Over the last four years of working here I have come to see the benefits of this to the child and have realized that the child suffers no great trauma because of it.

PR: How do you know about the quality of teaching and learning taking place in Hamilton?

MA: We monitor it, the three of us – myself and the two deputies. I think I had better explain the structure of the school. I've got two deputies because the school is on split sites. The deputies need to be able to manage and administer their buildings because there will be times of the day when I'm not there. For example, I haven't been to the other site all day today so my deputy has to take responsibility. To do so they need to have time and so they each have two days a week non-contact time to manage and administer their sites. Each site has a senior teacher and one other teacher who are on the management team. So our management team has seven members drawn from a staff of 36 teachers altogether.

The head and deputies are responsible for monitoring quality. We started four years ago with an appraisal system and have now moved on. This was quite a challenge because when I came there were not even job descriptions. We've had to move the staff a long way. We used the appraisal process to get the staff used to classroom observation, and a year and a half ago we started monitoring the quality of teaching and learning. The three of us go into classrooms and sit at the back and do an OFSTED. We devised our own observation schedule. We sit there, make notes and we interview that teacher at the end of the day and discuss the lesson we have seen.

In addition we have a regime of testing throughout the school. By analysing our test results we can monitor the development of children. The SATs are a part of this, but we also use NFER testing in years 4, 5 and 6. We use a base line test on the reception class when they come. Finally, we have the 12-plus, a selective test at the end. Our teaching has to be geared to preparing children for what they are going to go through, or it would be traumatic for them. I am concerned at how this Authority places children in its grammar schools and would love to see more dialogue with teachers in which our professional opinion is sought. There are children who go to grammar schools who we know will not perform, others who should go who do not because at the time of the test they are still developing. I am anxious about sections of my Asian community. Children with English as a second language who have the ability to benefit from a grammar place can suffer.

PR: What do you feel about the publication of results?

MA: I've been a strong advocate of giving parents as much information as reasonably possible, but I think people need to be made very aware that children start from very different base points. They need to understand the idea of value added if they are to make soundly based judgements. Why deny them information? But league tables as they are now constructed makes anybody who understands anything about education laugh.

PR: When did the school go GM and who took the lead on this?

MA: On 1 April 1993. It was headteacher driven. In my view it would be very unwise for a governing body to take a school into GM status without the head being convinced it's the right thing to do. I think it is right for us but have anxieties about it philosophically. There are schools, for example in inner city areas, which LEAs could support in the old days with extra resources, extra advisory time, and even, in pre LMS times, extra staffing. With LMS things are very different. On the one hand it can seem open and fair to everyone but it can disadvantage schools who need real and extra support. It is much harder for such schools to get this kind of support now.

In making a decision on GM I had to look at this school and its needs. Without doubt it was right for us. Without GM and capital work on our Victorian building the school would have altered dramatically. The Authority would never have supported the governors in this because it harboured a grudge going back 20 years. Perhaps I need to say something more about this. Hamilton has two sites – the original site was built in 1873. In the 1970s the LEA decided it had come to the end of its working life and planned to replace it. However, one of my predecessors decided otherwise. As soon as the new building was handed over he admitted lots of children and succeeded in filling both buildings. Relationships with the Education Authority since the mid-1970s have been fairly rocky. The only thing the Authority could do was to run down the Victorian building so the governors would eventually be forced to shut it. LMS, they saw as a godsend. It was a way of handing responsibility to the governors, who would then have to shut the building down because they could not maintain it.

If one of the school sites had closed we would have faced a significant problem. Many of the children who come to us from out of the catchment area are from families who are particularly supportive of education and look for the best for their children. To put this in context, you must understand Buckinghamshire. We work in a selective Education Authority with children at the end of Year 7 being deemed suitable for grammar school or not. So parents anxious to get the best for their child tend to regard schools according to their rate of success in 'passing' pupils into grammar schools. If we'd dropped from 720 to 360 pupils we could only take our catchment area children. This is typical inner town where a lot of the housing is run down. Much of the Asian populace in High Wycombe lives within our catchment area. They mostly come from two rural areas of Pakistan where there was little formal education. The parents and grandparents of our pupils love them dearly, but can give very little educational support. When we write home and translate our letters into Urdu we find that most find this harder to read than English. So if we had halved in size and became a catchment area only school we would find something like 70–75 per cent of our pupils would come from ethnic minorities. We would almost certainly lose out of catchment area families who can come in now and redress the academic balance, and, in doing so, raise standards in a way that benefits catchment area children.

It seemed vital we maintained the Victorian building. The governing body visited the Development Section in County Hall and argued the case, but unsuccessfully. The Victorian building must go. So the governors decided there was no alternative but to become a grant-maintained school, not least because this would allow a bid for capital funding to restore the Victorian building. In 1994 we received half a million pounds and the future of the school is now assured. We were forced to become grant maintained.

Buckinghamshire seemed an Authority keen on simple solutions. I couldn't understand an LEA which did not appear to have a philosophy. Take selection, it existed in some parts of the Authority but not in others. When I met its advisers, it seemed to me there was nobody with real fire, there was nobody leading, there was nobody I could describe as visionary. I had been used to advisers like that but they did not seem to be in Buckinghamshire. I made telephone calls, I rang County Hall and asked for support but never got it. I had no empathy with the Authority so when it became obvious that the only way really to guarantee the future of the school was to seek capital works, and the only way to do that was for us to go GM and make our own bid, I saw no alternative. I discussed it with the governors and said 'I've looked at it. Financially this is the only way forward.' We met the parents and talked to them about it. I said to the parents 'I'm not going to promise you anything dramatic other than maintaining the school's level of resources, but if we don't become a grant-maintained school we will soon have to start cutting things you take for granted.'

PR: What was the campaign like, and how did the Local Authority respond?

MA: It came as no surprise to the LEA that Hamilton was going grant maintained – it has always been seen as a privileged school in the town. It was the school that took the good kids who didn't go independent. As far as the LEA was concerned we weren't very keen on being a Local Authority School anyway. The Local Area Manager came to the open meeting and said 'We have to sit on the fence in these things.' The Authority had to be seen to be neutral because the County Council was Conservative controlled. We had the normal parent meeting with about a hundred present, not many when you think we have 550 families. Most who came were anti or anxious: it was a good meeting. We didn't really have a problem. It was an 80 per cent vote for 'yes' on a 70 per cent turn-out.

The governors trusted me and the parents trusted the governors. The staff were split professionally. They were asked two questions: 'Do you believe in grant-maintained status?'; 'Do you believe in grant-maintained status for Hamilton School?' They were 100 per cent on the second one, so there was no problem at all from that point of view. But our relationship with the Authority since then has been appalling.

PR: Has it been successful?

MA: Incredibly successful from our point of view. We got the capital bid. We have been able to make decisions in the interests of our children immediately instead of having to wait for the powers-that-be elsewhere to make them. Fortunately, three other primary schools in the town have also gone GM. There are now seven in the county. People sometimes say that GM schools are isolated. but that hasn't been a problem here. The LEA tried to do that to us by insisting that if we wanted to maintain liaison with other schools we would have to buy into something they call a core package. That would have cost us about £15,000 per year really for services we didn't want – back up services from the Local Education Office. So sadly we are not involved with our Local Authority Schools.

PR: What are your relations with your governors and how has that changed since GM?

MA: It's virtually the same governing body. Two have retired, one for business reasons and one has moved away. I don't think my relationship with the governors has altered. My appraisal focused on this theme, I hope it is going to be positive, but don't know yet. The biggest change has been the amount of time and energy I now have to put into working with the governors. We meet weekly in some form. The Finance, Building and Curriculum Committees, each meet on an evening once a month through the year. The full governing body meets twice a term and we have business meetings and development meetings. A week does not go by that we do not meet in some form. My secretary has become Clerk of the Governing Body. She has to be at these meetings. She takes the minutes and then we report back to the governors. This afternoon we are to be audited. This required getting out the end of year figures for a finance meeting next week. I sometimes feel frustrated at the time I spend on this. Mostly I am reporting on things I've already done. But much more often I appreciate the opportunities to talk things through and to plan with them. They're a vibrant group of people.

PR: Do they give you much discretion? Do they see you as their Chief Executive?

MA: On staffing I have almost total discretion. The governors only want to be involved at deputy head level. I think they see me as their Chief Executive. I involve other staff. At the Curriculum Committee I bring my curriculum people with me. As a young head I knew everything or pretended to. I would answer any and all questions. I don't pretend now. If you wanted to talk about curriculum development, I would have my deputy for the curriculum with me. If you wanted to talk about staff development and appraisal I would have my other deputy with me. That's how I work with the governors. They know I am not the fountain-head of all knowledge but that I am in control. If I don't know the answer to a question I have somebody who does in the school. They appreciate my skills as a manager, that's where my strengths are. The role of a head of a big school like this is to train people for their future development. My deputies are going to be heads. They are given every opportunity, I have learnt to step back. They work hard for me and enjoy their roles. They know I am here, and share everything with me. They are willing to make decisions; if they are anxious, they come to me before they do.

PR: Can you describe your chairman of governors?

MA: Dr John Preece was Senior Consultant at the local hospital. He led them into Trust status. He is Leader of the local Conservatives at County Council level. He is a very, very busy man. He has a great affinity with this school. His grandchildren, he hopes, will come here: he believes it is the best school in the town. He trusts me and I respect his judgement but I don't abuse it. If I think something is of significant importance, we discuss it. We have briefing meetings before committee meetings and before governing body meetings and I take him through the agendas. He then chairs them and he is very effective. He comes to the school on a regular basis. Usually at the meetings and prior to the meetings. He is very, very supportive.

PR: And your responsible officer?

MA: We've changed since the new Rainbow Pack. I was the responsible officer. That is no longer possible. None of the governors was willing to take it on. They maintain that it is a very onerous role and that you need to have a degree of expertise to do it properly, so we've appointed a chartered accountant to that role. We are just finishing an audit with Deloitte Touche who have been in for a week. The responsible officer then takes over at a finance meeting on Wednesday night and will be paid by the hour.

PR: How would you describe your managerial style as a head? Has that changed?

MA: I used, very much, to manage by example. I was on the shop floor and leading. I've always believed I needed to facilitate and enable people, but it's much more than that now. I get my satisfaction out of seeing others function effectively. I get great pleasure out of watching teachers get delight out of their children whereas before I liked getting that delight out of children myself. I haven't got a problem with that at all. I am sure you talk to lots of heads who bemoan moving away from the classroom. I haven't got a problem with that. I've had glorious times with children. They still see me as the giant and so I can still do assemblies with them and have fun with them but on the whole I am divorced from them. Now I know that they are getting an effective education because of the backing I am giving my staff. My role as I see it is as a facilitator and an enabler.

PR: I was reading some research recently which suggested long serving heads tend to become less flexible and more autocratic as time passes? Do you agree? Also, do you still enjoy headship?

MA: I don't think that has happened to me. I've tried to develop a system here which can work without me in all sorts of ways. My two deputies are working almost as headteachers and I delight in seeing what they are doing. Also I do still enormously enjoy headship. I'm at work at 7.30 am and leave when we are finished. I've a secretary who is equally committed so if we go on until six or seven o'clock it doesn't matter. I have found it increasingly hard to work at night. I used to be able to work late but I am not as good at that as I was. I can certainly work right through the day.

PR: You work a 60-plus hour week?

MA: Yes, and I will be in school Saturday and Sunday as well – probably only for a couple of hours. I am a clear-desk person. I go into some rooms and am horrified by the state of people's desks. I like to know that my desk is clear when I start my day.

PR: Finally, what's next?

MA: When I came here I told the governors I'd give them ten years, because I saw it as such a big job. Last year I started to think about what I would do when I become 55, I'm 48 now. I thought I probably ought to move on and let somebody else have a go at this job. But there is so much to do still – take the buildings, we've still got outdoor toilets. Curriculum wise, it's really exciting. We are beginning to get to where we want to be. We've cracked it in terms of schemes of work, and we're prepared for OFSTED when they hit us. I haven't got any problems about any of that. So it's really a question of whether the place will deserve somebody else and a change.

I then thought about what, at 55, I might want to do. I would still want to be involved with schools, perhaps working with prospective heads. What credibility would I have for this? Well I'm an experienced headteacher. But if I want to talk to people about managing schools, to be involved in training people for headships or deputyships, I'm going to need an academic qualification. I must be the only person in this place who still only has a Teaching Certificate – I don't think many realize this but it's never bothered me. I looked at an MBA last year and rang up an organization offering one. The professor was delighted and said 'It would be great to have you.' I said 'Aren't you talking about people who have got degrees and things?' 'No problem,' he said 'I need somebody like you to complement those doing Higher Education, I'll take you.' He sent me the reading list, and then the books hit me. I sat there looking at them, and then at the work I knew I had to do for school and I thought there's no way I can do this. I can't do it yet. I know I ought to do it and sometime over the next five years I will take something like an MBA. Then, when I am 55, I will say 'Right, thank you, I have got 30-odd years in, I've got a reasonable pension, a nice home, things are OK.' I'll go into some form of management training, if anybody wants me. If they don't I'll become a gardener. Can you think of a better second occupation for an educator?

CHAPTER 3

From Tigger to Eeyore: a headteacher's life

SUE BEESON WITH PETER RIBBINS

Sue Beeson is head of Greenholm Primary School in Birmingham. This is her second headship in the city. She grew up in Toronto and Durban before completing her education in the UK. Over the last 30 years she has been a full-time mother of two girls and has worked as a playgroup organizer, in two infant schools, and as head of infants in a primary school. Greenholm has gained awards from the National Primary Centre, the Business Partnership, and the Investors in People accreditation. She is a member of the DFEE Advisory Group for National Literacy Centres and Birmingham headteacher representative on the Basic Skills Agency advisory panel for the BSA Quality Mark. Currently, she is studying for a Master's degree in school improvement.

PR: Can you tell me something about your personal background and the people and experiences which have made you who you are?

SB: I had a rather atypical life as a young person. I went to three primary schools in Canada before I was ten. My parents are of a nomadic type. Then we moved to Durban in South Africa and I completed my primary education there and went to secondary school.

In terms of the personal influences I suppose I'm fortunate in having a very eccentric family! My grandparents on my paternal side were both musicians: my grandfather was a commercial artist, my grandmother was a music teacher. I spent a lot of my formative years visiting her and listening to music being taught in a very creative and unorthodox way. Her pupils were prize winners and over the generations she taught many children of former pupils. Although officially retired twice she taught until she was nearly 90. She had tremendous drive and energy, but was generally uninterested in her home, and, from my father's account, in her family! My uncle was a concert pianist. My father was an extremely talented pianist although he went into industry. My mother had been very shy and my father did a lot to build her confidence. They decided their children would not be shy, although we both showed early signs of this. They instituted a system where everyone in the family had to give an after dinner speech on Sundays. At the time I was three and my brother seven. We were encouraged to write our speeches down and read them out. They could be on anything that interested us. This gave us a sense of being valued and of our views being important. My parents also made sure we were included in 'adult' activities such as eating in restaurants – and we were expected to behave!

My parents were very significant in forming my view of management and how you deal with people in general. Moving around the world made us very close as a family and probably my peer group had less effect on me than they might have had we stayed in one place. I never had a peer group for very long. The longest I had in one school and in one house prior to coming to England was five years.

South Africa was a very good formative experience. There was no television and we learned a lot about entertaining ourselves. I became an avid reader and did a lot of painting. I was still shy and hated performing in public, but because the family was musical (I was the least so of the lot and usually ended up playing the tambourine), I was encouraged to perform with a family group. We played some awful country and western music! At that time all this was quite common, people entertained themselves in groups in local village halls and so on. I hated it but was made to do it. I found that a very useful skill. I still don't like getting up in front of people and performing, but I can do it and am improving, especially when talking about things I really believe in. I learned early on that there are tricks of the trade. People think I'm confident but I'm not. It's artificial, from my very early years. In my family there was always a lot of laughter, we found ways of making jokes about even quite serious things and of laughing at ourselves. My parents encouraged me to sit down and work out what was stopping me doing what I wanted to do and to find out how to do it. They were never conservative in their outlook. They would try new challenges and accept failure when things do not work. For example, I was born on a chicken farm which went bust after a couple of years. They just picked themselves up and started again. That was my model, if you want to do it, try it. If it doesn't work, learn from it and move on.

PR: It sounds like a happy childhood. Do you remember any disappointments?

SB: Not being given a horse! But I do remember feeling the most inadequate member of the family, everybody else was so talented. My uncle was very talented, as were my grandparents and my father. He ended up as managing director of a multinational company. There were high expectations. My mother was a talented mother, and did a lot of charity work. She was good at everything: making clothes, cooking. The perfect mother. My brother was much more outgoing than I, much more talented in drama and music. He has been very successful in the market research field. He was nearly five years older so I had great respect for him. We used to fight like cat and dog but I looked up to him. I always felt an also ran, the one who had not quite made it. I am still driven by the desire to be as good as the rest of them.

PR: What were your family's key values?

SB: Tolerance of others. Canadians tend to be very tolerant. People have gone out there to make a fresh start. My grandparents came from Birmingham. There was a feeling that you went out there and made a fresh start. That was an underpinning value through the whole of my upbringing. It did not matter who you were or what you had or had been, it was what you did that mattered. There was a tremendous sense of democracy on my father's part in the working environment. This didn't make him friends, in South Africa especially. He was a pioneer for his time. We moved to South Africa in 1957. He did a lot to try to establish training schemes for black workers. He made a point of doing what he had done on the shop floor in Canada: to go round and talk to the people doing the job. This was unheard of, you didn't talk to these people who were, after all, African workers. He gave us a sense of the equality of all people, which I hope I've brought into my adult life and to the decisions that I make. I've an American Indian saying hanging on my wall: 'Let me not judge another man until I've walked for three moons in his moccasins', and I try to apply that. I doubt if any of us can really judge what someone else is doing, we are not standing where they're standing, we haven't come from where they come, we don't know why they're doing those things.

PR: How did they regard education?

SB: A high priority. They were always very involved in the schools, particularly in Canada where there's a tradition of parental involvement and PTAs. They were not quite as involved in South Africa. Because of the distance we had to travel, the school was not as much a part of the local community. Also my brother and I were in those teenage years in which we did not encourage parental involvement much! When we came here, they were quite active in trying to get a PTA started at my grammar school. I think they were regarded with some suspicion by the people who worked there!

PR: You haven't said much about your schools.

SB: They are probably not as important to me as they might have been if I'd stayed in one place. My overriding memory is of continually struggling to make friendships with people who wanted to know you because you were the new girl, then wanted to revert to their original groups. You were the extra body. I never found work particularly difficult although I had to work much harder to succeed than my brother. I was a good B stream person. Once defending my brother against false accusations I slapped somebody and got into trouble. I was terrified of getting into trouble. I was never punished at home for getting into trouble, although I think if I'd gone home and said 'the teacher told me off' I would have got a second telling off. My parents' attitude always seemed to be 'we assume that you will do your best', that was a tremendous spur. It made it impossible for me to do anything other than my best.

PR: Did your teachers tend to assume that?

SB: I suspect they did. My report always said 'Susan always does her best'. I don't think they often told me I did my best. I was just one of the kids that stayed out of trouble. I tried very hard to please everybody, which probably shows some deep down insecurity in me!

PR: Do you remember the influence of any teacher from your school days?

SB: I remember my year one teacher as a very sympathetic person, very nice and kind. She involved her pupils in everything – we all got invited to a party at her house because she was getting married. I remember some of my South African teachers for their cruelty almost, two in particular were vicious – they would go round slapping everybody hard on the back and would force people to stand up. There was a boy with a terrible stutter. He was forced to stand up and read in class like everybody else. There was no sympathy. I remember being upset by that. I was quite frightened in a lot of my secondary schooling in South Africa. I remember a very kind English teacher in secondary school here who inspired me to read more English, to become more involved, and to study English when I went to college. I remember being told by another I was wasting my time doing art!

I found the school, a grammar school, rather repressive having grown up in two countries with co-educational comprehensive schooling. I was there for two years, and couldn't wait to get out. I went to the local art school against the advice of my teachers. I did a pre-diploma course in art and design. Originally I wanted to lecture in art, once I had got over wanting to be a vet! But the university entrance at that time required you to do an arts degree and to do that you had to have a second foreign language. I had learned Afrikaans for five years but had become so rusty that even if I had found somebody to teach me, I probably wouldn't have passed the exam. So I decided I wouldn't go down the university route after all, I would go to teacher training college.

PR: Do you remember any of your headteachers over that period?

SB: I remember my brother's head because he went to high school while I was still at primary school in Toronto. He was a very imposing man with a bald head. I don't remember my headteacher at my primary school or the head at the school in South Africa. I was only summoned to his office once and that was to tell me that my brother had been taken ill and I was going home early. The heads didn't seem to play much of a part in the school as far as I was concerned.

PR: They didn't leave much mark on you?

SB: No. But I remember my head at the grammar school. She was a strict and frightening lady, very small. I remember the head of my training college, also a strict, frightening and small lady. I remember the things she said you couldn't do. I couldn't see anything positive as a role model in them.

College was an interesting experience in itself. I wanted to get married part way through the course and this was almost unheard of. I was summoned to the head's office because I had to have her permission to get married! I had a stern lecture about how I was throwing away my career; if I got married I would probably fail the course. There was still a notion of it being a waste of public money if you got married and threw your life away on things like husbands and children. I went ahead anyway and decided I would prove her wrong, and I suppose in my last year I really set about that. I'd been doing quite well and had probably been averaging B-plus and A-minus and so on. In the end I came out with three distinctions and a credit on the teaching practice. The only reason I didn't get a distinction on teaching practice was that the tutors hadn't come out often enough to visit me. The head did write a note on the bottom of the pass list saying something about 'no other student has ever excelled these grades'. I did that not consciously to spite her but to prove I could do what I had been told I could not do.

Then I left college and went to the school where I had done my final teaching practice, in a not terribly salubrious area of Birmingham. At that time they were eager to have anyone who would teach in those schools, I was welcomed with open arms.

PR: Why did you become a teacher?

SB: I sort of went into it. I went through the vet thing and was told women did not become farm vets. I realized I would never stick a seven-year course. If I knew about myself what I know now, I would have gone down the fine art route. I had the chance to go to the Slade but lost my nerve. That was a parental influence. Moving around the world meant my mother tended to be anxious about my safety and well being. That communicated itself to me in a feeling it wasn't a safe thing to go off to London with all these strange hippie people. I was too easily dissuaded and should have given it a bash. Teaching was a 'safe' option, something that girls did anyway. It fitted in with a family, it wasn't too terrifying, until I did my teaching practice anyway!

PR: Why primary education – did you consider secondary?

SB: I was rather scared of older kids. I have never had an awful lot to do with children of my own age, I tended to want to be with my brother's peer group. I had one or two friends of my own age but didn't have any experience of younger children. I had done some work with cubs and brownies and felt reasonably comfortable with them. Beyond that it was not a conscious decision not to work with older children, it was just that maybe younger ones seemed less frightening.

PR: What was your first experience like as a teacher?

SB: I can't remember much except sitting in my own classroom for the very first time taking the register and the enormity of it hitting me. All of a sudden all the cushions that had been there were gone. No tutor was going to come in and see how you were getting on. I don't know if in those days advisers or anybody bothered coming in. It seemed as if you were on your own with little equipment and ammunition to deal with the things that would arise. I found myself dealing with my first real confrontations with pupils, children who would refuse to do something or have a tantrum. There was a very steep learning curve and no structure in place or any kind of support or mentoring. There were three newly qualified teachers (NQTs) and I suppose we became a self-contained unit.

PR No induction?

SB: It was just here is your register, here is your classroom. You can have your 24 cards for your alphabet. When I asked the head which two letters we should leave out she wasn't helpful! We found locked stockrooms, never enough equipment, an egg box mentality, making something out of nothing. There was a lot of camaraderie between us three NQTs. The person who showed us the greatest friendship was the deputy head who was very kind. She had always been at that school and was nearing retirement. The class-room assistant and secretary were also very friendly, I've always had a soft spot for classroom assistants and secretaries and perhaps that's why! They would give you lots of advice in an informal way.

PR: How many schools did you work in before your first headship?

SB: The first one was an infant school in Perry Common. The head did a lot of feeding of fish and watering of plants. She didn't visit classrooms very often. She used to pop into mine on a Thursday. She went to have her hair done and popped in on her way out because it was by the front door. That stopped when one of my children accidentally kicked over a bucket of paint on her pink skirt and she never came in again! Some suggest I set it up on purpose but I hadn't really!

I left after two years to have my first child and had seven years out. That is another influence of my mother I suppose. There was a very strong feeling in our family that you couldn't be a mother and work. I had many arguments with my mother before my first baby about whether I should have children because I was enjoying my career. There were some discus-sions about my perception of her role as a full-time mother. I said some unkind things which I know hurt her to this day because she told me. It wasn't such an option to go back in those days, people did tend to leave. When my youngest went to school I went back to teaching. I'd kept in touch with education – I'd set up a play group with a friend. I'd done a term of teaching, the teacher where my daughter was at nursery had a heart attack and they were desperate. I thoroughly enjoyed that. Then I offered to help at my daughter's school, at this time parents in schools were unheard of. The head rang up the office to see if it was all right. Because I was a quali-fied teacher. I was allowed in. Then she asked if I would do a term of supply teaching just before my youngest started school. I agreed and then applied for a permanent position at the school. I stayed seven years, mainly because that was where my children were. It was big enough for me not to have either of them in my class. They called me 'Mrs Beeson' when they saw me. It worked well because I could go in early and take them with me and they would play in the classroom while I got things ready. They would then come back to me at 3.30 pm.

PR: Did that work for them too?

SB: They claim so. There was no real conflict. My eldest never liked me leaving her. She cried each morning of the first three years of her infant schooling. I felt awful. She was a teacher's daughter and didn't want to leave me! She did that once or twice when I was working there. Perhaps surprisingly, she's probably more independent than the younger one; now she goes off all over the place on her own. It seemed to work quite well. There weren't the number of after-school meetings there are now, it was very much 'do your own thing in your own classroom'. I would work with them before and after school until about 5.30 and there were staff meetings once a fortnight. I was there for seven years.

PR: Did you take on any responsibility posts?

SB: I feel ready for new challenges easily. I began as resources co-ordinator, then became co-ordinator for science and environmental studies. I did a lot of other bits and pieces like music, and so on. I began to feel I'd outgrown what I was doing. The girls were older and the eldest had started at secondary school. I learned to drive – a very big spur to change because I'd been working at a school where I could walk to and from home. I decided at 36 that enough was enough, I couldn't rely on other people for the rest of my life so I learnt. I took great pride in the fact that I took my test in a Land Rover! I had learned to drive in a Fiesta but two weeks before the test the teacher told me I could not have it because he had double booked it. I took great satisfaction again in doing what people said I couldn't do. I guess if somebody throws me a gauntlet I tend to pick it up.

PR: What happened then?

SB: At the school we were talking about I had worked under two heads. That provided a bit of enthusiasm and change. The second head tried to persuade me to go for promotion a couple of times but I said I was happy where I was. But I began to feel she was making it difficult for me to do the things I wanted to do, and heard the odd comment that 'well you haven't got the rank and authority to do that'. On one such occasions I decided enough was enough, I'd go and get some rank and authority! I applied to another school for a Head of Infants where the head was someone I'd been to college with, and I knew we shared quite a lot in common. I went and did that for three years. It was enjoyable, a nice team of people to work with. I began to develop my notions of leadership. I began to have people working with me for whom I had some responsibility. I was in a position to make some decisions about how things would go. The head was great because in his view the Head of Infants was almost like a second deputy who made decisions for that department and as long as he was kept informed he was happy. That allowed me to develop many of my own philosophies. Interestingly, now I feel it important not to have two separate departments in a primary school. I am trying to establish a seamless transition from Key Stage One to Key Stage Two in my school.

At this time I had no interest in becoming a head, but one morning I walked into my class, I can't say why, I knew I wasn't happy. I had been perfectly satisfied when I set off for work that morning. I walked into the class and went through the routine of putting the chairs down, and I thought 'I don't want to do this for the rest of my life'. Maybe it was mid-life crisis. I was quite sure I couldn't be a deputy or a head, they were different kinds of people – they did all these wonderful things which I couldn't aspire to. I talked to the deputy at the school and she said 'it's not as impossible as you think it is, why don't you go for it?' Within a fortnight the deputy head-ship came up at a nearby infant school. I went and looked and thought 'I'll put in an application' and I got the job, much to my amazement! I have never not got a job that I have really gone for. It makes it hard to empathize with those who don't get them first time round.

That experience I found very frustrating. The head was a different style of leader than the one I worked for before. She was much more autocratic. It was a difficult transition because I found I had actually had more power, decision making and responsibility as a head of infants than I now did as deputy head. I faced a dilemma. I was drawn to the staff and their concerns and anxieties, yet knew my role was to support a head who I found hard to support in much of what she chose to do. That was the spur to move.

After a year and a half I applied for the headship of a church school. I was short listed but didn't get it. I found myself thinking at the end of the interview 'what will I do if they should offer me the job because I don't think I want to work here?' It was designed to be very heat efficient and there were tiny windows and tiny teaching areas. I thought it claustrophobic. Whether that coloured how I interviewed I do not know, but I was not offered the job, much to my relief. Shortly afterwards I applied for a combined school in Four Oaks. I did wonder how strong a candidate I would be. I was infant trained and had worked mostly in infant schools with little experience of juniors. The school adviser said they were looking for a manager of people, it didn't matter whether you had taught juniors or not. I got it. At the time it was very much a case of going for a job to get out of where I was. That is probably a very poor reason but I loved it.

I didn't really find out what I'd taken on until after I'd been offered it, then the adviser told me I ought to go to his office and spent an hour with him filling me in on what I'd taken on. After that I wasn't sure I should have taken it. It was a school full of conflict, they'd had a succession of heads following a head who had been there a very long time. The message was they needed 'somebody to get in there and drag it into the twentieth century'. I was the fourth in six years to try. Along the way damage was done – rifts between governors and governors, parents and parents, governors and parents. I arrived in the September that the National Curriculum became statutory, nobody had seen the documents.

PR: What have you learned from the heads you experienced as a teacher?

SB: I learned more about how not to do it. I wouldn't denigrate any of the heads I worked for because I think until you do the job yourself it's a case of 'don't judge people until you're in their shoes'. The climate in which a lot of them were heads was different and what is expected of heads is not the same. It tended to be assumed then you would and should control from the top. The heads I worked for were pleasant people I got on with quite well personally, but professionally perhaps disagreed with how some things were done. Some gave me examples of good practice in aspects of administration and organization.

PR: Did you prepare for headship in any formal or informal way?

SB: I did not consciously prepare for headship. I just reached a point where I felt 'I can do that'. When someone once told me 'you will be a head someday' I said 'I won't, I don't want to do that' then all of sudden I found I did want to. That was my preparation. I had co-ordinated every subject in my teaching career, including PE which I hate. I guess I began to see that as a preparation for understanding the workings of a school. I had done a counselling course. I had kept coming up against situations where I wanted to talk to parents about the difficulties I might be having with children and would end up with a parent in bits about what was happening at home. I felt very unqualified and unprepared to deal with this except on a personal and passive level. The counselling course was probably the most significant piece of professional development I ever did.

PR: Was it relevant to your headship as well?

SB: To my headship, to my understanding of the difficulties parents face, to the difficulties staff face. It enabled me to learn how to let people open up, not something teachers do easily. The person leading the course reckoned many teachers were not good counsellors because they were too good at telling people what to do instead of listening to what people wanted to do. That is still something I have to make myself remember.

PR: Counselling is mostly one to one, and teachers' great skills are with groups of people.

SB: As a head a lot of my work is one to one. It is with individual parents or members of staff and certainly with individual children. There are tricks of the trade, key phrases, aspects of body language that enable people to feel more comfortable and to talk. I find it very useful because it helps to open up the real issues which may be getting in the way of somebody teaching or working with their child as well as they might.

PR: Can you remember what headship was like on your first day, first week?

SB: I knocked on my own door for a long time. It was ages before I just walked in without hesitating to knock. Although I make a joke of that it was quite serious. That told me something about what heads should not be. I don't feel people should have to knock on my door to come in. My view is if it's open, come in. But I also I felt very optimistic. I suppose when you don't know what can go wrong you feel you can do anything. I hadn't really had many knocks up until then, I'd got most of the jobs I'd gone for. I'd had odd disagreements with the people I'd worked for, but there had never been anything serious that undermined my confidence in myself. I would say I am not a confident person and yet I am confident in a lot of things I do. I always question whether what I do is right, in that respect I lack confidence. I never believe that I have made the right decision. If someone questions it I always assume they probably know better than I do. Looking back, I suppose I have got a certain confidence in that the things I have done have gone well for me. That builds confidence.

In a way it was easier going into a school which had a lot of problems than into one that was successful. Going somewhere where the experience of headship had been negative meant I could have gone in with three heads and horns and people would still have welcomed me as long as I smiled and said 'you're doing all right'. That was all I had to do in the first few months, reassure people they were not bad teachers and say 'do things your way and we will look and see what needs to be changed if anything'. They had lost confidence in themselves. They'd lost the ability to know if they were good or bad teachers. Most could not see anything good in their practice. It was easy to find good things we could build on. In some ways it was a success story. I started from the position that you 'don't judge people, you're there to support'. Over three years we built up a very good team. It was a small school, which helped because I could get to know people on a personal level. The counselling skills helped because I found I could listen to what people were telling me about their self esteem, and how that had taken knocks and why. All this helped me to avoid some of the pitfalls my predecessors had fallen into. The school began to get noticed – I think I do a good PR job maybe – because some good things were happening there and I had a super staff who did some amazing things once they'd been liberated. We brought in a few new people and there was a sense of optimism in the school.

These are things which I have begun to think about. I've been through some of the same things in my second headship. You get it wound up to the point where it's in danger of exploding. I am becoming interested in finding out more about how organizations work. I suspect they must go through some kind of cycle of fairly low output and energy and then something happens that begins to wind things up. It may be a new head, a new member of staff, anything. You build confidence and excitement and expertise, but you can get to the point where there is too much going on, and something has to give. Maybe a key member of the team leaves, or maybe there is a big conflict. I wonder whether it's the big conflict that might be on the horizon for me at the moment.

PR: Can you take me through your career as a head?

SB: I get restless. The only place I stayed any length of time was because of the anchor of my children being there and I couldn't drive. After three years in a small school I began to feel I had done as much as I wanted to, if not as much as I could. There were personal changes in my life at that time, I split up with my husband. A lot of that was to do with my career and the longer I was in headship the more obsessive I have become about the work. I felt I had to do the best I can all the time. My children probably needed me less and I think my husband was the one to suffer the most. In the end I felt my life had gone off in a totally different direction from his and it didn't seem fair to keep him there, so I decided to make a move. Moving school was part of making the final break. I left in October and applied for a job a year later and got the first headship I applied for. I decided I wanted a bigger school – something very different.

PR: What was it like when you took it over?

SB: A good school, without the kind of conflict I had inherited in the other one. In a way that made it more difficult. The previous head had been there for 14 years and had run an extremely good school, very well thought of in the community. It had a stable and happy staff. A lot needed doing to the fabric of the building, to the resources. The previous head, knowing she was going to retire had, thoughtfully, not made decisions about changing the building. That gave me a good start because I could make visible changes without upsetting any real apple carts. But I was told by the advisers the school was only about 80 per cent effective. There was work to be done, although everybody's perception inside and out of the school, except the school's advisers, was that everything was going well. It was a traditional school which prided itself on its commitment to the three Rs. Everything else was peripheral. It had some parent involvement. Against this background, there didn't seem a lot I could just go in and start blasting away at, which I wouldn't have wanted to do anyway. I knew I had to be cautious. You must be careful you don't just go in and challenge or ignore people's history and culture.

PR: Did the fact that this was your second headship make a difference?

SB: It was much more frightening. I was far more nervous. Perhaps this was because this was a different kind of school. With the first I felt that really I could hardly lose, so much had gone wrong almost anything would be an improvement. It had seemed easy to build a happy and effective school out of the rubble. This time I knew that things could go badly wrong for me. I could be seen as a new broom wanting to change just for the sake of change, yet I knew I had to effect change. I was much more aware of having to establish my credibility. It does not matter how successful you were before, you are seen as a beginner. There was so much more to learn, it was twice as big, there were twice as many people to learn about and twice as many children in a complicated building. It seemed much more daunting. I remember after about six months saying 'I will never do this again' – it's a bit like childbirth! I can remember being totally exhausted after the first year of my first head-ship and thinking I could never do this again just like when you have a baby but then you forget. It wasn't until I was doing it again that I remembered!

PR: Can you say something more about the pressure and workload of head-ship?

SB: I have tried to work out how many hours a week I work and given it up as an awful task. I get to work at about 7.45 am and rarely leave before 6.00 pm and take home two to three hours work most nights. I give myself Saturday off usually unless I'm going to a conference or a lecture, and work on Sunday from about 1.00 pm until 9.00 pm with a break for about an hour for something to eat. That's a regular working week. I don't know what all this works out on average but it is a long week. In week-long, half-term breaks I work two or three days out of the five. And the thinking goes on all the time. I am rarely conscious of being without a thought of school for any length of time, when I'm driving, sitting reading there will be something that comes into my head. I go to sleep thinking about school and I wake up thinking about school. I suppose I'm obsessed with it really. I find it very difficult to be in a position where I haven't got to think about work, I feel guilty if I'm not thinking about work.

PR: How long have you been in this headship?

SB: I'm in my fourth year as head of this school. In another couple of years I would like to retire. Whether I will I don't know. The more you know the harder it gets. I would be 52. I think I'll be burnt out by then and probably the school will be ready for somebody new. I might eat my words!

PR: How successful have you been in developing a vision and implementing it?

SB: If you'd asked me after my first headship I'd have said very successful. I felt successful although I don't think I was terribly good at communicating it. I remember getting very passionate and saying something about a vision for the school, and a member of staff said 'What is it then?' That brought me up short. I thought I'd communicated it but had not. I started making a greater effort to do so. I suppose at that level my vision was that it should be the best school it could possibly be, and that is still my vision. It should be a place where everybody is learning. You refine this as time goes on, I am clearer about what I mean by the best it can be. It is a school where every-body accepts everybody for what they are. I suppose it's Utopian, but it would be wonderful if everybody could see the value everyone else has – the qualities and skills. If people could acknowledge that the best reason for being there is to learn, whether they are parents or teachers or governors or children. I have a long way to go in communicating such a vision and am only just becoming able to articulate it myself. When I put it into words it sounds so airy fairy that I'm not sure people take it seriously. The hard part comes in putting it into practical terms, to explain what it might look like. I get very frustrated when people make me realize they don't know where I'm coming from. I know that's at variance with my saying I ought to know where they're coming from.

PR: *What kind of leader do you see yourself as, has this changed over time?*

SB: I suspect it's always developing. If I get to the point where I think 'I know what kind of leader I am' it's time to get out. It all comes down to this learning thing. I keep learning more about myself and my effect on the institution and the institution's effect on me. The more I find out about what I'm trying to do, the harder it gets and the more it changes me as a leader. I get a bit complacent and think 'I'm democratic, I believe in other people, I believe in delegation, I will shoulder the responsibility if things go wrong.' Those are the messages I give people, but if I am honest, I recognize there is a stubborn streak in me that wants my own way. If I feel I'm being challenged, or told I can't do something, I set out to prove I can. That could be a bad thing for a school, I mustn't let the need for winning take control of a situation if it compromises what is right. It's a difficult balance between your expectations and how you want to work with people.

PR: *What do you do about those who don't meet your expectations?*

SB: I try again. I rarely resort to conflict. I don't think it's constructive. I was brought up in an argumentative culture, but in a positive way. We used to have wonderful debates about anything under the sun. If I said something my father would challenge it. He would prove me wrong then say 'Shall we do it the other way?' He would prove me wrong again. He taught us to be arguers, to enjoy an argument. I try to explain my point of view. I hope I can compromise, if they persuade me their point of view is valid then I will move. I have very high expectations of myself, my institution and other people and find it difficult when I let them or myself down. If I do I try to go back to the drawing board and start again. There's a growing tension between what I feel is expected of me as a head and what is possible. I had more patience with people before I felt as accountable as I do now. People are human. They can't always function perfectly. But it seems I am now expected as a head to act as if I believe they can.

PR *How do you enable other people to lead?*

SB: You can't have an effective school unless everyone else is taking a leadership role of one kind or another. But the bigger the school the harder it is to manage without many others leading in it. I delegate, I try to give people a clear idea of what I'm delegating to them and what is expected of them. I don't give too tight a framework, that inhibits their creativity. I say 'This is an area I would like you to work with, come back with a plan. If you have trouble doing the plan we'll sit and do it together.' I try not to say 'This is what I want you to do, I want you to do it like this.' When things go well, they should take the credit because they did it. If things go badly I take the blame because I asked them to do it. I felt I had established this in my last school and I am getting there here.

PR: You've stressed the importance of enabling the highest reasonable quality of learning within your schools. How do you go about this?

SB: That worries me. I visit classrooms a lot. I try not to interrupt. I don't go in just to deliver messages. I visit and see children and the staff have become used to that. I usually talk to a child, look at a piece of work, pick up a feel for what that classroom is like. I carry out formal monitoring where people know I'm going to come and watch a whole lesson. I ask staff systematically to evaluate what they are doing themselves and that is beginning to improve now. I encourage staff to monitor what is happening within their curriculum area by looking at books, watching lessons. I try to couple monitoring and support. We have got good at identifying our strengths and weaknesses. But the more weaknesses you identify the more sense of urgency there is to do something about it and the harder it becomes to be objective and pragmatic about plans for improvement. If, for example, you know you have weaknesses in eight aspects of the school, you can console yourself with the thought that you can plan for some of these for next year, but I find they still play on my conscience. That's the down side.

PR: You've taken a lead in implementing approaches to school improvement – why?

SB: Two reasons. One is to get an outside view. I can be a good sales person. I don't want people to believe the school is good if it's not. I need an external measure. We can all persuade ourselves we're successful, but you've got to have someone else come in and take an objective view who might say 'Do you know you've got a gap here?' or 'Yes, you are as good as you think you are.' Birmingham's Quality Development process helps. I find it so useful to keep going back through the cycle of where you are, where do you want to be, how you are going to get there, where you are going next. I cannot imagine school development without it now. This you can do for yourself but it is worth bringing in an outside agency with no axe to grind. It can give credibility to my claims to the staff that we are getting things right. Also if someone comes in and say 'This is not up to scratch' I can more easily say 'What are we going to do about this?'

PR: Who are you accountable to?

SB: I feel accountable to myself to get things right. The accountability that can be in conflict with my personal belief and with the way I work comes mostly from the DFE. I find the LEA currently very supportive. People there inspire me to feel while it's a heck of a mountain to climb, it's worth climbing. Others I find supportive if I have a problem. I don't care much for other kinds of accountability. It may be that is what I work towards with my style of leadership. I want people in my school to feel they are letting me down rather than that they are not coming up to scratch. If you could achieve that kind of accountability in everyone you'd have a stunning school.

PR: You used the word 'currently', does that imply there was a time when it wasn't like that?

SB: The LEA at one time was a very distant bureaucracy. They asked for lots of information without telling you why they had to have it. They didn't consult at all. There is a feeling now that if we are asked to do something we are told why it has to be done. The LEA now has got to be a service I want to choose to use. It has changed dramatically for the better. This has made me think more on leadership. There has been a change of leadership in the LEA I have found inspirational and empowering. So I have to try and translate that in some way into what I do in my school.

PR: What do you see as the role of parents?

SB: In general they have been underrated and undervalued educators of their children. I am committed to working with parents. It is growing in our school. For many years the cultures in most schools were that parents were a necessary nuisance. Parents have had a bit of a raw deal in the past. I think they've been manipulated by the media and some political bodies to join the teacher bashing brigade. We've work to do on two fronts: help them work with their children and with schools to educate their children, and help them see the ways in which teachers are represented is not always right. We're currently working on various fronts with parents, we have a huge range of parent training in place which meets what they tell us they want. This ranges from a family literacy group for parents who want to improve their own skills so they can help their children to a group of parents who are studying for NVQs. There is a tremendous sense of confidence amongst those parents who are doing those courses. I think this will slowly make an impact on children's education. I would like to think we work very closely with parents but we've got an awful lot to do yet. We're only hitting at most 80 parents out of 350.

PR: Who's been doing the teacher bashing and why?

SB: The cynic in me say it goes back pre-1988 when, maybe, there was a political decision that teachers and LEAs had too much power and were hotbeds of left-wing dissent. I try not to get too embroiled in thinking about the politics of all this but cannot help feeling there has been a systematic undermining of the profession and what it stands for so that certain things could be achieved. The Labour Party claims it will value teachers and education more than the Conservatives but I am not sure how true this is. Political parties can call the shots more easily if they have a weak profession which cannot stand up for itself. We've allowed ourselves to be pushed around for so long.

PR: What do you feel about the argument that levels of achievement are significantly lower in the UK than in many other comparative countries?

SB: I'm suspicious about statistics. I want to know what we're measuring. I wouldn't argue that we've not been doing for some of our pupils what we should have been doing. With so many young people out of work there is an argument to be made that whatever we've done hasn't prepared them for the economy that we're in. It's got to be looked at in the whole context of social change and economic decline and recession which is happening across the world. I don't think we can get away from the fact that we should always be trying to do better than we're doing. I am interested in whether our children are doing better than they did last year. This should not be too narrow. I wouldn't want them not spelling accurately and being numerate, but I believe many other skills and achievements like verbal communication and adaptability have been sidelined.

PR: How do you cope with stress? How do you keep up to date?

SB: I do not find this difficult because I am surrounded with up-to-date literature although I do not have enough time to read it. I'm currently taking an MEd in School Improvement. I like to go to conferences and seminars where I meet people from different schools and aspects of education. I love discussion about education because I learn something new. I like reading – I went on a fast reading course which helps. Some documents I don't bother to read, I think I'll read them when I need to know about it. I want to keep up to date with things like thinking on where education ought to be going and so on.

I'm not very good at stress release. Having counselled teachers in stress, I know the theory. I don't put it into practice much. I have become better at planning and prioritizing and being realistic about what I can achieve. I do not have a mini nervous breakdown because there's still 18 things left on my list, I just leave some of them until they're out of date and they can come off the list. I take my dogs walking short distances. They give me very great pleasure. I find them uncompromising friends! Talking to people, to friends also helps. I've only got my daughters as close family in this country so I can't rely too much on my family for support and stress relief. I laugh when I can. When I cannot laugh at myself it's time to jack it in!

PR: What part of the job do you least like?

SB: Letting people down. Not meeting their expectations of me. Making decisions that I know are right in the long term for the school or for the children, but in the short term will disappoint or upset members of staff. Letting down my family sometimes when the demands of the job mean I have to be there rather than somewhere else.

PR: Has headship changed in the last decade or so?

SB: I went into it knowing it was going to be different. There had been plenty of talk about the National Curriculum, LMS and governors and the involvement of parents, it was all in the melting pot. In some respects I went into headship with my eyes open. It probably hasn't changed as much for me as for those who were heads before me. I never knew anything different. I can't help thinking that many of the changes are for the better. Especially if you look back 20 years to a time when headteachers could be paid head-teachers' salaries for appearing to do very little. I might be maligning people. They might have been doing huge amounts I wasn't aware of – but it certainly never showed. That has made me aware of the fact that I do have to show people what I am doing. I'm getting the biggest salary in the school and therefore maybe I'm accountable to them as well. I don't hide away in corners when doing work, although a lot of it is done without people seeing it. I make sure they know what's going on though. In that respect it's better – it can't have been right that people took so little part in the education of children once they had become heads – or that's how it appeared to me.

PR: Some argue it is harder to be an educative leader than it used to be?

SB: Heads used to teach more, I wouldn't say that was being an educative leader. Now I tend to have very specific reasons for why I'm teaching. I occasionally do first line cover but I don't think it's an effective use of my time or teaching skills. It is a way of monitoring and I do it sometimes for that reason. It give me an insight into how the teacher organizes the class and if the children are responding as they should.

PR: Some argue that it is harder to be an educative leader because the legislation has forced heads to become accountants and/or administrators?

SB: It is an enticing argument. But I believe we don't have to spend all that much time being administrators. I have a highly competent and efficient administration assistant who does the majority of the work for LMS. I plan and monitor the budget with her but she's trained to highlight when there's a specific anxiety or concern we need to look at together. Some heads do see themselves as administrators. They have chosen to do so. If they wish to follow the paper route they can.

PR: What of marketing?

SB: We need to market the school but haven't we always? Schools have always depended on the good will of their community and that requires a certain amount of marketing. It's all about educating the children and in doing so working with the parents, understanding what they want. To me that's a key part of the learning that has to go on. If we know where children are coming from and what aspirations their parents have of them and of the school that should help us to be more effective as educators than just assuming pupils trundle through the doors every morning and go home at night. I would argue that all this makes for better schools and enables heads to take a lead in education.

PR: You have always wanted to follow the people route?

SB: I follow the people route but set time aside for the paper, like evenings and half-term holidays. Because I have been following the people route for the last half term there is a small mountain of paperwork awaiting my attention on the desk, some may be out of date. I've never found it mattered that much. If it is really urgent, someone will phone.

PR: How do you manage your time during the day?

SB: The night before I will run through diaries, an annual one and a daily one, and plan all the meetings, assemblies, etc. All phone calls I have to make go in a separate column. Also a certain number of tasks. Some tasks stay on week after week because they're not urgent. I try to allocate a number of tasks to the day. It looks wonderful at the beginning of the day because it's all planned out, but it rarely works! I let people hijack me. I have a framework file with all the details and dates in. If ever I lose it I shall shrivel up and die. I don't carry anything in my head. It's not productive to send somebody away if they have plucked up the courage to ask 'Can I have a word?' My heart beats when I have to ask somebody in authority, 'Can I have a word?' I send them away only if I have a commitment to the children or if I already have somebody with me. So my planning sometimes goes out of the window, but so far I haven't come too badly unstuck.

PR: A case of paper in your own time, with most of the day devoted to people?

SB: That is when they are here. I know about good time management, I have been on the courses. I know you're supposed to have 'red time', when nobody phones or comes. I can't do that. I don't think I'm really ideal head-teacher material. Colleagues I know and heads in the past keep saying things like 'You're not paid to be liked.' I can never subscribe to that. Sometimes I have to and that is hard. I have a desperate need to please people. Therefore, I can't shut my door if there is someone who needs me.

PR: What marketing do you do and why do you do it?

SB: I like staff, pupils and parents to feel appreciated. There is a limit to how much I can do this personally. Also they perceive real acknowledgement as coming from outside as well. I like to invite people in to say 'Look at this wonderful teacher here' and 'Look at this wonderful project there.' I'm not consciously marketing but it does market the school because it brings people in who then go out and say 'I saw this good thing at this school.' It also bene-fits the school because it makes the people in it feel valued. I guess I'm also looking for the pat on my back. Maybe that's true of all heads. I don't really expect staff to tell me that I have got something right because I don't think they expect that I need that. But sometimes I do need it, and may go and look for it.

PR: Schools must now survive in a much more competitive environment?

SB: I've never consciously marketed for that reason, although I am aware of the fact that good and bad vibes going out from the school can affect what parents think and whether or not they bring their children to the school.

But I can't bring myself to go down the road some people have of making openly derogatory remarks about other schools in the area or even just little sideswipe comments. I don't think you should have to market a school in this way when it is striving to do its best and is achieving something. It should market itself. That's not complacency. I'm not going to go out of my way to have the best prospectus in the area, or the glossiest brochure or the most meetings. We have our induction meeting when it fits in with the diary and when my teachers feel most comfortable with it. I might feel differently if my rolls were falling. I've been fortunate in both schools. Although the rolls were down at the beginning of my first headship they did nothing but climb. Even so I was very conscious of every time a child left. They always left for the right reasons, for example, moving from the area. The rolls have climbed in this school too from 398 to 427, but I am conscious also that that's not all to be explained by the fact that we are a successful school, it's also demographic. It doesn't hurt to be aware of that, so when a family is going to move out, I always ask myself first of all 'Why are they moving?' If they are not moving out of the district I will look at what we did that's made them want to go away. In this school, I have only lost two families to other local schools and that was after a great deal of work with the family over issues to do with children's behaviour. The parents in the end were in conflict with the parents of another child and decided a fresh start was better. I agreed.

PR: Are any of your local headteacher colleagues aggressive marketers of their school?

SB: Yes, one. I know them all professionally. We generally try to work together. In this head's case it's more things I hear about rather than know directly. Parents tell me what was said at the induction meetings. Some of the things are untrue or exaggerations. It tends to come indirectly so I don't put a huge amount of value on it.

PR: What do you see as the responsibility of the governors? How do you work with them?

SB: They have awesome responsibilities for volunteers. I think I work well with governors, but don't always get it right. The governors in my last school were much more aware as a body of their power than the majority of my governors here. I don't think they were that aware of their responsibilities. They exercised their power, and I sometimes found that difficult. I found it difficult to be challenged about mundane everyday operations, the classic being 'There's dysentery in Birmingham, it's in the paper, have we got enough toilet paper?' I found that level of involvement annoying and intrusive. One who was also a governor at another school was not always discreet about what was happening in both schools. We heads used to ring each other up and say 'I've just heard this of you, what were you told about me?' One or two governors made a point of eliciting information from staff about issues which maybe were quite sensitive or were things that weren't on the open agenda yet. The governors at my present school are fine. But we are having to work quite hard to keep them involved. Some are very supportive. The chairman is, he comes from an educational background and understands the issues. I find that very helpful. It's a very useful relationship for me because he offers a sounding board, and he will challenge me and I need that.

PR: How has primary education changed? To what extent has this been for better or worse?

SB: I think the notion of whether or not education has changed is an interesting one. I think education has to change. It isn't education if it isn't changing. How can you be educating children in a changing world if you're not changing the way you do it? Some of my colleagues find such a notion of change difficult, and are very resistant to new styles of things, to new reasons for doing things, to new technology. I can't help but think that the way we were taught didn't prepare us for this, so what justification have we got for maintaining such a style of teaching. Yet I see people doing it all the time, still teaching the way we were taught to teach 30 years ago. This just can't be right. We're two generations on from there. My children are in their twenties, I don't think the education they received really prepared them for the world they are living in. What has prepared them tends to be the experiences they got outside school. Yes they've taken the academic route to certain jobs, but they haven't been prepared for the fact they may have to change their jobs several times in their working life. They weren't prepared for being well qualified and out of work.

PR: What would you have felt if one of your daughters had said she wanted to be a teacher?

SB: They both wanted to be teachers originally – I talked them both out of it! I figured that if I could talk them out of it then they weren't really committed. I wouldn't like to be a teacher at the beginning of my career now. That may be a sign of old age and cynicism. I have a theory about Winnie the Pooh. I feel that heads probably all started out their careers as Tiggers, and they are on a continuum towards Eeyore. I'm fairly close to Eeyore now. When you get to Eeyore it's time to hang up your boots and call it a day.

PR: Of all the many heads I've talked to, you have used the word teaching less than almost any other – why do you think that should be?

SB: That's interesting. Maybe it is because I see myself as a learner not a teacher. I don't know whether I see myself as a teacher. I'm not sure I know what a teacher is. The term teacher is restrictive. It shouldn't be. I'm not sure that I even perceive as much difference as many might want me to between the teachers and the other significant adults in the lives of children within schools. When I talk of my staff, I am talking about everybody – teachers, classroom assistants, integration assistants, secretaries, administration assistants, dinner supervisors. I see them as a whole lot of people engaged in the education of children.

PR: What do you see schools like in the next millennium?

SB: I don't know – I go to IT conferences and video conferences. They excite and alarm me. I would like to think there will still be schools if only so that there will still be places where children can go to learn about interpersonal relationships. If there is going to be a major change I suspect it may be towards having more significant adults in classroom and fewer teachers. If we're going to improve such things as ratios and class sizes it won't be with more teachers, it will be with more adults assisting. Perhaps I haven't talked about teachers because I'm aware of the fact that that's not a popular notion. I'm still struggling with that one in my school. Some teachers feel uncomfortable with the notion that classroom assistants can be as valuable contributors as everybody else.

PR: To what extent is headship itself also problematic – are heads necessary?

SB: I think it's important that someone at a local level has a vision for what is being strived for. In the short term I'm not indispensable. If I don't go in the school will still function providing my teachers and classroom assistants are there, and the toilets are cleaned, etc. In the longer term, I suspect the success of the school – defined in terms of whatever goals there may be for children's learning – is influenced by having heads who know what it is that they are trying to achieve, and who are struggling with the vision. I have access to information that teachers don't have time to access because they're busy doing their job in the classroom whilst I am doing my job in the school.

A Coda (several months later)

PR: Is there anything you would like to add to our initial conversation?

SB: Thank you for the transcript. I found it a sobering experience to read. I feel brain dead at the moment having just survived a short notice OFSTED inspection. There has been so much to do following the inspection. The draft report has been 'gone over' and I have tracked down all the data the inspectors lost and asked me to reproduce for them (but that is another story). I am now able to start to give my attention to the real world again.

I can't help considering how far I have moved in my thinking since our interview. So many things have altered, if only slightly, in how I am thinking and acting as a head. I have finally come to realize that however much I believe in the infinite capacity people have for improvement and in the central role of staff development, I can no longer allow teachers who are not giving our children their educational entitlement to continue to progress slowly. The children have such a short time in school that we must capitalize on every year and not accept 'fallow' spells. How hard I am becoming! Having said this, I am still deeply upset by the inevitable consequences of this thinking when I have to accept resignations from people whom I like and respect as human beings whatever their capacities as teachers. At times like this I don't feel I have what it takes for this job.

CHAPTER 4

Thriving in the face of insurmountable odds

DAVID DAVIES WITH PETER RIBBINS

David Davies is Head of Blaengwrach Primary School in Neath, West Glamorgan. He was born and received most of his schooling within a few miles from where he now works. Initially, he went to a teacher training college in Manchester because he wanted to study horticulture. Teaching practice persuaded him he wanted to be a teacher. Although secondary trained, an opportunity to teach temporarily in a primary school led him to his ultimate vocation. After working in a number of primary schools, finally as a deputy, he was appointed to Blaengwrach where he has now been for six years. During that time Blaengwrach was one of the 11 schools identified by the National Commission on Education as 'thriving in the face of insurmountable obstacles'.

PR: Can you tell me something about your personal background and education? Could you identify some of the people who have played a part in shaping what you have become?

DD: I was born in Skewen, a large village ten miles away. My father was self-employed and very supportive. He believed life should be enjoyed and education was important, but not the most important thing. He had a big influence on my outlook. He spent a lot of time working with disadvantaged children. He always had time for children.

I didn't go to nursery although this was available – I started school at five. I can't remember the infant school, only milk every day and having to go to sleep for so long in the afternoon. I can't remember the names of the teachers but I do remember several at my junior school. I hated it.

PR: Why?

DD: It didn't stimulate me at all. The only thing I liked was maths, which I was fairly good at. I disliked every other aspect of school. I would have been regarded as a remedial child – I couldn't read until I was eight. I had plenty of help at home from my parents. My mother would do spelling exercises with me, and tables daily, she would read to me and try and get me to read but I had no interest at all. I found school a barren place. At home there was woodland, ponds and lakes within walking distance. I thoroughly enjoyed that – there were people around who used to be ex-poachers or worked for those trying to catch the poachers. I enjoyed being in the company of adults doing things: my parents, grandparents or any of the local characters. I failed the 11-plus: did very well in maths but atrociously in English. I went to a secondary modern school and started to work only in the third year. Two teachers, Mrs Stone and Mr Lewis, one took maths and the other gardening, cared about children, all children, not subjects. I spent most of my time doing my exam studies. We studied with these two rather than the subject teachers who, unlike them, cared about their subjects not children. If you were good in their subject you were a star pupil, if you were not you were ignored.

I ended up getting 13 O-levels or GCSEs, more than any of my peers who had gone to the local grammar school. I went to the grammar school at 17 and found it very boring. I was given vast amounts of paperwork when I arrived to do A-level botany and zoology and was told 'If you learn this you will pass.' They let me do my own thing, the teachers didn't want to know. I found that very disturbing. I spent a year there and decided to leave. I left in July but decided in August to go back after all. I spoke to the headteacher. He suggested I considered going to college instead, which is what I did and ended up in teacher training college.

PR: Even though you hadn't enjoyed your own schooling, you still wanted to be a teacher?

DD: I didn't want to be a teacher. I was keen on horticulture and was going to study this but then thought 'No, that's not the most appropriate sort of course.' My headteacher suggested a teaching course with horticulture as a subject. That is how I came to choose teaching. I had given it no other thought at all. If that hadn't happened, it wouldn't have come about any other way. I wanted to get a further qualification, teaching was one way of doing it. If I am honest, initially, the holidays appealed, so I went in through the back door. I taught biology, my subject, and for my first year that was what mattered to me. It was only when I realized I was doing what those who had taught me, who I had condemned strongly, had done that I began to take a more child-centred approach.

PR: What were the values that informed the schools you went to?

DD: Most of the teachers in those schools had come into teaching after the war – they were only concerned about their subject, they had barren classrooms. In the junior school we had maths all morning and language all afternoon. You had art on Wednesday and were told to paint a picture. If you finished, you were told to turn it over and paint on the other side – no value was put on what you were doing. I developed a hatred of art. If we were lucky we'd go once a month for games on a Friday. I remember one person who had travelled the world in the war had his map of the British Empire.

Everything he did was linked to the British Empire. Until he retired his classroom stayed the same. It's very sad that children were exposed to such education. It did little for me. What I did was off my own back with the help of two members of staff who had encouraged me.

PR: What made them different?

DD: They cared about all children but not in a soft way. They were perhaps the strictest teachers in the school. That didn't matter – they cared. They cared about me as an individual, whether I was successful or not. As it happened, because of their care, I put much more effort in and did very well in their subjects. They were the ones who went on residential visits with you, stayed behind after school to run clubs for you and gave up their time for you. You responded to what they were doing for you.

PR: Do you remember any of your headteachers as a boy?

DD: All of them. We rarely saw the infant school head, she kept herself to herself. The junior head's office was upstairs; he'd come down for assembly or you saw him if you were naughty, and at no other time. He gave me a hard time once for something I never did. I would never accept the blame for something I wasn't guilty of. I told my father who spoke to the head, and he came and apologized. He said, 'Why didn't you tell me who your father was? I wouldn't have given you a row.' I thought that disgusting – you should treat people fairly whatever their background. The head of the secondary school was a keen angler. I won a national competition and after that he spent a lot of time with me and I appreciated that. I felt it was something I had achieved, not been given because of who I was or where I came from. The head of the grammar school was very fair. He was seen around the school a lot. He tried to encourage the pupils. Whatever your strengths, sport, science or humanities, it did not matter, he was supportive. I remember him with the greatest affection. He helped me to make one of the most important professional decisions of my life. If he hadn't suggested teaching I would not have done it. It hadn't crossed my mind.

PR: Why did you choose to teach younger children?

DD: I was secondary trained to teach biology. I'd come back from Manchester and applied for a couple of jobs. I was short listed for a secondary school to teach chemistry which wasn't one of my strengths. I just wanted a job. Then a lady who lived in our road who knew I was looking, told me there was a post going in their junior school. I had been working in a shop just to do something. She asked if I would be interested for one term. I said I would consider it and went for interview. I turned up for interview, parked my car and went to the head's office. We had a little chat and the conversation went something like this:

    'Do you play Rugby?'
    'I play Rugby.'
    'Do you?'

'I played for the grammar school.'
'A very successful side.'
'Oh yes?'
'I played for my college.'
'Excellent. Do you play cricket?'
'I've never played cricket.'
'Are you prepared to learn?'
'I wouldn't mind learning.'
'Can you start tomorrow?'

It was as farcical as that.

He turned out to be brilliant, passionately interested in sport with nobody in the school who could offer it, so my sporting background got me in. I was given a J4 class. I found it strange for a couple of months. Then I started taking children out on visits. Once, when the headteacher was off sick, the deputy called me in and said 'You can't do this, there are serious insurance implications, you must stop taking them out.' When the head-teacher returned he explained there was no insurance implications but the deputy's concern was that if I started something like that the rest of the staff would be expected to continue it. I learnt very quickly not to follow the rest but to do my own thing. I was there for five happy years. The head retired and a new one came in. Numbers began to drop and I thought that I would go. But he didn't work on the principle of 'last in, first out'. He said 'If you want to stay I will stick by you, somebody else will go.' But I was offered a post in a school that had just been built. The Advisers had told me I would have more opportunity there and to go for it. So I went to work in a primary. During these years I had taught every age from 7 to 11, and assisted with all the younger classes.

As time passed I became aware of a local Adviser: John Jones. He had started in West Glamorgan on the same day I had. I didn't see much of him at the junior school. He only once came to visit me as a probationer. The only advice he gave me was to use an old string vest to clean my black board. But in the new school he became far more involved and gave me great help in developing my teaching methods. He introduced me to others who shared our views. I have always spent much of my time taking children out on residential visits, at least three a year. Then we'd have activities after school, at least three evenings a week. I also took them out on the weekends. I have always found that if you spend time with children, they will respond enthusiastically.

PR: An active approach is ...

DD: Very important. I believe in a discovery-based approach, an experiential approach to learning. There were always lots of animals in my classroom. This was to enable children to develop the concept of care, to make them involved in what's going on. It is also important to involve parents at an early stage so they know what's happening. That is the sort of philosophy developed in my second school.

PR: Were they both village schools?

DD: They were both village schools – one in Skewen where I lived and one in Cilffriw, a much smaller village. It had a split catchment area: a new and affluent housing estate and old council housing. But the split didn't matter. You still had people who cared about their children. The first had about 150 children when I started and had dropped to 120 when I left. The second had 114 primary pupils when I started, it was a brand new school, and 219 when I left. From that school I started applying for deputy headships. I applied for Crynallt School which, with 350 junior pupils alone, was the biggest junior school in the county. I was successful and very pleased. It had been acknowledged by the Director of Education as having received the best HMI report the county had ever received.

PR: What interested you in becoming deputy?

DD: I increasingly found I didn't agree with some of the practices I saw going on in some classrooms. I wanted more of a say in how children should be taught. For that I needed a power base, a position of strength from which to argue my case. Before becoming a deputy I had been involved with *my children*. That was fine when I was with my class but what of other classes and what happened if my class went to a poorer teacher? They were all still my children and were losing out. I realized I must become more involved in the overall running of the school. That's why I set about finding a deputy headship. In Crynallt I worked with several outstanding teachers. The minute I walked in I knew what I had thought was a good school previously was poor in comparison.

PR: What was the difference?

DD: The level of work the children were producing; the quality of work expected of them; the standards expected of them; the time and the effort teachers put in, both during school time and after; and the organization within the school. In my previous schools maths and language were very much the main focal point of our work. I had thought its standards were acceptable but they were nothing like Crynallt. There a typical piece of written work from a good J4 child could be six or seven A4 sides of high-quality language work. Crucially, they were encouraged to work from their own experiences. The curriculum was geared to the local environment. The children went out into the environment and the environment was brought to the children. If they were doing a stream study they would go and visit a stream, they'd do their science based on the speed of the stream, they would do their art work and would sketch it, they'd do batik work on it, they'd do silk screen printing on it. I thought that wonderful. Teachers were encouraged to go on courses at the highest level and bring back lots of new skills and disseminate skills and good practice amongst the other staff. They worked very closely together to encourage and help each other. This atmosphere was wonderfully conducive to children's learning.

PR: Why do you think that happened?

DD: The head had a wonderfully clear perception of how children learn. He knew his most important resource were his teachers. He knew he had a difficult school to turn around and that this would take time. He knew if things were rushed this would not allow the staff to come to terms with what needed to be done and to make the changes, *their* changes. He also knew that he had to resource people, to let them go on courses and when they returned to consolidate what they had gained. So he gave them a chance to work with smaller groups and the resources they needed. It was clearly thought through and well organized.

I didn't agreed with all he did. In some respects I'd seen better practice from my previous heads. They all had their strengths and weaknesses. The first cared a great deal about the individual and family. If there was illness he would send them home. He knew they couldn't be at their best if they were concerned about their family. The second would be upset if staff took a day off for any reason. I began to realize all my heads had their own style and strengths and weaknesses. I wanted to develop a style with a concern for the needs of everybody – children, parents, governors, teachers, cleaners, caretakers and the kitchen staff – if the school is to be effective they must all be catered for.

PR: How influential was your head at Crynallt in appointing you?

DD: It was his decision: apparently 74 applied but only two were short listed. He made me feel welcome when I went to visit the school – I seemed to give him the answers he was looking for. He said 'When you are appointed, and I hope you are, we will do this together' – it was very much a 'we', a partnership, and being made to feel wanted from a very early stage made you contribute that much more. I like to think he appointed me for what I was doing in my previous school and the reputation I had earned for the way I worked with children. He wanted to develop a more experiential approach to learning in his own school, to take the children out and to give them more residential experience. He had developed a very good standard within the main curricula areas, but felt that there was more that his pupils could take on board.

PR: At what point did you realize you might want to become a head?

DD: It was during my time at that school. I wanted only to be a deputy because I did not want to leave the classroom. In practice, I was released for two days a week because the head worked for the Authority. I was respon-sible but couldn't make changes. He was definitely the head – he would listen but he made the decisions. He would take advice but would have his own way. During my third year he left and joined the Advisory Team. I was in an 'acting' capacity from September through March. I began to realize the vast array of problems that face a headteacher which I had not been aware of as a class teacher or even as a deputy. In the past if people had a problem, they knew that although I was there Tuesday and Wednesday, he would be back on Monday, Thursday and Friday and would keep their problems for him. It was much the same with parents. Everything seemed to happen at the beginning or end of the week – I thought this was the norm. But on my first day in post 30 parents came to see me. Some had children coming in from the infants, they wanted their children put in one class rather than another because they'd heard she was a good teacher. I found myself trying to explain that you can't have 350 children in one teacher's class – it was impossible. I was in school until 6.00 pm most days meeting parents with problems. I had not experienced this as a class teacher. It was during this time that I began to become aware of what headship was about.

During the Christmas period they advertised for a new head. I was asked by the governors to apply and told the job would be mine. I don't believe in internal appointments. You need people bringing in a fresh impetus from outside. So I said I wasn't going to apply for the job. I persuaded a good friend of mine to apply. He was more experienced – already a head. He got the job. I had somebody coming in who I knew I could work with. But within two days of being back in the classroom I knew I wasn't happy. I was glad to be back with my children but I had far less of a say in the running of the school, and they were all my children. It was problematical at times, but I thoroughly enjoyed headship. I was challenged; I could have a bigger input into what was going on; I was stimulated; I wanted this. I started applying for headships straight away.

PR: How useful a preparation was acting headship for headship?

DD: As an acting head your hands are tied. If the head is coming back, you can't do anything much new. At the same time you have a responsibility for the children and must cater for their needs. I was given freedom by the governors to run the school as I saw fit. It was definitely a beneficial experience. It made me aware of the changes taking place with regard to Local Management of Schools, of the problems a head faced, an insight into what was going on in headteachers' meetings, etc. If nothing else it gave me an advantage when I was being interviewed for real. It also made me very aware that each school is different, the way you can manage one might be totally different to the way you manage another. Acting headship was a bonus.

PR: Did you get a headship easily?

DD: I tried for three. The first a teaching headship in a small school and the Adviser said to me 'Don't apply for that, there's something better for you coming along.' I don't like to be told where my career should go, so I applied anyway. There were six on the short list and I got to the last two – we went to County Hall for the final interview and I wasn't successful. I felt disappointed but the next day the Adviser said 'Don't worry, that wasn't for you.' I said 'I should be choosing what is for me, not you.' He said 'No, no, there are better schools than that for you.' Shortly afterwards I applied for another, a very good school. Again, I was told 'Don't apply for that, it is someone else's job you have no chance of getting it.' I thought 'I'll give it a go.' Again six were short listed, three got to County Hall and I wasn't successful. The very next month the Adviser came to see me in my class-room, and said 'Have you applied for Blaengwrach?'

'No, I haven't applied for Blaengwrach.'

'Why haven't you?'

'Because it is at the top end of the Neath valley and I don't like the valley, I don't think I want to work there.'

'Yes you do, apply.'

This was a Friday morning – 'I'm not applying for it.'

'Apply for it. You go and look at it over the weekend then fill in that application and get it in my office by Monday morning.' I had never been in the village before. I looked round the school, it looked OK. I felt there was potential. There were lots of natural resources near by. Also I thought I had better apply or I might not get another chance. So I applied, got on the short list. I found it soul destroying when I walked through the door for interview to hear a governor speaking to another candidate, a good friend of mine, saying 'Don't you worry, the job is yours.' I then heard another governor say to a second candidate 'I know you are in the Chapel, the choir, the opera, you will have this job.' I thought I may as well go home. Anyhow we had the informal interview in the school where we spoke to local advisers, members of the LEA and governors. They asked lots of questions, about children in particular, which I was pleased about. I could tell the governors were very supportive. They were very proud of their children. I had to acknowledge that there was good work going on, but there were also a lot of weaknesses. I don't think they liked it when I told them this but they had to accept it because I could give them specific examples.

PR: You talked about this at interview?

DD: I told them 'There is some lovely work going on here but there are weaknesses – here, here and here. Don't pretend otherwise. It would be wrong of me to say anything else. I am sure we can raise the standard and I am sure you want your children to achieve at least what others do. We need to take this school forward.' On the next day I went to County Hall. There were seven governors and nine or ten councillors there. I was success-ful. I heard later from the Chair of Governors it was a unanimous decision, which pleased me immensely after hearing those comments when I came to the school. All the governors came up to me straight after the interview and made me feel very wanted, very welcome. I came into school the following Saturday morning. By 9.00 am two parents had come in – one had rung me up and the other had come into school to meet me, and asked me up for tea and toast – they made me feel very welcome in the community. I got the job I wasn't going to apply for and I was happy to do so.

PR: The Adviser played a crucial role in all this.

DD: Yes and he was very supportive during my first 12 months. Cut backs meant he was asked to retire. His was the greatest influence on improving education in West Glamorgan over the last 15 years. He has set up his own business and still offers a great deal to education. The LEA don't like that: they think we should stay in-house, but I don't. I must bring in the best support I can afford whether local or 300 miles away. The children must have the best.

PR: How did you prepare for headship?

DD: I had no formal preparation. I had no support from the heads I'd worked with. That was wrong of them. The Authority now has courses for deputies preparing for headship and courses for newly appointed heads. None were available when I started. My preparation was to clarify my philosophy. To be clear about why and how I had achieved promotion. I concluded I had been promoted for doing what I believed in, because this catered for the needs of all my children. I then drew up a list of criteria I felt important and fitted this into my philosophy. This is what I took to inter-view. I've been successful. I got the second deputyship I applied for and the third headship having been told I was not getting the other two. There's no big secret. We deal with children not bottles or car parts. We must ensure they have the best possible opportunity at all times. It's simple really. How you make the most out of the resources available is a different matter. Even so, catering for the needs of children is what headship should be about. I do the best I can for my staff but what I am most concerned about are the chil-dren.

PR: What have you learnt from heads you worked for?

DD: One was always talking about 'When you become a head.' He was very positive which made you feel confident. I came to see this was important. You must make your staff feel a vital part of the school. My last head believed strongly that you must 'Make the most of your resources; make sure people work to their full potential; you can't do it all yourself so ensure you are getting the best out of them.' My first head felt everybody would respond better if you thought about them as whole persons: their and their family needs. Some wanted parents to come in to be a key part of the set up; others wanted them to be kept at a distance. You have to sift through what you saw them do and take on the good points and leave behind the bad ones. You need to use what is appropriate to the situation you are in. My style here is totally different to the style I would adopt in any of my other three schools at the time I was in them.

   I find it very confusing that the government seems to think it can so easily compare schools with one and other: every situation is unique; every child is unique; every school is unique – they shouldn't be treated as if they were the same. If you mass produced ten thousand cans you can have them all the same – you can't with people. We talk about special needs for chil-dren; every child has special needs. How you can best cater for these depends upon individual circumstance.

PR: What do you advise those who come to you saying they are thinking of headship?

DD: My deputy will get one soon. I have three others who should apply for headship in due course. When I came the school was fair; I had some potentially good teachers. I was lucky to be able to appoint two teachers within a fortnight of arriving. I've a superb staff now, the best I've ever worked with. Of the six here now, I have appointed three.

PR: What do you hope those who might become heads have learnt from you of headship?

DD: Most importantly that you cannot rush change. You must first develop a common philosophy, until that is truly shared by all members of staff you will not as a school be as effective as you should be. You've got to give them time to try out what you are trying to implement: they may try to do things because you have asked, but they will not succeed unless they really believe in and understand what you want. If necessary you must bring in people to help them, you must send them on lots of visits to see what you want happening in other schools. We believe in an experiential approach in which the children are actively involved in their own learning. We use this in everything: literacy, numeracy, even morality. With this you have a firm foundation on which you can build. Without this everything you try can topple very easily.

PR: Are you saying that it is more important to have a philosophy of education than a vision for headship and that if you have the former then the latter will come?

DD: Headship is just one aspect of providing for the children. In a way my cook's job is as important as mine. If anybody does not contribute as they should the children suffer. It's a three way partnership: the home, the child and the school. If there are problems with any one of those parts the child suffers. Within the school every member of the staff is of equal importance: they don't work for me, they work with me. We work as a team. It is my intention that they have a major say in what goes on. Ultimately I am responsible but there have been times when I have accepted what they've wanted to do. Sometimes they are right and sometimes wrong, that applies to me. As head you have got to be prepared to be flexible, to let them work alongside you.

PR: What did you do on your first day as a head? What was the first week and month like?

DD: I had make the staff realize I was going to lead by example – that was vital. So I spent lots of time going into the classrooms and I still insist on visiting every classroom on a daily basis. In term I do not like being out of school. I enjoy being in the company of children. So I went into classes and talked to staff, spoke to the children, began to get them comfortable in my presence and not feel I was watching everything they did. I would go in sometimes and ignore the teacher and just work and talk with the children. I began to break down the barriers.

I believe in an aesthetic approach to learning – why should children only communicate through speech or writing. Some communicate wonderfully using other media. When I came this was weak. I had a stroke of luck. British Gas came into the community, there was no gas in the village. They approached us and asked if we would be involved in a project on 'Gas in the Community'. The staff said they didn't really want to. I said 'I would like to do it, let's have a go. We'll take something simple – like the gas flame.' That was six years ago and the first thing we produced is still on my wall. I persuaded the staff to let me work along side them. We used 27 mediums for producing the flame. I promised during the first two terms I would mount and display all the art work myself. Bit by bit they started to say 'Can I give you a hand with this?' or 'Can I be involved with that?'

I did all this in various ways. First by putting on a display in the local village. There were several other schools involved. I spent a fair sum buying some lovely drapes and bird of paradise flowers which linked into the colours we were using for the gas flame and displayed this along with a variety of other artefacts. I spent two days on this and then took the staff along two or three at a time to see it. Compared to the other schools it was outstanding. One of my more formal teachers was standing there looking at this display when some of her friends from the village walked past. She tapped them on the shoulder and said 'My children did that.' There was a sense of pride which hadn't been there before. It was reassuring for them to know I would support them and that together we could make things work. It told us that the limits of what we could achieve together were restricted only by the extent of our own enthusiasm.

They soon began to realize that if they called on me for something I would do my best to do it. I spent the first months as a handyman. If at all possible, if they asked me for something on Thursday evening, I would get what was needed that night, come in at six o'clock the next morning and have it up by the time they came. When I was asked could we have this or that my answer was yes, yes, yes, yes, yes, yes: I tried never to say no. I paid for this from capitation, our parents, local industry, friends of mine or myself. The staff were well supported and in return they began to break down barriers, relax, accept change. If I now suggest a change is necessary, rather than question it defensively, they usually begin with a positive attitude. A very important example is the debates we have had on how children learn and what can we do to ensure we support this as effectively as possible. To help us with this we have brought in, especially at the beginning, lots of outside agencies. I would start such debates, then rely on one or two of my stronger teachers to take it up and then bring in outside agencies to progress it.

PR: What kind of outside agencies?

DD: We use John Jones Educational Associates. They talked about the early
years, for example, and good practice. Then they took us to other schools,
not just in this county but in Wiltshire or Yorkshire, to show us good practice we could relate to. They would say 'This was regarded as good, they got
a superb report, do you think you are doing better or worse?' 'We do better.'
'Of course.' That was wonderful for confidence. That was how it started.
Once I got through to them we began to change the philosophy of the school.
I did not try and rush them and I'm glad I didn't. I have tried to protect
them from some of the worst effects of the implications of national educational reform and the ways in which this has been changed and changed
again.

   We could have spent a lot of time and effort on this but we didn't. I have
tried to get a new philosophy in place first and develop policies which the
staff were committed to. I was very keen to get the staff taking the children
out. We have three residential visits a year and lots of extra curricular activities for staff, parents and children: canoeing, pony trekking, badminton,
water skiing, surfing. I got staff to get qualifications in these activities so
they could lead on them. But I would be here five nights a week hoping to
make them think 'If he can do it, I can do it.' For the first two to three years
change was very slow. I then had a stroke of luck. I appointed a superb
teacher, one of the best I have ever worked with, who gave as much time as
I did. She revolutionized the early years department. She brought the
parents in and made them feel important. We did not just involve them in
menial tasks: that snowballed. Other teachers began to do the same and
then rapid change began to take place. If staff feel things are coming from
them rather than from the head they will make things happen much more
quickly. You may have to manage this a bit, I am not saying I am under-
handed, perhaps I am a bit tricky. I sew the seeds but try to make them
think it is coming from them. I'm willing for them to take all the praise for
the things that go well. One or two are a bit more astute now. They know
what's going on.

PR: What kind of a leader are you?

DD: I like to think I lead by example, by my commitment, dedication and
enthusiasm. I hope I am aware of the needs of all my staff, parents and children and that as a result I have produced a real community school with a
real family atmosphere. A school that is seen as safe, welcoming, rewarding,
caring, sensitive and within which every one feels welcome. As the head I
am just playing my part – a cog in the wheel if you like.

PR: What do you do about teachers who don't come up to your expectations?

DD: When I came I had one or two. As a teacher I always thought that as a
head I would simply say to weak teachers 'You are not doing the job,
change.' It doesn't work. They all think they are doing the job to the best of
their ability, even if they are not. I realized very quickly that unless they are

appalling, where you may have to go for dismissal, you have to make the best of every member of staff. This may mean losing many battles before winning the war. You may need to get to know them and their problems. Take the case of a teacher who is off every few weeks. I find this difficult to tolerate. You may feel she should be in school but she feels she should be at home. You may have to give her time for a while until she begins to realize you are on her side. There are times when you have to give to hope to be given back. You've got to win them around by giving what they need before demanding what your school needs.

PR: Your account of headship sounds very demanding. Do you find time for any other life?

DD: I try to go home and switch off from school completely. I could not keep up that level of commitment 24 hours a day. Lots of my colleagues take their problems home and worry about them all night. I will not. I solve school problems in school. After I have left, I have left. Having said that, I try to get into school before 8.00 am every day so I can spend time before anybody else comes. I leave school on a Monday between 5.30 and 6.00 pm. Tuesday is an fairly early night for me, I leave by 5.00 pm. Wednesday I run extra curricular activities: canoeing from 4.00 to 5.00 pm with the children; snorkelling with the children from 5.00 to 6.00 pm; sub-aqua with the parents and staff from 6.00 until 7.00 pm. I take a badminton club on Thursday which keeps me in school until about 6.00 pm and on Friday I finish round about 5.00 pm. In addition, I do three residential visits a year with the children and take them for extra activities in the summer months to the local beaches. I will take them away at the weekends as well when the opportunity arises. Other than that I do not do school work – I've got to have a break.

PR: That makes you sound like a workaholic.

DD: I umpire badminton internationally, I travel the world for this; I keep a large collection of reptiles, I travel the world with that; I'm very involved with sub-aqua. So when I am in school, my mind is on school, I'm refreshed and full of enthusiasm for school. When I leave school I switch off from school and my batteries are re-charged.

PR: How do you know what happens in your classrooms and what your children achieve?

DD: First, I try to delegate a great deal. I do so for a number of reasons. First, it gives all staff an opportunity to put in place what they believe in. We've all got our strengths and we teach best to our strengths. Second, all curriculum areas are covered by designated staff responsible for them – I don't take responsibility for a curriculum area. Third, we are a very close-knit staff – we meet regularly to discuss what's going on. Fourth, I go into classrooms on a daily basis. Most staff talk to me about what they are doing. I encourage involvement in how they are going to teach aspects of the curriculum. This is particularly true of science and IT. I like to be involved in the planning of what's going on. I can keep an eye on what's going on. Fifth, I go around the school every evening to look at what's changed in the classroom when the staff have gone – not in an inspectoral way but to keep in touch with what's going on. Sixth, we have systems which enable staff to communicate and plan together from nursery right the way through J4 and these are usually effective. I am involved in many of those meetings, so I know what's going on. We are always trying to raise standards in every curriculum area: we keep abreast of good practice both locally and further afield. We attend lots of courses. Well, the staff attend lots of courses. They visit lots of schools, I bring in external agencies who inspect my school on a regular basis and report back to me. It is easy to become blinkered by your own perception of what's going on. I try to keep abreast of things in all these ways.

Why do we put such emphasis on extra curricular activities? I once heard a head claim that the so called 'better schools' – the schools where the parents can afford to send their children at whatever the cost – offer this as part of the curriculum. I was struck by this. But if these activities are being offered in the so called 'better schools', why aren't our children having them? My parents can't afford them, but I am determined my children will not go without them. But not in place of other important things. We ensure our children get a broad and balanced curriculum, both within the accepted curricular subjects and in the extra curricular activities. By involving children in a wide range of activities you increase the chance of their experience success in something and they may transfer this to other areas in which they may be struggling. I have found that they are more ready to react positively to criticism when they can say 'I might not be the best in maths, but have you seen the award for my art work?' They must have success.

PR: Do you encourage the staff to observe each other in classrooms?

DD: If there is a specific need. For a newly appointed teacher I release more experienced staff to work with them. I also try to release new staff to work with more experienced members. I do that by teaching classes myself when possible or if there is money in the GEST budget I bring in a supply teacher. If I have to split a class I do. If I think a member of staff needs to acquire certain skills then I will release her or him to observe or to work alongside colleagues.

PR: Do you monitor with reading tests or in other similar ways? What of SATs?

DD: No. We are not a believer in the National Curriculum and don't agree with SATs, so we do not prepare for SAT tests. Having said that, when they have to have the tests, and the pupils have only had them so far in the first year and last year, in between staff were boycotting the SATs, the children have come out of the SATs far better than we would have expected. It is lovely to see that the way we teach seems to prepare the children for whatever they encounter. I see that as vital. If you teach to the SATs and they meet different kinds of problem, they cannot cope. If you teach them to cope with life and problems, they can apply that knowledge and skills to what-ever they face. We do not prepare children for the comprehensive school; we do not prepare children for the next level or the next test they will encounter; we prepare children for life and do so at the age they actually are. We have a duty to do that. If they are fulfilled at this stage they will cope with the next stage very easily.

PR: You mentioned to me earlier that some of your children seem to have problems when they go on to secondary education?

DD: I also said that the biggest problem I've got is to get them out of the prevalent attitude of parochialism I find here. This raises a difficult ques-tion. Do we have the right to change their views? I don't really know the answer. I do know I have a duty to educate them to what is available. After that, they must make up their own minds what they want. In terms of them moving on, more and more have had the experience we have tried to give them over the last six years. Those who have had this seem to be able to cope a lot better than those who did not. Those who have been with us for some time are used to mixing with others, they've been taken out and mixed with others, they have been in all kinds of projects and activities, they are used to achieving success.

PR: How do you manage the transition from primary to secondary school?

DD: We are in close liaison with the comprehensive school. We use their facilities: their pool for canoeing or snorkelling lessons, their science facili-ties, we bring in their members of staff to assist with things like gymnastics or to work with children in science or art. So our pupils become familiar with their teachers early on. They go to the comprehensive for a full day in their last term where they run through an example of the timetable that they will experience when they transfer. They take part in sporting events – they go along for the netball tournaments, rugby tournaments, athletics tournaments. Their deputy heads take assemblies for us. So there are lots of regular meetings between their staff and my children and my children and the comprehensive environment. We feel that is a step in the right direction. The Deputy comes in and explains things to them, he meets my J4 teacher, he meets me, there is a dialogue going on all the time.

PR: Your school was commended by the National Commission on Education. How did you come to be involved?

DD: I was approached by Alun Evans of Cardiff University to ask if we would take part, my first reaction was why us? He said they were looking at schools succeeding against the odds. I said what makes you think we are succeeding? His response was headteacher colleagues in the Authority had suggested us. That was nice to hear, but I didn't feel it was enough reason to be included and suggested he come in himself and spend a few days going round the school seeing what was going on, speaking to children, staff and parents and if he still felt we were succeeding then go ahead. I felt it would be wrong of me to say we were succeeding, all I could say was that we are making progress: how you compare against other schools is for somebody else to say.

PR: What did the Commission mean by against the odds in the case of this school?

DD: The school is located in a mining community. It has changed a great deal the last few years, there used to be an old tip as you come into the village. The coal lorries used the local road showering dust everywhere. More recently there was little in the community – it was in the process of closing down – at one time there were 29 shops, now there are three. The people were moving away. There was almost no work locally. Those were the odds we faced – a village community in the valleys with very little going for it. What we tried to do was to show the parents there is a big wide world out there, that there are alternatives, that the expectations they have adopted are often not realistic. I'll give you an example. In my first year I was invited to a presentation dinner of the local Rugby Club for the youth teams. The Chairperson got up and said 'All of you here now, all you've got to achieve in life is this' and tapped his chest. I asked myself 'What is he talking about, a strong heart?' 'This,' he said, 'this badge you get for playing ten games for Cwmgwrach Firsts.' This was the ultimate ambition in life. I thought that typical of the community. It seemed an inadequate ambition for the boys, and what of the girls? I was asked to speak and said 'I've heard your Chairperson. I agree with a lot he said, but I'm sorry, I can't agree with everything. He talked about achieving, life is far more important than ten games for the Firsts. If Rugby is your ambition then the very least you should aim for is a British Lions' Cap. Not everybody achieves their ultimate ambition but you must set your sights high. Rugby is an aspect of life, life is far more important. You've got to go out and experience the whole of life. You must fight against the attitude which you find from some within the village who seem to believe in little more that staying close, staying local and going to the Rugby Club.'

I remember asking a very good girl during my very first year 'What would you like to do when you leave school? What is your ambition in life?' She replied 'My ambition is to get a flat of my own in Glynneath.' Glynneath is a village a mile up the road. People who live there think it wonderful, but that is no ambition in life. Those were the kind of odds we were fighting against – very low parental expectations, low local self-esteem. There was great belief and a pride in a very close-knit community. But take the people out of that community and their confidence goes.

Mr Evans came, he looked around and spoke to the people I suggested, spoke to parents, spoke to staff, spoke to whoever he liked. He felt the school was succeeding and offering a very good level of education in all curricular areas. He brought in other educationalists, interviewed me for three hours on three occasions; interviewed all my staff; interviewed lots of children; spent lots of time in classes watching children work; interviewed several governors and parents; he was happy that we were succeeding. I said to him and to many others that we were succeeding no more than many other schools in West Glamorgan who had been given the same kind of support. We try to give a lot more than the formal curriculum. There are many extra curricular activities.

PR: What did you feel about the report?

DD: I thought it very fair. It highlighted what we were doing. That we are innovative in many ways, a close-knit community who work together and do our best to encourage parents to come and join us. We've a supportive governing body and parent association. This can be tremendously helpful. For example, we have bought two mini-buses. We make good use of them. You've seen the hall, there are a lot of bags against the back wall – £1200 worth of snorkelling equipment that has just been donated to us. We received four new canoes last week. We approach lots of agencies. Many don't want to put money into education – we should be paying for books. I say 'We are not asking you to pay for books but you can give us other things we can use.'

PR: You have been good at this?

DD: We've got to do it. But my aim there is to make our children realize that this school does not finish when they leave at 11 – we still care and they can come back to us. We have children up to 15 come back and take part in various activities. We have no graffiti and no vandalism. We run clubs for them outside school, so we are part of this community. It's vitally important they feel part of us, this is what this community needs.

PR: You also encourage your pupils to look outward?

DD: By focusing them here first, we can encourage them to branch out. They can take part in competitions, activities with other schools. This includes schools from the more affluent parts of Swansea. So they meet children from different backgrounds and don't feel out of place. They don't feel looked down upon. We encourage other schools to share the resources we've got so there is this mixing all the time.

PR: Are you opposed to competition for pupils?

DD: Behind you is a cabinet full of trophies. Pupils participate in competitive, mainly sporting events. They also take part in *Wales in Bloom*, a horticultural event. The school has won the West Glamorgan heat every year it has entered, and the national event this year. So there is competition in all aspects of life.

PR: What about competition between schools, for pupils for example?

DD: I would like to think we are not competitive in this. I don't agree with that. Children do come here from other schools and have gone from here to other schools, but we've not lost a child to another school because the parents aren't happy with what we are doing. But we do have a lot of children coming in because their parents aren't happy with other schools. I am not happy with this. I insist that these parents speak to their present head and try and sort out problems they may have. But competition does exist in this Authority and lots of my colleagues are very aware of it. The nearest school to us is a mile and a half up the road, a Welsh school is also a mile and a half away, another school three miles down the road. Parents, if they choose to, could take their children elsewhere. I am not worried by this. I honestly feel we couldn't be offering their children a better education than we do now; I'm not saying it can't be improved, we are making progress all the time. The ethos and atmosphere are there and the care and sensitivity are there and the curriculum is improving daily. There is a very good standard being achieved, better than the majority of schools in our Authority. Parents are realistic. They know well if the children are happy and achieving. We do our best to make sure every child is catered for in a wide variety of areas. Not just in maths and language, although they are vitally important. If you can provide an environment that makes children want to learn, they will cope with maths, language and everything else.

PR: Who manages you? Who are you accountable to?

DD: First to myself. If I felt my children were being let down I would be more upset than anybody else. Second, to all my pupils. Third, to every member of staff. Fourth, to my parents. I am answerable to them because I have their most precious commodity under my care. I suppose the logical answer is I am answerable to my governing body, but they believe that I and my staff are professionals and know far more about education than they do. They are involved in everything that goes on; they want to be aware of everything that goes on, but they do not feel they should dictate how things should go on. I've got to agree with that. I involve them with a lot that goes on. It is essential that decisions are shared. But as to the best method of making progress, once they've been informed of the options they usually say 'You've given us the options, you are the professional, what do you advise?' I appreciate that immensely. I have a great deal of freedom in one sense, but I don't want to abuse that freedom.

PR: What of your Chairman of Governors?

DD: He comes from a working class, an engineering background. He's a self-made person, a very strong-willed character who is involved in local government. He thinks a great deal of the school; he's English, I don't hold that against him – I'm only joking – I'm not at all a Welsh Nationalist. He came into the community and made a name for himself. Some like it, some don't – the latter tend to think he is far too outspoken. As far as the school is concerned he has been very supportive: he played a major role in enabling us to obtain 95 per cent of the additional funding we received. I tell him what I want; he tells me who to get in touch with and he sows the seeds in the right places. I have a great deal of time for my Chairman. Perhaps he, and the governing body, put too much responsibility on the school but if that's the price I must pay for the support I receive then I will live with that.

PR: What do you mean by that?

DD: For example, when it comes to the Chairman's report for the Annual Meeting he always ask me to write this. I think that should be his report, his perception of what's going on in the school. He should be given the facts and make his own report on them. He relies very heavily upon us at the school and it's nice that he trusts us but I would feel a lot happier if I had a second viewpoint on some things.

PR: Does all this take up a lot of your time?

DD: The governors are of the opinion that the staff's time in school should be spent with children and I wholly agree with that. We had one meeting per term plus the Annual Meeting which is not excessive, this has become one per half-term.

PR: Are there no sub-committees?

DD: There are, but we meet as infrequently as we can. The Finance Sub-Committee meets when the budget is given to us. The other Sub-Committees are the Appointments Committee, which only meets when appointments are to be made, and the Curriculum Sub-Committee, which only meets when something major is to be considered. Other than that they have one long Governing Body Meeting at which curriculum matters are discussed. All in all, it doesn't take up too much of my time. But I acknowledge that perhaps, with a view to our next inspection, I should insist they become more involved for their sake rather than for mine. So it is my intention as from September, by which time four of the governors will have retired, to double the number of meetings per year in order to make them more involved, to bring them into school more. They do come in occasionally. As it happens, most have children in the school.

PR: How do you regard your local authority?

DD: I've always been within West Glamorgan. They changed West Glamorgan just before I started from the old Glamorgan Education Authority. West Glamorgan ceased to exist on 1 April 1996. We then went into Neath and Port Talbot. West Glamorgan has been tremendous. I would not criticize it, they have been very supportive, they had a superb philosophy prior to National Curriculum. A philosophy which valued children. They ran courses to allow staff to develop this philosophy. They resourced us far better than most LEAs. We cannot complain. They've tried to preserve their 'message' within the restrictions of National Curriculum. There has been something of a mixed message of late. That's unfortunate, but they've tried. They say we should be putting children's needs first of all as the main message, but cut backs have meant they have lost some of their best Advisers and replaced them with Advisory Teachers on a short term basis. Advisory Teachers are usually subject centred and, as such, are more concerned about fulfilling the needs of the National Curriculum for music or art or whatever than preserving a holistic approach to education. That has been disappointing. The Senior Advisers who haven't left their post are still giving us the old message which say 'Don't worry, the approach you've been using caters for 90 per cent of the National Curriculum. Remember what is really important is the children receive the kind of education we really believe in.' The Advisory Teachers are less committed to this view. They lack this philosophy. They are too concerned with attainment targets rather than children. You are not going to tell me a child is of less value because he cannot obtain a certain attainment target – that's rubbish. Try telling his parents he is of less value. Some will achieve National Curriculum attainment targets, others will not. We have a duty to try and prepare them appropriately but these targets are not realistic in every situation. Those who can afford to send their children to the top schools are not subject to the National Curriculum, so why is it so wonderful? It has restricted some wonderful teachers and done far more harm than good in good schools. I have to acknowledge it has done some good in picking up the poorer schools.

PR: What about LMS – how has West Glamorgan implemented this?

DD: They've tried their best to retain control while delegating as much as they feel they should. I understand what they are doing – the partnership of schools is important. Their policy has been shaped by the political persuasion of the county more than anything else. But I don't care which party is in power. As long as they cater for the needs of everybody that's fine – unfortunately none do. The LEA being 110 per cent Labour believes in a sort of brotherhood idea which they control. I think they have to be realistic and loosen the reins a bit more. When they had the funding to maintain top quality Advisers and top quality courses and cater for our needs, that was great – we could be happy to stay within LEA control. But they haven't got that now. The people whose services they offer are sometimes good but some Advisory Teachers are nowhere near as proficient as my own staff. How can they hope to offer my staff useful support and training? The money I am given to spend on such services is wasted and I would much rather bring in outside agencies. I've long been very supportive of the Authority but in recent years I have become less so. Nowadays, because of restrictions they tell us are imposed by central government, they cannot offer the quality of services they once did.

PR: Arguablely LMS has given more autonomy to individual schools and heads?

DD: In theory you're right. I define management as having the opportunity to make your own decisions. In practice the size of the budget doesn't allow you to 'manage', it allows you to 'exist'. If I was given my needs plus £20,000 I could decide whether I wanted to put this into extra buildings or a teacher to allow my staff more non-contact time. If I had this I could manage, I could make decisions based on sound educational principles and put them into operation. In practice that does not happen. You have enough money for the staff you've got, to maintain the cleaning services you've got, and four to five thousand pounds for resources. That accounts for every penny. So what has really happened? A system has been put in place by a government who decided we should have LMS but has not funded us sufficiently to allow us to manage. I know in England they get far more money per child than the Welsh schools, so they've a distinct advantage. Lots of our English counterparts run nursery nurses or ancillary helpers. We would love to be able to do it – give me the same level of funding and I'll do it!

PR: There are vast variations in England, some of the poorest English Authorities are at least as poor as the poorest of the Welsh Authorities in terms of unit resource per pupil.

DD: If so how can you publish league tables that claim to compare like with like?

PR: I'm not defending it, only saying that such variations existed long before LMS.

DD: Even so, if that is the case, how can you publish league tables claiming to compare like with like? For this to be possible comparisons must be made on a common base. As things stand, how can it be fair? How can the parents in this community, who scrimp and scrape to make ends meet, compare with parents in Swansea who are nearly all professionals? I've got three professional parents in my school. It is so unfair.

PR: Do you share Wragg's view that you have to be mad these days to want to be a head?

DD: I don't. I wouldn't do anything else. I thoroughly enjoy my job. We are very privileged to work with children. I know I could earn far more doing something else but there is nothing more rewarding than working with children. As a head I have a far greater say over what happens to the whole spectrum of children than I would as a class teacher. Headship is a very special job, I wouldn't change it for the world.

PR: I think he is arguing recent changes make it much harder to be an educational leader?

DD: Wragg is right, but who is to blame? We are. If we allow this to happen we voluntarily sacrifice our beliefs. I've got paper work to do. Today, I put it away because you were coming. My priority is children – if you believe this it will remain your priority. There are many times I haven't sent forms back as required – if you let yourself be dictated to by the system then you are doing your children a disservice. If you believe your children have priority then give them priority and everything else falls into line.

PR: Brian Sherratt, head of the largest school in the UK, claims heads who allow themselves to become administrators do so because they want to not because they must.

DD: I agree with him entirely. At the end of the day some get out of the classroom because they can't teach the children. That's not what it should be about. Headship is about children – schools are about children. Forget everything else – at the end of the day that is what it boils down to. I agree headship is more difficult and the amount of paper work is totally over the top, I see no need for it. The changes made over the last three years have done nothing to improve the system. They don't even know what they are trying to improve. I find it farcical that we can have comments like 'The standards of numeracy and literacy have dropped drastically over the last 20 or 30 years.' When I was in school we did maths all morning, language all afternoon. I wasn't doing the nine other subjects they do now. They expect our primary children to be more proficient than I was in many subjects when I was in the third year of secondary school. It is all so unrealistic.

PR: And to do it whilst resources are squeezed as well?

DD: Exactly. You've got to be realistic. You've got to do the best you can – you've got to manage your time as well as you can and in doing so to be at peace with yourself.

PR: How do you keep up to date with all the changes that are taking place?

DD: I'm not looking for many more changes. I still say from the first to the last school day, we are here for children. Lots of ideas are brought to me from people who attend courses and we discuss them. I go on courses when I feel it's relevant. I rely a great deal on people like the Adviser I told you about who was very much into the current educational debate. He knows my emphasis so he keeps me aware of things I might not otherwise be aware of. I have headteacher colleagues who have a similar philosophy who make me more aware of what's going on. So it is a mixture but at the end of the day I don't feel that that is where my main responsibility lies – that is in my school and with my children.

PR: At the national level, are things done better in education in Wales than in England?

DD: I've been inspected in two schools and in my experience, I haven't been inspected under the new regime yet, the Inspectors were very fair. They supported good practice. They said I do things correctly but did offer constructive criticism which enabled me to make progress. I feel that people will usually play fair in education if they know you are doing your best for your school and your children. What they don't like is people who make excuses and are not doing their best and why should they? Even so, I think at times the community is unrealistic in what they expect. There are far too many changes being made. One example is the teaching of Welsh in the schools in Wales. We have got to be compared with English schools. That doesn't worry me personally – it might some of my staff – but the point I make is that if we are teaching Welsh for approximately 20 minutes a day, one and a half hours a week, 40 weeks a year, 60 hours a year for eight years, 480 hours in all. Now if you give me 480 hours more of maths time this is bound to influence what can be achieved. People don't think about things like this. This is unfair. I don't think such comparisons should be made. I've said all along each school is different and so each school should be judged on its own merits.

As for inspection, I don't like the idea of being told 12 months in advance that you are being inspected. They should knock on my door and say 'We are here to inspect your school.' This would mean that rather than trying to paper over cracks in anticipation, schools would be inspected on what they are actually producing day in, day out. If this were done we would see where the good schools are and which are the ones which just work like mad for 18 months and have done very little for 30 years previously. I think children deserve the best so they should be having the best all the time, not being served a rich diet for the benefit of the inspectors. Children deserve more than that.

PR: How has primary education changed over the time you have been in it?

DD: If I compare my own with my son's primary education, he is far more knowledgeable and has a far better understanding of every aspect of school life than I ever did. I was quicker with mental maths, but he understands the concepts behind the subjects far better than I did. I didn't like school – I would take any opportunity to have time off school. I've tried to ensure that all of my children enjoy school – I always had a very high attendance in my classes, and this school enjoys a very high attendance figure. When we take them away for a week's residential visit – they come home at two o'clock on a Friday afternoon and we say go home have a wash, you're tired. They might go home and have a bath but they are back in school at half past two not wanting to miss the last hour. They must be happy to be in school. Their parents are happy. I haven't had five complaints from parents in the six years that I have been here. I had 30 in my first day in my previous school. You've got to ensure parents know what's going on, that wasn't the case in my day. The partnership must go forward together. As long as every-body knows what's happening and why they all feel certain you are working in the best interests of their children. That is philosophy – I hope it will always be. I know I can't teach all my children myself. My staff have that responsibility. I've got to ensure they have a positive attitude towards the children and want the best for them. I'm lucky I'm in a school where all my staff think like that. It was very frustrating when only some did.

PR: What major changes and developments can you see taking place in primary education over the next decade?

DD: I don't know. There have been so many changes recently I dread to think what it will look like in ten years. What I would like to see would be a period without change, a period when primary education was valued rather than condemned. Too often now we are compared with other countries who are said to be doing far better. But people from every other country I've been involved with or spoken to envy our educational system. I don't see why we always knock ourselves – it's a silly British trait. Let's appreciate the good practice that exists here; let's build on that good practice. More specifically, I would like to see smaller classes and I would like to see greater funding. I hope that's the road we go down. Whatever happens, I expect the next ten years to be interesting and stimulating. I won't try to be too prescriptive. I don't want a system where every child in every school does exactly the same thing: you can turn out robots in a factory, we are dealing with people not robots. Children must unfold in their own way, we should not attempt to mould them. They've got it inside them and we've got to bring it out of them. I hope we are given the opportunity to play our part in doing that.

CHAPTER 5

Demonstrating that learning is for life

Michael Gasper with Christine Pascal

Michael Gasper is Head of Leominster Infant School in Hereford and Worcester. He has been teaching for 25 years, 17 of them as a headteacher. After experience in middle and first schools, he moved to his present post following research in early childhood education. He has developed that research interest over the last six years, achieving an MA(Ed) Early Years in 1995. With Claire Mould, he produced the teachers' booklet to accompany the child development programmes in the BBC *Start Right* series, published and broadcast in 1996. He is also currently participating in a European Comenius project on early childhood. Michael is married with four children.

CP: Can you tell me about your personal background and the people and experiences that have shaped you?

MG: I have to say that overall I was very lucky because I enjoyed my education right from the beginning and that did have a major influence on where I ended up. That's not to say that all those memories are positive ones. If I go back to the earliest times, I started pre-school in a private nursery in Wolverhampton, and I hated that. I just hated being taken out of my home, and having to start with all these people I didn't know, in an environment that I didn't like, having to do things that people said, when they said and so on. I found the whole thing was very threatening. There was also one individual child called Roger who I was frightened of, and who I reckon bullied me. I do not know if he did or not, but I was very fearful of him and my memory of it is of fear.

When I moved into infant education I took a long time to settle. This may sound as if I am saying the opposite of what I started saying, but I remember distinctly in my first class at story time refusing to come down from the top of the climbing frame. The teacher ignored me completely, carried on with the story and when I started to come down said 'No you can't come down and join in the story, you have got to stay up there.' My introduction sounds as if I started off on a dodgy basis, but from really very early on I discovered drama and acting out stories. I loved stories, and I discovered a talent for play acting, and throughout my primary school, which was in Wednesfield, Wolverhampton, that talent was recognized and the school brought it on. I always knew everybody else's lines as well. In one play I played three different parts, because different people were away, just at the drop of a hat, I had a moment's notice.

CP: How did your family and relatives prepare you for school?

MG: Well, my father was a GP who had emigrated from India at the time of partition in 1947. My mother followed on to Britain afterwards and I was born in 1948. Dad's qualifications were not recognized here so he had to re-qualify and do his final housemanship again. We started off in accommodation which we didn't own, a rented flat and Dad was taken on as a junior doctor in Wolverhampton. I was born in Leicester. My mother and I were living at the time with an aunt and uncle, who were a service family in service accommodation, a Nissen hut. I've got very distant memories of that. I have very distinct memories of using a pop gun to shoot daddy longlegs on the wall with my cousin. My mother and I then followed Dad to Wolverhampton, where we lived in rented accommodation. I have memories of a dark hallway and a sinister landlady. Dad was, of course, incredibly busy and I didn't see a lot of him even at weekends. He always seemed to be on duty, or at least that is my perception of him. Later on, we had a cousin of mine living with us, who effectively was an older sister to me. That was an interesting dimension, because I started off as the oldest and then there was a period of time when I wasn't. Home was very supportive. Dad had a very strong work ethic, and there were times later on, when I was a teenager, when his views and mine didn't actually match. Both of us are very strong willed and as I grew older conflict was inevitable. I guess we grew farther apart, I think it would be fair to say that. I mean I don't want to suggest that he wasn't loving or caring, I think he was and is, but I would not say we were ever very close, and we came into quite major conflict later on.

CP: Was your closest relationship with your mother then?

MG: Yes, very definitely, and I wonder whether my conflict with authority early on was linked to that. In secondary school I was in a private school as, what was called, a day boarder. I stayed in school at the end of the day, had tea and did prep in school, and then went home. It was a really long working day but I was very interested in rugby, and that was all I lived for. I always talked about being a doctor. It was the one thing I wanted to be. I got streamed out of sciences, and I felt a failure and I can consciously remember thinking this and that I had let the family down.

CP: How old were you then?

MG: Thirteen I guess. There was a very strong ethic about the eldest child and family tradition so I thought about what was an equally prestigious occupation on the arts side. That was law, so then I talked about becoming a lawyer. Dad, not surprisingly, thought I wanted to become a lawyer. I left school at 19, because I stayed on to do a third year in the sixth form. The school had asked me to be head prefect, which was a great honour. At that stage I was very conformist and I knew it was important to uphold the school tradition. Then I did two and half years as an articled clerk in Dudley before I left the law and went into training college to be a teacher.

CP: When you were streamed out of the sciences at 13, how did that affect your self-confidence?

MG: It wasn't a surprise to me because I was not very good at maths and I got streamed out of the top set. I ended up virtually in the bottom set at maths, and in fact I haven't got O-level maths still. It amuses me every time I look at the school budget. I think of all those teachers turning over in their graves. But there were one or two teachers who had been quite sarcastic. The geography teacher who later advised me about primary education was very unkind. I remember distinctly when we were being selected to be put forward for O-level or A-level, he said 'Oh I shan't be sorry to lose you Gasper' and I thought 'right mate', and was delighted that I got one of the top grades in geography O-level in the group. Perhaps they should all have done that but I wasn't surprised in the end to be streamed out of sciences. There was a feeling that science was for the brainy people, and arts was for the also-rans. It is an interesting perception of arts education generally which persists even today, it's the poor relation all the way.

In secondary school my interest in drama had waned as I went through early adolescence, when I wouldn't go on the stage for all the tea in China. Later on that changed. In primary school I also had a teacher who hated me, and I think it was connected with the fact that my father was an immigrant. He would go out of his way to find fault and ridicule me, and of course there was physical punishment in those days, so I used to get the ruler regularly. I put down some of my difficulties in spelling to that, because I was fine with spelling until I got to his class, and he would deliberately find fault, and even if I had only got one spelling wrong, that was it, I got the ruler.

CP: These experiences didn't turn you off your schooling and education?

MG: No, not at all. I had been on the receiving end of hardship, but I had also been in a position of authority. There was a sort of natural leadership there, and I recognized that within myself. I also had an ability to perform, to relate to others and to get things out of other people. So all those things sat comfortably together. Not comfortable in the sense that you curl up in an armchair and go to sleep, but comfortable in a sense that I felt 'Yes, I can work within this situation. I don't feel threatened, I don't feel undermined. I know that I can go out and do things.' I also found that I got on very well with children with learning difficulties. A number of our friends had got such children. One friend in particular had a handicapped daughter, and when we went over there for meals and so on, she would sit at my feet and I would tell her stories. And whenever groups of people were together, doctors particularly, I would be the focus and organize the other children. It wasn't conscious, it just ended up that way. Sometimes it was a pain because I wanted to be with the adults. Later on I recognized that it was a strength within my own personality. I also cared about people so there was a people element.

Looking back, the aspect that is coming through to me now in terms of management and leadership is that while systems and results are important, it's how you encourage that without losing the first element – the social dimension. But I would have to admit and recognize that I am more socially orientated, I am a people person first and foremost, rather than a systems and results person. I believe education serves a more fulfilling purpose and if you only approach education with a systems orientation you are in grave danger of losing the bottom of the pyramid. You've got the top and it's up there in the sky, but it has no secure base. I think the danger is that you end up with something that looks brilliant on paper in terms of results, but you are only looking at one dimension of the whole. Questions occur to me when I see that an individual's results are absolutely brilliant, brilliant O-levels, brilliant A-levels, went on and got firsts at university, but my immediate question is – what are they like as a person, what contribution do they make to the world in general?

If you look at my school reports I was a dead loss but I was lucky enough through my primary and secondary schools to have key figures who encouraged personal growth. There were a number at primary level who were either friends of the family, or were just very nice people, and were also people people. A couple of them were also results orientated and made me work and that was no bad thing. One of them is still in touch with my parents even now actually. At primary level my old headmaster was a key figure. He was a wonderful man and I still have him in my mind. I think of him taking assemblies and going round the school as well. He was very human. One day I took a cap gun into school and let it off in the lesson. I got sent to his office and I was just reduced to a blubbing mass. He didn't actually say anything to me. I think he said 'Oh Michael, oh dear, oh dear' and walked past, leaving me outside his room. After I'd been stood there for half an hour he just said 'You won't do that again' and he was right. At secondary level I had a particular teacher called Colin Cope, who was an eccentric. I had quite a lot of eccentric teachers in my secondary school, actually. He was a semi-aristocrat, had been to both Oxford and Cambridge and was a classicist. He looked after us very much as 'his' group of boys (it was a single sex school) and he was wonderful, because education wasn't just lesson time, it went beyond. He was a big influence and he helped me look beyond, and, because he was a classicist, he would always be quoting Greek and Roman traditions. He was a historian too, he gave you a sense of your place in a much wider continuum. My old headteacher who took us for French was also a big influence on my life. Again, despite the fact that I was terrible at French, I did French A-level and though I was always the one whose work came back covered in red, he made me head prefect. I remember distinctly being called into his office and he said 'Garsper', because he would never pronounce a short 'a', 'would you be prepared to take on the honours and the responsibilities of being head prefect?' I was absolutely gob smacked but it taught me that education was about more than just results.

When I left school and went on to study the law that was the big crunch time because I came face to face with the realities of life. This was pre-legal aid so you would say to somebody who came in, 'Yes I'll listen to your story and that will cost you ten guineas. I'll write a letter and that will be another ten guineas. I'll read the reply and so on.' I couldn't reconcile myself to this. I can remember the day when a battered prostitute arrived at the doorway and the office girls called me down and said 'Will you go and see her?' This poor girl had been messed about by her pimp and she had absolutely no chance and I had to turn round and say 'Look love, there is no way we can help you. Grin and bear it.' I would say that was a major turning point. The practice I was in was very old fashioned and not very enlightened. My actual mentor was superb and I am still in contact with him but I came face to face with the harsh economics of life and I didn't like it. I then made the conscious decision to go in a different direction.

Even though I had always talked about the law I had always hankered after teaching. I looked at teachers and the life that they led and the nature of what they had to do and it had its attractions. I always thought that I would either end up as a priest, an actor or a teacher and in a sense teaching combines all of these. Religion has been a fundamental thread all through my life. I think through my parents' influence initially, including being forced to go to Sunday school on a Sunday morning. I believe very strongly in a spiritual dimension. I think that is fundamentally important and that people without a sense of spiritual identity are shadows of what they could be. That is fundamental to my beliefs and the way that I go about my job. Why did I actually turn to teaching? Again, fate has been kind to me. There have been certain things that have happened to me for which I really recognize something of influence beyond myself. My boss in the law firm fell out with me and at that time my girlfriend, now my wife, was applying to teacher training colleges. I did try to get other articles of clerkship, but when they heard who my boss was no one was interested. So I applied with her to training college and that caused a major confrontation with my father. It was a major turning point in my life. There was no alternative, it seemed the right thing to do and I was quite certain of that. I was very disillusioned with the law, and I wanted to work with people, helping people and education seemed the best way forward.

I went to Saltley College in Birmingham and when I was interviewed I told my story, much as we are doing now. It wasn't an interview, it was just a conversation and he said 'I think you should go for primary training', and I was quite happy with that. So I entered primary teacher training and those were the days when training courses were good. Saltley was a particularly good college and we spent time in a nursery in Birmingham and an infant school. I had kids crawling all over me and I loved it. I remember a little girl who was fascinated by my beard. The teacher said afterwards that before he had watched this child sit with me and just feel my beard, her concentration span had been non-existent. This was a formative experience because the teacher said I had shown him that she could do something. We were given experiences like this all the way through and I enjoyed being with young children. I found myself gravitating towards the younger group, rather than the 11-year-olds. I have always been interested in how children actually learn, so you tend to want to go earlier and earlier.

CP: What was your career from training to headship? How and when did you decide to become a headteacher and what are your views of headship? Were the heads that you worked with influential in shaping you?

MG: I have never been content to stand still and when I joined the profession we were still in the age where the logical thing was, if you were any good, you looked for promotion. So there was an in-built expectation. Having said that, I didn't actually look for promotion until I had been teaching for two or three years. I was influenced by the headteachers I worked for. The first headteacher I worked with was at a middle school in Halesowen. He was a character and a half and the staff made fun of him a lot. I was only there for 12 months and it seemed like years. I can remember almost everyday. I think that is probably true of your first year in teaching. I remember we had a sports day and I felt a real affinity with those children because I was closer to their age group. I corresponded with a couple of those children for years afterwards. Anyway, I saw young people on the sports field outperform even their wildest expectation because I was encouraging them and that was both exciting and terrifying. Afterwards the staff were talking about which team had won and the head said, 'You know why they did that, it's down to him' and he pointed at me. I think that was a moment of revelation. The fact that this figure of fun should be able to make that judgement, put it in a different perspective. I realized during the course of that first year that teachers can have a profound effect on the children in their charge and headteachers, similarly, have a profound effect on the staff they look after. Now, whether the staff appreciate it, or even realize it, is another matter. Other things also left their mark. I used to turn up to school in a cord jacket and one day one of the children remarked because I went in wearing a suit. They said, 'How smart you look', and I realized it made a difference to them how I looked, which was again a terrifying thing.

During that first year the deputy and I had a major confrontation. I can't remember what the issue was now, but she put pressure on me to do something I didn't like and I said I wouldn't do it. She said, 'if you don't do that I will make sure you will never get another job anywhere else again'. I said, 'fine, you do that'. I wouldn't be bullied, I don't know where I found the courage to do that, I always think it was pure stubbornness or a sense of justice. I went back to her later and apologized but made the point that it was not an apology for what I said but for the way that I had said it. I learnt again how it is possible to compromise. You know how important pragmatism is to me as a life skill. So, I started off in teaching in middle schools and I was generally supported by colleagues.

After one year at this school, fate again played its part. Halesowen at that time was in Worcestershire, but it was splitting off. We were given the option to apply to other Worcestershire schools, so I applied to a middle school in Redditch. There were several jobs and I was lucky enough to get one of them. This middle school was quite large, and got larger, so I was working with a much bigger group of colleagues and the collegiate atmosphere was important. I made some of the most awful mistakes which could have had me thrown out of the profession. The head supported me through all of them, bawling me out, quite rightly, for being a bloody idiot, but he didn't kick me out. That school allowed me to make mistakes and to learn from them. They also allowed me huge opportunities to succeed. In only my second year of teaching I put on a school production in which every child in the school took part and it involved each of the year groups.

As I went up the ladder I became a deputy in a first school. I worked for somebody who viewed her role as head as being to train me for headship. I don't think I had that in my mind and certainly, at the start, I wasn't necessarily imagining that I would be a headteacher. I think that when I was a deputy, the job was absolutely thankless, it was the worst job on earth. Once I realized that, it was inevitable that I would go for headship. My desire of headship was certainly influenced by other heads I had seen and the way they operated, but it was also a need within me. I didn't like being in the position where I was the pig in the middle between the staff and the head and didn't have ultimate responsibility or control over where or when things were going or how they were done. I wasn't afraid of the responsibility. I was actually called arrogant in an interview and I agreed!

It has to be the supreme arrogance to believe that you can be a good head. You are either supremely self-confident and a very good judge of your own abilities, or else there is an element of arrogance in believing you could make that assumption. You have got to have a belief in yourself because you won't last without it. Once you are in that position, all the circumstances conspire to shoot bullets at your own belief in yourself and your ability to do the job. The world around and circumstances are constantly trying to undermine you and if you have the slightest lack of self-belief, you shouldn't even consider it. The heads I'd worked with knew what they were at, you might not have liked the way they went about it, it may even have been ridiculous in the funny sense of the term, but they knew what they wanted and how they were going to do it.

CP: Can you tell me how you prepared for your first headship?

MG: It is quite interesting looking back. I was very fortunate because Pat Lewis, who was my head then, groomed me for headship. She was very inclusive in terms of problems that occurred within the organization or the culture of the school, between members of staff or their career prospects, or the way that they were organizing their work and on discipline issues. I had a lot to do with the PTA and she was quite happy to leave that to me entirely. That was good experience because I was working with parents and hearing what parents said and often they forgot that you were part of the staff. The head helped to push me in the right directions. She was great because she allowed me to make mistakes, helped me to discuss situations, but also sometimes left it entirely to me and said, 'No, it's your problem, you deal with it.' I guess it wasn't mapped out in a clinical sense, but all of the basic areas which are involved in organizing a school were actually covered. The only area perhaps that we didn't really cover would be the political aspects, but we are going back now to the 1970s and although changes had started and we were becoming more responsible for larger portions of our budget, it was still very much LEA controlled. I met my first HMI when I was a deputy. There were a couple of aspects of our school that were very formally organized and they really hammered us for this because it was not in the early years tradition, but the head and I knew that they worked in practice.

So I did consciously prepare for headship and eventually I was an acting head for a term at a totally different school. It was a two-class village school and an ideal position for me to take on at this point in my career. Somebody else had been appointed, but could not take up the post for a term, so I had a job to go back to, and yet I could get all this experience of running the show without having to make any long-term plans. It was wonderful. The LEA and the local inspector in the area knew this position was coming up and they found a suitable young person to go into it and that person was me.

CP: So how did you go about moving from that into your first headship? What was the process you went through and how difficult was it to make that jump?

MG: It was very difficult really. I actually had 13 interviews for headship within a matter or months, in some cases it was two a week. Extraordinarily, nobody ever came and saw you in your job in those days. I suppose there was still a lot of influence from the LEA inspectors who did know you and they certainly had seen me in action and they knew what I had done in the acting headship. The procedure was that you went in the morning and looked at the school and you had the interview in the after-noon. Sometimes I didn't actually want the job, but I didn't know whether it was politic to withdraw or not, so I sort of went through with the thing, but deliberately sold myself short and I knew I was doing that. I think now that if I was in that situation I would say I am ever so sorry, but I don't want this job.

Finally, the patch inspector in my acting headship came and spent an afternoon with me. He was a fearsome man with a terribly severe reputa-tion within the authority of being an absolute tartar. Oddly enough, he had been responsible for passing me after my probationary year. He spent the whole of the day with me and watched me work. Once I had settled the chil-dren down he started asking me questions and he tutored me. Now at that stage I had one more interview. It was the thirteenth coming up and it was for a school within the area that I was working. It was a peculiar place because it was a village school that had then expanded, so in size it was like an urban school, but the setting was totally rural and the aspirations were rural. There were a lot of families there who were children of prison officers, so there was quite a lot of social difficulty amongst the clientele and the local villagers and the prison families didn't always mix. There were some wonderful elements of conflict. Without his help I wouldn't have got that job and that job was my first independent headship.

CP: What do you feel about the interviews and processes you had been through as a way of selecting heads?

MG: There was a hierarchical structure. If it was a small headship, you went along to the school and saw it in action in the morning and maybe you met the chairman of the governors. Then you went back to the council offices in Worcester and you went into the interview room one by one. You had members of the governing body and county councillors on the interview panel. It was always chaired by a county councillor and there was a representative of the LEA to advise. If it was a bigger headship they were just adopting the system where you spent a day, or part of a day, looking at the school and then on a second day the interviews were split. In the morning session you had a series of mini interviews with a longer list of candidates, which was then whittled down and the afternoon session was the formal interview along the same lines as it always had been. I still felt that there didn't appear to be a lot of consideration of heads' track records. Although there may well have been behind the scenes, it was not made apparent. I think a lot of the decisions were down to the inspectors. It certainly worked, but whether it could have been done better is another matter. Practicalities come into all this and at that time there were a lot of jobs that came up and there was no other way for the LEA to get through them all. With the best will in the world we are all governed by practicalities.

CP: When they actually offered you the job, what were your feelings?

MG: I was delighted, speechless and really elated. It was a definite achievement and I felt that now I had really done myself justice. The other thing was that you knew a lot of the colleagues that you were up against. There was a sort of college of candidates and camaraderie amongst us and I was up against a number of people I knew and whom I respected. I felt to be appointed for this post instead of these people was really good. There was an acknowledgement there that lifted me.

CP: Did you feel prepared for the job? What are your memories of the first days?

MG: The first day I remember distinctly because I sat in my office thinking, 'Well this is very nice.' At that stage you could see the table, so I pretended to play about with a bit of paperwork, but there wasn't much because I was new to the job. Then I thought this is no good, I can't just sit here, this is ridiculous. I thought, 'I must get to know each of the teachers better and I must get to know the children.' So I went down and wandered round the classes. I now know that wandering around is a perfectly respectable management technique but I honestly did not know what to do. I just sat there, with nothing to do. I was slightly phased by this because I don't know what I had expected, but I hadn't expected to be sitting behind a desk doing nothing. I just don't operate that way, I think there was a bit of guilt maybe. Over the first three days that very rapidly disappeared and as I got a feel of the organization, strategies suggested themselves to me. It was very much flying by the seat of one's pants and fortunately I'd had a reasonable amount of training and experience and my instincts were good. Also the kind of problems that came up were really just ones I had come across before, but in a new setting, so I had confidence in dealing with them. As time went on that changed, I had some of the political naiveté knocked out of me.

CP: What would be your advice to someone now hoping for headship?

MG: It would depend on what they thought headship was about, because I think it is ever so easy for people to get a false impression of what the job is. One thing for sure is that it is no longer about day to day contact with children. When I moved into this job I found it totally different and nothing that I had done previously actually prepared me for it. The best help I have had was through the college management courses I have taken since I was appointed. These forced me to take a step back and to think much more carefully than I had ever done before about what I was doing, what the issues were and how to address them. I think for anybody new approaching headship, they would have to be very clear about why they wanted to become a head. There has to be some element of enjoying moving things around because that is basically what you have to do. The problem with it is that there are so many other factors coming in that force you to change what you have planned to do, that you have got to be adaptable. If you are the sort of person who finds it difficult to operate in this way and to cope with sudden change, then you will find the job very difficult.

CP: How would you describe your career as a head?

MG: Very enjoyable, despite everything. You have got to have a totally bizarre sense of humour to succeed as a head. You have to appreciate the totally ludicrous range of things you will be asked to do, from considering a budget, deciding on teachers' futures, working out whether children are going to be scrunched together in a large group or spread out, to being out in the pouring rain with your hand up a drainpipe. You have got to have the sense of humour that can cope with that. I know continental colleagues, and particularly those from the USA, who come over and are mind blown at the range of what we have to do.

CP: Do you see your career developing in a progressive way?

MG: I think there has been a definite progression but it's in an odd way. The more I am in the job the less I feel I know. Teaching is like that anyway, if you get to the stage where you think you know it all, then you have gone beyond your best. You have passed your sell by date. The way that I approach the job now is quite different and rightly so. I think there are specific skills that I have now got that I didn't have before, but it is just the whole way that I approach the job which is so different. With that first job everything was inspirational and not planned in the sense of me standing back from things a lot. I think I developed some of that then, but now it is much more conscious, and I am much more strategic. Finance and organization tend to dominate and have to be balanced against educational beliefs. Working in my last headship I learnt how to co-operate with colleagues because you have to do that if you are in a small school. In this school I try and operate with a much more collegiate approach with my staff and with other headteacher colleagues. That has been a development which I have acknowledged within my own mind much more clearly.

CP: How has your vision for each of your schools developed?

MG: I have to go back to my basic values in that case because I am very much a people-centred person. Justice is important and I want people to do themselves justice. I have always been interested in those who were not achieving their full potential whether they were very bright or not so bright. I think I have encouraged people to do themselves justice, to be more assertive and to stand up for what they believe in, in all the schools I have worked in. It is very important that schools are social places. I acknowledge that they are academic and, of course, the academics are important, but unless your academic skills are intermixed with social and personal confidence, then there will always be limits to success. No matter how good an individual looks on paper, when it comes to the crunch, their applications will be as weak, or strong, as their confidence. This vision has run consistently through all of the schools where I have been head.

In my present school, I am actually saying to people, 'Come on, what do you believe in?' I am trying to get the staff to be explicit about their values and judgements. I am confident in myself, I know where I am at and I know where I am coming from, but I am now saying to other people, 'Define where you are at, find out about yourself because you will be able then to do your job much better.'

Going back to my first headship I see that I just burst into it, and I spent certainly five years or so of the ten that I was there, enjoying myself, leading and getting people together and enjoying the events of the year. Then, because the school shrank, and I moved from being the non-teaching head to being a teaching head, there was a change in the way that I approached things. I had to be up front leading with clear directions. This changed again when I took over this current headship.

CP: What kind of a leader or headteacher are you?

MG: I think any head has to have a certain amount of personal charisma, dynamism, call it what you will. There are those who can go about their job very quietly and get it done, but I think you are up front and your presence has to be felt, but I am not necessarily saying you have got to be loud. I would describe myself as being somebody who likes to know where I am going. Yes, I can be adaptable, but I don't like a constant situation of adapting where you end up feeling that you are in total chaos. So I am somebody who likes control. I do think it is reasonable for people to expect traditional leadership models from leaders, so there will be times when, and I have to judge when those are, the staff will expect me to say that this is what we are doing, at this time, in this way. But, there are also other times where I have got to take a backwards step and let them influence the direction we take. However, I don't think you can have total equality in a school situation. So yes, I am the head in the school and there are expectations that impinge, from the parents, the children, as well as the staff.

I have also learnt over the years that whilst sometimes it is inconvenient to consult and it takes time, you can end up in a stronger position by finding out what people feel about particular issues. If you have actually been consultative and you have got everybody together and there is the professional agreement to go in particular directions, then you will get them working together and this allows you to achieve much more in the long run.

CP: Do you think headship has become less difficult or more difficult?

MG: I think the nature of the job has become more difficult. I think actually if you start looking at all that you are supposed to do it is impossible. But because it is so impossible, you have got to decide your own priorities. This is what I have been saying to my own staff. I think that what we have been asked to do is totally impossible, so we have to decide what we are going to do and why. Now somebody can come in and say you should be doing it in a different way, or argue over the fact that you have got no plan, or that you are somehow sinking in the morass. But, if you have got a clear idea, a clear philosophy, a clear plan, they can't argue with that. They may wish it to be something different, but then they have got to put an argument against you. And for me too, I have got to recognize the elements of my job at any one time that are a priority and that are achievable and focus on those.

CP: How do you enable effective teaching and learning to go on in your school?

MG: I would say that over the last five years I have been very tied up with organization, management and restructuring. We have lived through redeployment and redundancy and we have not really looked hard enough at the curriculum areas. I know that there are things going on in some classrooms which we need to discuss and develop. We have begun with a collegiate approach and we have now actually defined curriculum aims. I also set up an adviser to come in to start our development in this area. I have found an independent third party can be very helpful in opening up discussion, and my role then is as a facilitator for the development which must follow. I wish I could do much more but I can't, time doesn't allow. I also have built in meetings with senior management staff and those tend to be strategic.

We have to face the fact that there are strains undermining what we are doing. You sometimes get the feeling that the world is conspiring to undermine everything you believe in or think you should be doing. The day to day, week to week activity is very much reactive, rather than proactive, unfortunately. Again, we are trying desperately to lift ourselves out of this. In my depressive moments I think it is all hopeless, but when you start looking carefully at what is going on I would say there are a lot of positive things happening and I can see that we are gradually lifting ourselves out of the morass.

CP: To whom do you feel you are accountable?

MG: I am accountable to those little children that I stand in front of every Monday morning and at intervals during the week and that's my bottom line. If I feel I have done them justice, my conscience is clear, I can sleep with that. Looking beyond that I have got a responsibility to my staff, as colleagues and as fellow professionals. I feel accountable to them. I feel the need to explain to them why we are doing things or how things have arisen or why I believe we should go where we are going. Every now and again I will go in and make philosophical statements to them, because I feel I have to, I feel I owe it to them. They are purely personal, based on my assessment of where education is going and our place in it. I hope they are relevant and they certainly are underpinning our strategies in my mind. I also want people to think for themselves and not just 'do'.

I think the accountability with governors and parents is much more of a two-way process. I think it is a different accountability but I also think the parents bear an accountability too. I have to be able to explain coherently to the parents what it is we are doing and why and how it affects their child. As a parent I would expect that. But also, I want to know what parents are doing to back me up and to back up my teachers and support what we are doing. I think the best way to achieve this is through personal contact, face to face. I think realistically, parents find it difficult to come to me, not because I am not approachable, but it's just the mechanics. The first point of contact tends to be the teachers, quite rightly. I always say my door is open, if you want to say something, come. I am around at the start of every day, I am around at the end of every day. Accountability, answering for what we do and how we do it, of course I am accountable to parents, and I accept this wholeheartedly.

CP: What about governors, the LEA, DFEE and other agencies?

MG: It's curious isn't it? Increasingly the governors are supposed to be the people bearing the responsibility. A lot of the areas that headteachers were traditionally responsible for, and in practice are still responsible for, the governors now bear the ultimate responsibility. There have been an increasing number of cases recently when I have turned to my governors and said, 'It's your problem not mine, I will advise you but you have to make this decision.' I think the accountability to the LEA is much more in terms of whether I and my school are broadly within the band of acceptability by LEA standards and that I am not doing something so outrageous that they can't approve of it. It works at that sort of level. The DFEE are so remote that my accountability to them operates only on a very distant level. I am much more concerned about fulfilling my responsibilities to those who are in my immediate circle of professional activity: the children, their parents and the staff.

CP: How do you maintain your own professional well-being and development? Who do you look to for support?

MG: I suppose on a day to day level I look to colleagues who are close to hand, particularly my colleague at the neighbouring junior school, Ian Foster. He and I often have conversations, but I'm also in reasonably close touch with other colleagues in primary schools nearby and through our professional association, the NAHT. I suppose it's also true that there is a certain amount of support still available from the LEA through our inspectorial staff, most of whom I've known for a good many years.

In a wider sense I have found that the professional relationships which have developed with friends at Worcester College have been a tremendous source of inspiration and support and have kept my professional development on track in recent years. It sounds a bit of a contradiction in terms that further educationally based study or research helps you with your well-being and professional development, but it does. During the whole of the time that I've been in my present post I have been undertaking courses of study leading to various qualifications. That has been a terrific support and has largely been responsible for my own personal professional development, whilst also benefiting my school. My whole approach and way of thinking has become deeply influenced by the reading I have been able to do. This has been focused because of the courses of study and by the very nature of research itself. I find my approach to day to day problems is much more analytical, more clearly focused and that the quality of the questions that I ask are far deeper and penetrate much further. I do consciously try to relate the courses to tackling the practical issues I face in school and to our shared philosophical base. All that development is really down to the contact I have had with the college and, through this contact, with other professionals. I have been very lucky. I have been privileged to work alongside staff from the Pen Green Centre, and with people like Margy Whalley and Tina Bruce. It really is both very exciting and challenging to be in their company and to be sharing their professional development as part of one's own. But I suppose the core of support and development lies with the colleagues at the Centre for Research in Early Childhood at Worcester.

CP: What changes have taken place in primary education? Do you feel that these are making things better or worse? What do they mean for you as a head?

MG: I think while I have been involved in primary teaching the nature of it has changed out of all recognition. In the period since 1981 when I became a head, I've seen changes which have led to far greater control, or attempts to control, what actually goes on in classrooms. Whilst there might well have been some powerful arguments for some degree of standardization in curriculum content, what we've ended up with is so rigid and so regimented that it has killed inventiveness, imagination and the personal qualities which I have described as having been so important to me and to my development. These are completely at odds with what is now demanded of teachers. This has been compounded by changes to teacher training, where courses have now become fixed around the National Curriculum, as if nothing else mattered, and areas such as child development and thinking skills have been sadly neglected. There is a move to revive the whole area of moral and spiritual education but the fact that you should have to emphasize those areas just goes to show how far the curriculum has become regimented away from such important areas. The latest changes which have been put forward impose on the youngest children a style and ethic that is quite inappropriate for them. I believe if we are not careful we will end up with teachers of the young simply putting children through hoops, so that you have the surface appearance of children being able to do certain things, while there is very little foundation for real, experiential learning underneath.

Organizationally, there have also been phenomenal changes. We have moved away from a situation where schools were responsible for only a very small part of their current budget to purchase books and equipment, to a situation where schools are virtually responsible for every aspect of their financial management and planning. Indeed they can choose now to become completely independent of LEA control. Now originally I would have to say that I welcomed greater financial independence, which was fine while there was a degree of financial flexibility and a degree of resourcing which allowed real choice. Unfortunately the reality of practice has meant that resources have shrunk and finances have become so tight that there is no flexibility or room to manoeuvre, and finance dominates all else. We are reduced to having to make the same choices that LEAs had to make in the past of where to cut so that it will do least damage. This has been compounded by the changes in salary structure for teachers, which mean that a graduate who comes in at point 2 on the salary scale has but seven years to reach their maximum salary. Now if the majority of your staff under a county's financial system are above average earnings, you are effectively penalized because allocations are based on 'average' costs. That means that other areas within the total budget lose out. It also means that after seven years, staff who are just reaching a stage when they understand what education and teaching is about and are still young enough to have energy and enthusiasm are already too expensive to employ. The other insidious change has been a series of government reports which have resulted in legislation which carries the glorious misnomer of being 'enabling'. In other words it says what you must do but it doesn't actually give you the resources to do it. This happened very early on with the Warnock Report on special needs and has been repeated several times with other areas, such as that of setting up the National Curriculum and testing. In these cases it has been extremely difficult to get resources or, in respect of testing, resources have only been made available as a bribe in order to impose unpopular decisions about the publication of results. That's another whole area of detrimental change. There has been an awful confusion between assessment and testing and the government has resorted to techniques and tactics which would have been utterly condemned in any aspect of public life but a few years ago. It has not simply been the case that they have manipulated statistics but they have compared things which are not alike, as if they were. The tests themselves have been changed year on year and yet the results have been compared as if they were exactly the same. So I guess the political influence has increased hugely and, to my way of thinking, detrimentally. The whole idea of imposing the ridiculous notion of 'key stages', as if somehow learning was hierarchical and structured like a step ladder, has been damaging. These impositions have come along to the detriment of the children, and with the 7-year-old children we lose effectively at least one and a half term's worth of important teaching time because so much emphasis is now placed on the tests. And bear in mind that in my own school we try to resist teaching towards the tests or laying too much emphasis upon them.

I suppose another area of change in my time as a head has been the demise of HMI and the reduction of what was a well respected body which had authority, not simply by statute, but by the authority which is born of professional respect. This has been eroded and replaced by a system which is not respected because of its insensitivity to educational issues, its inability to understand the pressures that are on teachers, and its change from being apolitical to being perceived as entirely political and serving blatantly political ends. The independence which underpinned and strengthened professional trust and respect has vanished.

I think the really sad part of all of this is that there are elements in some of these changes which were necessary and which could have been so much more positive if there had been proper consultation. The denial of the value of teachers' professional judgement has been an insidious and poisonous pressure which has directly contributed to the early retirement of many capable, experienced and valuable teachers. If the process of change had been proactive rather than imposed, and if there had been a willingness to listen, particularly to those closest to the children, teachers would have felt valued, trust could have been strengthened, and the profession encouraged to be positive about their development towards the millennium. An important opportunity was squandered.

What do these changes mean to me as a head? They mean a lot of extra work, often for no particular reason other than that I am told to do it. They mean that effectively, when a newly qualified teacher comes into school, I have to start retraining them in what I would consider to be the really important aspects of teaching. They mean that I have to try and manage a budget knowing that if I hold onto my more experienced teachers I am creating problems for the school as a whole financially. They mean that I have to put up with being closely inspected by people whose qualifications may not actually be as good as those of my staff and who are not, in fact, accountable to anyone for consistency, accuracy or fairness in their pronouncements. I suppose they also mean that I look back with a certain amount of nostalgia to the times when things were just beginning to change as a sort of 'golden age', where you still had the freedom to choose what to do, when being professional meant that you gave careful thought to what you provided and how you provided it, and when you worked together as a staff to plan your work. I believe what we provided then was differentiated, though we might have used other words, it was assessed, though maybe we wouldn't have known what was meant by 'success criteria' and it was based very closely on what we knew about the children rather than about subjects, although we all had training in subject areas. All this may sound rather gloomy but it isn't. It is realistic and serves to remind me how important it is to hold onto the principles which I believe in and to keep a balance within my school, rather than to be forced into following one pathway.

CP: How do you wish your school to develop over the next few years? What changes would you like to see in primary education? What do you see as the future role of heads?

MG: I want my school to continue developing as it has started. We must be clear about what it is we're trying to do and why we believe in the things we believe in. Then we must look to see how those things will work in practice. This is not to say that we can't be critical of what we are doing. We must be sure that we are covering the main areas of learning and development – social, academic, moral and spiritual, physical and philosophical but all of this must be in a context that acknowledges that we are dealing with very young children. What we do in practice should be consistent with good quality early years' practice. We should be looking more at children as individuals, as we do when they come into nursery. We should be giving them challenges which will help them to achieve and to gain confidence from their achievements. We should be making them want to achieve even more, and helping them to respect each other and other people's achievements, so we must give them all an opportunity to celebrate their successes. I suppose ideally I would like to see our school become a 'centre of excellence' but we have an awful lot of work to do before then.

What changes would I like to see in primary education? Well, I'd like to see a restoration of the balance in our work, and an acknowledgement of teachers' professional ability to make judgements, rather than being limited to what has become an increasingly narrow curriculum. I'd like to see success measured in much wider terms than narrowly academic key stage levels. And above all else I'd like to see a system which allows children to be children and not be seen somehow as having to be 'old before their time' or to have undue pressures put upon them.

As to the future role of heads, I think the underlying aspects of the head's job of being a facilitator, an enabler, having the vision to lead, being a 'pebble dropper' who can stimulate argument or discussion or interest, I think those areas will always be there. But I think increasingly, heads are going to have to be more political. They are certainly going to have to either be accountancy wizards or know someone who is. I think one of their key roles in the future will be to remind everybody that we are dealing with young children who are growing and developing as people in their own right, and who have the right to be treated as individuals, not as empty vessels to be filled up with any current politically popular theory. I believe it is going to be up to primary heads to fight for recognition in the minds of all people that the early stages of education are just as important as the later stages and require the same level of funding and resourcing. And whatever else, I think heads are going to have to be able to retain their sense of humour come what may.

CHAPTER 6

Raising children's expectations

SUE MATTHEW WITH CHRISTINE PASCAL

Sue Matthew is head of St Ebbe's CE (Aided) First School in Oxford. She was born in Ohio, USA and educated in a number of states due to family moves. She completed her first degree in political sciences at Duke University in North Carolina, and then trained and worked as a teacher in a girls' boarding school in Tanganyika, East Africa. She met (and subsequently married) a Scot while in East Africa, and then came to England, where she had her three children and retrained for primary teaching. She worked for 11 years at St Barnabas First School before getting the Headship of St Ebbe's First School, where she has been for eight years. For eight years she was also the Teacher Member on Oxfordshire County Council.

CP: Could you begin by telling me about your personal background, your home, school, and the people who have shaped the kind of person you are?

SM: I was born in Ohio in the United States in 1941 into a very close family. Mother was a teacher and my father was in business. Dad worked for a large American corporation which meant we moved quite a lot. Looking back it was an important influence for both my sister and me in that we moved pretty well every two years, which meant new friends and new environments. This does make you flexible and helped to develop a more outward looking approach. It also meant that we got to see more of the states. We lived in Ohio, Colorado, California, Illinois and Indiana. The United States is such a big place. Such a diversity of environments was an important influence on me as I was growing up. This wonderful close family has been supportive to me and Billie (my sister) throughout our lives. We also had a fantastic maternal grandmother who was absolutely committed to education. The reason for this was that she had had to stop school when she was 12, and to all her numerous grandchildren she would always say, 'I never had the chance to go to school beyond 12, but you do, and mind you read those books!' She was an avid reader and very committed to the view that education was important, not just to get on, but because she had seen how it would feed your personality and your lifestyle during your whole life.

The other great thing about her and my granddad, who was a carpenter, was that they built their own house in California. Anybody in the family who wanted to go to California would go to their place. Our cousins would meet at their house in San Clemente Beach. We had happy summers with up to 20 of us all sleeping in their 'lanai' – a sort of veranda. That experience has kept us close and we still have reunions of the Richardson clan about once every five years. My grandmother had six children, and those six children have generated quite a large family, and quite a lot of teachers amongst them. So you can see that my grandmother was quite influential to all the grandchildren. It is remarkable that in our very diverse family everyone has carried on their education in one form or another. Grandmother Richardson would be absolutely thrilled that she has done that. They were such a wonderful pair, my grandparents. She was tough and determined and had to take in washing to look after her six children and was a classic American pioneer type. My granddad was the sweetest person ever. He wouldn't correct us about anything, he thought his grandchildren were wonderful and he loved us deeply but in his wonderful quiet way. He was a very different sort of influence on us. So I think we were really lucky to have such a good family.

Even in those days the number of American families who actually stayed together was quite low, but there was no question of that in our family. There was a very deep love between my mother and father. My parents were the best parents I can imagine. They gave us love, freedom, encouragement and a zest for life. This 'zest for life' was enhanced by a bizarre experience that happened in California. I was down on the beach early one morning and a 16-year-old tried to murder me. Later on I found out about his background. He was angry with the world and had the 'urge to kill'. He chose me because I happened to turn up. He held me down in the water until I was unconscious and then left. Fortunately, someone called an ambulance and I was taken to hospital for an emergency tracheotomy. A very crusty old German/American doctor there firmly believed I should realize what had happened and make sense of it. He gave all these reasons why I should have died and then said, 'Now look, you haven't, so don't just take this life you have for granted.' I think the result of that experience is that I still see every day as a gift. I think this carries over to my feelings about young children. They see each day as precious. They do it naturally. Children live in the present. My yoga teacher says, 'Don't think about what you have just done or plan for the future, teach yourself to live in the present.' In a busy life you have to think ahead a lot and you do lose the pleasure of the moment. We don't have enough time in our professional lives and that is a challenge, not to create time because that's impossible, but somehow to create the illusion that we do have time to savour the moment – to listen to the children, to allow them to teach us the preciousness of 'now'.

As to my school days, I had lots of different schools. American education in those days was very much about problem solving. We were set problems and we dealt with some of them through role play. I remember a wonderful mock United Nations assembly. They were positive influences and I was often actively involved in activities and had some excellent teaching. It was not always the sort of excellent teaching that you would have understood at first. With some teachers I thought, 'What is she trying to accomplish?' but then things became clear. I have some quite clear memories of teachers, some very positive and one very negative. The negative one was Mr Taylor and he made me feel I could never learn mathematics. I always say to the children in this school that they are so lucky because our teachers at St Ebbe's make you love numbers, and that I would have given anything to have a teacher who made me love maths rather than one who made me feel I couldn't do it.

When it came to choosing a university I made a difficult decision. We had lived in various parts of the United States but we hadn't lived in the east coast or south. I was attending high school in Illinois. It was not a high-flying school but basically it was a good high school. I had done well on various SATs (Standard Achievement Tests) and in my high school courses and so they were trying to encourage me to go to some posh eastern school, but I said I didn't really see myself as a posh easterner. I went down south to look around and just fell in love with Duke University in North Carolina, because its environment was beautiful, with trees and a sort of settled peace about the life that I hadn't seen before. So I chose to go there and read political sciences. Looking back this was quite selfish of me because it is a private university. Subsequently I found out how much my parents were having to pay, but you don't think of that at the time because they say 'Well you choose, go where ever you want.' When I got there I found out that the peaceful exterior at Duke was a shell. The south in the 1960s was not peaceful. You probably don't believe it now, but at that time Durham, North Carolina was still a segregated city. I had seen racism up north, but at least people were allowed to go to the same shops, restaurants and sit anywhere on buses. In Durham for the first time ever I met with a very clear political choice that I had to make. I certainly didn't go in thinking 'I am a crusader', all I knew was I couldn't believe what I was seeing happening around me. Some other Duke students and I joined with some students from North Carolina College and targeted Howard Johnson's Ice Cream, one of the American 'great symbols'. The idea that we couldn't go into an ice cream parlour and have ice cream with friends who were black was unacceptable. So we just went in quietly and sat there until we were arrested. Even when we were arrested I was put in a white woman's jail and the black students put somewhere else. Seven of us were kept overnight in jail. That was a learning process too because we found two women in there who had not been read their rights or been allowed to phone a lawyer. So when we got out we talked to our friends at the university and we got things done about Durham jail. Sometimes I think people go though their life without having to take sides. I think anybody seeing that situation would say that this is something that is wrong and we must take action. The excitement was to see that you could effect change. Sit-ins were happening in other southern towns and segregation was stopped eventually.

Duke was a good university. I had some very good teaching and the chance to develop ideas and skills. There were clever women there who formed a very special group of friends. Through the various links with friends, not only in North Carolina College but also in other aspects of my student life, I became involved with various groups. One of these groups provided the key to my future teaching career as it has turned out. I went on a summer programme to East Africa called 'Operation Crossroads Africa'. The programme was run through a wonderful minister in New York who was keen for black and white students to have the chance to work in East Africa. Our project that summer was to build a school for the Wa-Arush people. I loved East Africa! So when it came to the time that I started thinking of what I would do after graduation I had no qualms at all in going to my adviser and saying 'I don't care what I do, but I must go back to East Africa.' I remember him taking out a book, flicking through the pages and saying 'Oh, here is something called Teachers For East Africa, would you like to be a teacher?' and I said 'I will do anything to get to Africa, even being a teacher!' Yet the great thing about being a teacher is that when you do it, it is one of those professions that you know is right. I am so lucky that Africa got me, because I think part of me was thinking that because mother had been a teacher and my sister at that time was a teacher, I thought maybe I should try something new, but I loved it. The Teachers Programme was very interesting, it was a precursor to the Peace Corps by just one year. Other Americans came over later for the Peace Corps Project. The good thing about 'Teachers For East Africa' was that we were seen as civil servants working for the Tanganyikan government – not the USA.

CP: So that was your teacher training?

SM: We did our PGCE at Makerere University in Uganda, with practice teaching in African schools. This was important as we were better qualified than American teachers who had just dropped in to Africa through the Peace Corps because we had had our training at an African university. Then you were posted to a school for two years. I was given to this amazing government girls' boarding school, 5,600 feet up on Kilimanjaro in Machame, Tanganyika. It was just wonderful! The children were so dedicated to the learning that they were offered. The school children here get tired of me going on about caring so much about education but African children would walk as far as 15 miles to get to their first schools, and their mums and dads had to work day and night to find the school fees. Nyerere, the President, came to see us there one day and he sat down on the ground with the children and talked to them and said, 'Look, we are investing in you, you are our future, don't you dare forget what these people have sacrificed for you to come here.' So it was absolutely wonderful teaching experience.

CP: You are emphasizing the value of education and the importance of communicating this to children. Is this what your African experience gave you?

SM: Yes. They believed passionately in education – and what it could do for a young nation. I am forever grateful to Africa for all it gave me. It was just terrific! Africa also gave me my husband. I met Colin there. He was also on the TEA Project, the British side, which was sponsored by the Ministry of Overseas Development.

CP: What happened at the end of your time in Africa?

SM: I had seen a lot of my friends getting married straight out of university and then resenting the fact that they hadn't done things, so I had promised myself that I wouldn't get married until I was 36 or until I had travelled the world on my own. So at the end of my two years teaching in East Africa I made my way through India, Cambodia, Thailand, Singapore, Hong Kong and Japan. Then Colin and I were married in Indiana in December 1966.

Colin, my husband, wished to do an MPhil in history, so we came to Oxford. I did two part-time, wonderful jobs. One was in the morning, editing the Salisbury Papers in Christ Church Library. In the afternoon I was working at a private nursery because nobody else would accept my qualifications. Duke University is a good university but they would not accept my degree, and nor would they accept my Makerere PGCE – an external London University teaching qualification. Later on I did various research projects. I helped with 'African Affairs', 'The History of East Africa' and 'African Law Reports'. We had our three children, David, Lucy and Oliver, during this time. Fortunately I could combine family and work.

CP: Until this time had you always taught older children?

SM: Yes. In Africa I taught at both GCSE and A-level and when I got back to the United States, even though I was only there for a short time, I did supply teaching again with older children. So I didn't teach young ones till I got to Oxford. The extraordinary thing was that this private nursery school took me on even though I had no qualifications with young children. I couldn't believe it. While I was doing this I realized that I'd much prefer teaching young ones but I knew that it was absolutely essential that I be retrained. I decided to do a course of primary teaching at Westminster College, which I very much enjoyed. I was then fortunate to get a temporary job at the local primary school called St Barnabas where my own children attended.

In the end I was at that school for 11 years! I loved St Barnabas. It was very interesting teaching in a school when you live in its neighbourhood. A lot of people say you shouldn't do this but in fact the children were wonderful and so were the families. Nobody ever pushed me into what I would have felt was an unprofessional position. The children in school always called me Mrs Matthew and they would meet me around tea-time and it would be Sue. There was never a conflict really, I found it wonderful because I was a well informed person in the school as the neighbourhood children tell you everything. I was there for the first nine years as a classroom teacher and the last two years as deputy head. The head retired and a new head arrived who was wonderful and you could just feel that the school was going to be secure and happy. I think that was the first time I thought of leaving. I wouldn't have left before, because it was too important to me to keep in that community, but when Hilary came and the school continued to thrive, it gave me the confidence to think of a move. She was splendid to work with as a deputy head and I am very grateful to the governors for giving me that chance.

CP: What do you think prepared you for your own headship?

SM: My own head was encouraging and supportive. Also throughout my career, and this probably goes back to my African links, I have been very keen on equal opportunities. I was part of something in Oxfordshire called the Equal Opportunities Network, which a group of us started up ourselves. At that time the statistics in Oxfordshire were that 75 per cent of the teaching force were women and 75 per cent of heads were men. Fortunately things have got much better. I encouraged other women to go for headships and one of them said, 'Why is it that you are always encouraging us, and you don't go for one?' I said, 'Well, I have an American accent and it wouldn't be fair for a school to be stuck with a loud-mouthed American.' They said, 'Why don't you give them the choice?' I remember ending up saying to this friend, 'OK, if you ever find a school that it is small enough to know all the mums and dads and the children so I can feel like it's a family, that has a multicultural and multisocial mix, and that is a bicycle distance from home then I'll go for it.' Then I got this phone call saying 'I've found a school.' My decision to finally go for headship, and then getting it, is interesting and I think I was surprised I got appointed because I hadn't come through the normal career route having done a lot of different odd jobs. I went for the interview feeling very positive but had I not got it, it wouldn't have upset me to be honest because I could have carried on being a deputy in a school I loved. I almost said to them when they offered the job to me 'Do you really want me because I have disabilities? Not only am I foreign and outspoken, but also I don't drive and I am almost partially sighted, and that is not easy with all the reading you have to do and the computer.' But they were willing to take on a partially sighted American. I also think back to Tim Brighouse, who was our Chief Education Officer. We were so lucky to have him for ten years in Oxfordshire. His vision was inspirational and he was so supportive of all of us. I remember chatting to him once about headships becoming very administrative and about budgets and how I felt people come first. He said, 'It's got to be people first' and I said, 'If you promise me it is going to be about people, I can do that.' So there were questions in my mind and it is interesting that it just came all together and made me think that I could have a go. I am so pleased I did because looking back, although I was being prepared for it in a sense, I didn't realize that there were all these challenges ahead.

CP: What did you learn from your previous head?

SM: Her positive approach to the children and her calmness. When I got the headship I asked her for some specific advice and she said three words, 'Sleep on it!' I wrote it down and I still have that piece of paper – Sleep on it! It is so important having just a bit of time to reflect. So I tend not to make immediate decisions unless I have to. I sometimes say to my colleagues, 'Don't make a decision now, everybody go home and think about it and then we'll come back tomorrow and decide.' She was also very keen on working together. In terms of style, St Barnabas relied very much on teachers working together, it was a democratic team approach, and when I came here I tried to carry on that tradition. I told the staff here, 'I have only ever worked in teams, I am coming straight from being a class teacher and I like working in groups. Please don't expect me to make pronouncements, we will take advice, and on the whole we will decide it together. Of course there will come times when governors need to advise me and we will have to make a decision but it is never going to be without consultation first.' Looking back, I think that one of our problems was that I didn't make it clear enough to them that I really meant that. Some of the staff were wary and wondered in some cases that I really had a hidden agenda, and I didn't! So that has come out eventually, and I try to do better now to communicate my priorities and my hopes but also my needs.

CP: There is a fine balance between collegiality and the need for teams to have a leader sometimes.
SM: Absolutely and I think probably one of the needs that I still have is that sometimes the teachers would say 'Please, take a decision on this and lead us through it' and what I needed was for them to say that they would take more responsibility themselves. But, there comes a point when they say 'Please tell us!' and you have to respond. It's finding the right balance.

CP: Looking back, what are the things that best prepared you for headship and what advice would you give to others who are thinking about taking a headship?
SM: I left out some of the crucial things that were such a help. One was being a governor myself of St Barnabas. Being a governor is so good because it gives you a new perspective. I also gained new perspectives as Teacher Member on Oxfordshire County Council. At St Barnabas we were all complaining because the policy makers didn't ever seem to understand what teachers really needed and somebody said, 'Well, you can always say what you think, why don't you go and tell them? We need a teacher member for the Education Committee, let's put you up for that.' So I agreed, they sent my nominations paper in. One of the official candidates of the Union didn't get their papers in on time and because of that I was chosen as the NUT's candidate and I won! I represented all Oxfordshire teachers on the Education Committee for eight years. It gave me a view of what our local authority has to do and a great understanding and appreciation of the difficulties they face. This is why it makes me so angry that some people can consider running an education service without the local education authority. That is absolutely not fair to anyone, especially the children. Not only did it give me that understanding, but it also gave me a much wider view of

the issues that were coming up at the time. I kept all the papers and one day I am going to write it all up because it was really interesting. We went from a one party dominated council to a balanced council. It was a time when Tim Brighouse was our Chief Education Officer. One of the first campaigns I saw as a teacher member was the fight to save nursery schools. Can you believe that? It was organized by mums and nursery staff who had never taken any political action in their lives and it was wonderful. There is no doubt that getting yourself wider perspectives in whatever field is so important because it gives you more space to understand where you are at. I was also fortunate in that St Barnabas put me on a senior management course when I shouldn't have really but the deputy head argued, 'Every teacher in small schools is senior management, so go on it.' It was a joint Buckingham/Oxfordshire/Berkshire course and was very good. It was very important to me at that point because it put me in contact again with new groups of people and gave me skills and confidence to think about management issues.

CP: What you are talking about is breadth of experience.

SM: Yes, even though you are in one school, you can gain this. I don't think you necessarily need to have been in six different schools to have a broad perspective.

CP: Given that you have been in this headship for seven years, how has your own career and professionalism developed during that time?

SM: Before I even knew I was applying for this job, I had already decided to take another course. This went on earlier in the year before the headship post came up and it was an excellent, six week, GEST-funded course. I found great satisfaction in reading about educational issues and taking time to reflect and to have a bit of time out of the classroom. So I was then looking for other opportunities to continue this and my tutor at good old Westminster said, 'Well, why don't you think about a part-time MEd?' and I said, 'You know I would really like that after this six-week course' and so I got a place on that. I was going to do it with another friend from St Barnabas because they liked us to do it in pairs. That was all set and then I got this headship. I remember saying to my tutor there, 'You know, I can't be a new head and a student at the same time' and he said, 'Of course you can, it would be good for you.' In fact it gave me the reputation in the first year of my headship for holding the fastest staff meetings ever. I had to be picked up for my lift at 4.30 pm and so we met from 3.30 to 4.30 pm and all the business had to be done before I zoomed off to my course work. My MEd thesis was also very useful as I did it on how we can use volunteers to help children with special educational needs. So it was basically, interviewing volunteers and it meant working with children, parents and some teachers. It was fascinating and I learned a lot. All teachers should have the chance to be teacher researchers!

CP: So again you were getting different perspectives there?

SM: Yes. I was developing new techniques but in fact what I was doing was changing our procedures here at school at the same time. It started as a case study and ended as action research.

CP: So the MEd was giving you a vehicle to go on developing and reflecting?

SM: It was. It was hard work but it was interesting and research is such fun. Every little bit of evidence can generate so much thinking and I still have all these ends that I want to tie up.

CP: Can we talk now about what you are trying to achieve at this school, and how that has changed over the years?

SM: When I first came to the school I think a crucial influence was an exceptionally supportive governing body. The Chair of Governors is one of those amazing women who has real breadth of vision and energy, and rock-like support for the school. Everybody would say that she is an amazing woman and gave firm support from the beginning. There were new staff, new children, new families and a lot of challenges. I think that the early vision I had when I came here was of just opening the school up and turning it to look outwards, because when you look outwards from here what do you see? The wonderful city of Oxford, the nature reserve is close and we have a super community in South Oxford. I just felt there was too much looking inwards, so by opening it up and by taking advantage of the people and places in Oxford I felt we could achieve a lot. There are so many people who think young children's education is absolutely crucial. We have the most wonderful people coming in and supporting us and helping us and all you have to do is ask. Also I think part of my vision was a fairly political one. I have many qualms about American education but class is not an issue in American society. When I came here I couldn't believe how some families had no expectation of higher education for their children and I could not understand why. I remember saying to the mother of one bright child I was teaching, 'You know, she has got a real gift for English' and this mother said 'Well maybe she'll be a secretary.' I said 'No, I was thinking of her studying English Literature at university.' The look on this woman's face was a picture and it made me think that I wanted to do something to raise expectations. These families were living on the edge of a university and the children didn't realize it could be for them, nor indeed, did the mothers. So I get a lot of people from the universities to come in to school and we have good links with the educational departments at Oxford, Brookes and Westminster. But you can't generalize, certainly a high percentage of the Asian families are absolutely committed to education and would, like my grandmother would always say, see it as the way forward. It is wonderful to support that.

I think that was the vision and we are still working towards it. I also believed that we had room to grow. When I came there were 91 children but by the end of this year we shall have 168, which is good. I am sure that if you get a group of people working well and create an environment that is interesting then people want to come. There is no doubt that we felt we had capacity for more children to share our lovely hall, the best cook in Oxfordshire and wonderful teachers and I wanted to utilize all of this better.

CP: Have your strategies had to change to achieve this vision over the years?

SM: I certainly have had to adjust and learn to be clearer in communication. Also to help people realize where we are going together and the importance of learning together. So yes, I think I probably have adjusted. I have a feeling now after seven years that I have a bit more time and space now than I did as a very new head because I was just trying to come to terms with so many things. Now I know the amazing support the staff, parents, children and governors give to our community. So from that point of view the job has become easier, but during that same period it has been more difficult because of so much change imposed from above. Even so, I have been able to take on extra responsibilities. I am Vice Chair of OPHTA, which is the headteachers' group in Oxfordshire, and that is a big commitment. It is not until talking to you that I thought that through, but maybe I feel that I can share a bit more of my time and energies now. I don't think it's because the demands are less, because there is no doubt that, in terms of not just government initiatives but also family needs and children's needs, these have increased considerably. Children and families need increasing support. People sometimes think there are fewer problems in Oxford but we are second almost to London now in the poverty tables and some parents are very young. Also there are increasing demands on many of our families. They need our support more and more.

CP: Let's look at you as a leader and as a manager. What kind of leader are you and has this changed over time?

SM: I do believe that six or seven minds are better than one in tackling problems. I like to think I listen more than I did sometimes, and I think a listening, democratic style of approach is the way to do it. But at the same time you have to keep the energy going and make sure you have clear frameworks for people to work in. It's no good if you want to have a democratic, consultative model turning up at the staff meeting without an agenda. From the very beginning, we have been focused and that means there is a business element to all our meetings. In many ways the frameworks are quite clear, I hope, and in some cases, tight about what we need to do. I think I have a clear focus and direction but a democratic approach to management. It's also about making use of other people and I am happy to allow other people to do anything. I can never understand when people say 'You are so good at delegating, I can't delegate.' I say, 'What do you mean?' and they say, 'Well, I just worry that if I don't do it, it won't get done.' I say, 'I'm so grateful that somebody else is willing to take it on.' There are very rare occasions when things don't get done and well. So what? On 99 per cent of occasions they do.

It also applies to the parents. We had a couple of parents who came to me and said, 'Have you ever thought about after school provision? We really need it.' I said, 'I have often thought about after school provision but I'll come clean, there is no way I can add that in to what the school currently offers. But, if you're keen and you want to set up a management group and there's a member of staff who's really keen, she can go to London and learn about after school provision. If you guys want to do it, do it!' That was the starting of our wonderful after school club called Eberneezers, the children named it. It now runs every day from 3.00 to 5.15 pm, staffed by wonderful young workers. It is great for our children and the teachers have been really good about putting up with people sharing their space. So that was about having complete trust and faith. Of course there's been some problems along the way but it's done so well for our children and is an important part of that vision about Equal Opportunities. We wanted to be very clear that our after school club wasn't just for two-parent working families who used it as a convenience. We wanted it for anybody who needed it and we have been lucky to get money through Children in Need, and the Lottery for subsidized places. We have ten free places a week and parents come to me and define their own need for a place. In some cases it's students who need to carry on with their courses, in others it's a mother who just needs relief. Whatever the self-defined need is, we have always been able to meet it so far. To have an excellent resource like that which can benefit everyone should be possible everywhere. This happened because I was confident to say 'Go for it!' I think that's also been true with our Learning Through Landscapes project, which has led to developing the outside environment. Two teachers have taken this on and have organized working days for families. People take on responsibilities and things get done.

CP: What you're talking about is an approach that's democratic and empowering of your colleagues, allowing them to take the lead and take the responsibility.
SM: Yes, and it's the same with parents and governors. I think that it is such a good way of working.

CP: Do you think that way of working has got easier over the last couple of years or harder?
SM: Well, I think it's a necessity and I can't see how people who try to do the old hierarchical model would survive, they can't – the volume of work is too great. There are so many people here who understand the difficulties and are ready to help. I think it does depend on trust, but also if you keep children at the heart of the process, if we're all thinking about that little child who is learning, then the goodwill and the determination to make things work for that little child will work. Problems come if you lose the vision of the child at the centre or decide that you always know what's best for that little child.

CP: Let's now focus on teaching and learning and the role you play in that. How do you work with your colleagues in the school to ensure that this is effective?

SM: One of the pressures over the last six years in the role of being a head is that I feel I'm increasingly out of touch with the curriculum on the ground. There should have been more 'ownership' of the National Curriculum from the beginning – more involvement from teachers and heads. Dearing fortunately made some constructive changes. My role is now more about overseeing and monitoring the curriculum but I really feel the people who are best able to do that are the curriculum co-ordinators. We have been developing ways of supporting co-ordinators to monitor each other. One of the problems about being a non-teaching head is that I have lost the immediacy that I had when I was a new head. I had 'street cred' then because I had come from being in the middle of it but now with implementing all the changes in school I am unable to be as committed to the knowledge of the curriculum as I was, yet this should be my major work. I know that our LEA and lovely advisers here will help us. In terms of basic strategies, we first developed our whole school aims together and then went on to develop individual policy documents. Because we are a small staff we were able to do that as a whole and we didn't have to break up into small groups for this. From the policy statements we have been working as a team to release teachers to develop schemes of work which then have to be relayed back to the policies and back to our aims. In theory that's how the curriculum has been developed. We also work together on the planning sheets which come in to me before each term begins. I look through those and on the whole they look wonderful but what we keep having to ask each other is 'How do we know that the planning sheets, the policies and the aims are being put into practice?'

CP: How do you ensure that the planning is put into practice effectively?

SM: I am happy to go into a classroom with a clip board and observe what is happening, in fact, that's what we end up doing, but I think it's going to be more the subject co-ordinators who need time to do this. Appraisal is helpful too. We have carried out appraisal throughout the school. Another thing that is helpful is that, as long as my life doesn't get madly busy, I cover so that each teacher gets a morning out of the classroom once every six weeks so that they can get on with their co-ordination or monitoring. It also means that I'm teaching around the school regularly. We don't have enough money for supply when teachers are on courses and I cover for that too. It's important to do that and I see that as natural monitoring because when you are teaching the children you are getting a real feel of what the children are doing on a day to day basis. This year for the first time in appraisal the teachers asked me to look in depth at the children's written work and to come up with some ideas of how that might be developed further. If that works we might take a joint decision for me to look at different types of written work from all the staff, for example, written creative writing pieces or maths or science. It may be that the co-ordinator does that but it will act as a dip stick on the quality of the work. Also, we ask advisers to come in on a regular basis to carry out observations of what we do. It's a sort of pre-inspection/health check and to help us with some ideas on how to monitor the curriculum. We are so lucky in Oxfordshire that the advisers always give us that support whenever we ask. Also the Diocese and the Board of Education people have been such a support and have great expertise. I am lucky because I am doubly loved or doubly served. We have natural checks too, through working with our nursery colleagues. They come up and keep in contact with their children and there's a sort of monitoring there. We try to work closer together and give each other feed back, and it's the same with our middle schools. It is an area that needs a lot of thought.

CP: Would you say that the role of the head in monitoring has changed?

SM: I think you need to be on the ground, because then you feel safer, but more and more you have less time to be on the ground so you must help others to do this. The best monitoring I have known happened soon after I got here as a new head. This was Tim Brighouse's Self-Evaluation Process. It was a very rigorous audit and made us look at what was happening in school, what the needs were and how we were going to put them right. That was a long time ago, seven years, but because we had ownership of the process we felt very positive about it. The LEA gave support, local council-lors came and visited and a report was presented. It was an excellent process. We all learned so much and it worked so well. I was upset when colleagues started reporting back to me how the OFSTED inspection process was not proving positive for them, whereas self-evaluation had been so helpful. Even friends who have had very good OFSTED reports said that the process was unhelpful. People were off sick and there was stress and upset. There wasn't the feeling that the external inspectors were there to help you improve. With self-evaluation we were able to see the way forward and we knew the LEA would give us support. The other great benefit was that the LEA knew your school well and they could encourage you to add in strands of development which you might not have seen. We were very keen on devel-oping Equal Opportunities and I'm sure we managed to implement policies before they were insisted on, because the LEA made sure it was a strand in the self-evaluation process. A lot of support was given for this through the courses, the LEA people and the Teacher's Centre. What I have seen of the OFSTED process (we haven't yet been inspected) does worry me and the inspection process is so expensive. Self-evaluation wasn't expensive and it was effective!

CP: Can we now explore your sense of accountability, who do you feel accountable to and how do you manage this?

SM I know it sounds corny, but I think I am accountable first and foremost to the children. They are our focus and they are such direct witnesses. They will soon let you know if you are going wrong. I am so lucky again in the size of the school and also the wonderful natural mix of the children that are here. They do tell you, and so I try to be with the children often and to talk to them and find out how they feel they are getting on and what they think we could do to help them more. When new children come to our school we have a 'welcome tea party' and I always say to the children, 'My name is Mrs Matthew, do you know what my job is? It's to make you happy and to help you learn. Please, if you ever need me, come and see me, that's my job.' Then I think there's this wonderful sort of interrelationship between all the people involved in the school. Every strand of accountability has an exact strand of support to match it, and thank goodness for that. There is the staff network, the governor network, the parents, the LEA and the Diocese. They support me and I am accountable to them. Each new step we take as a school we try to keep open communication to all of these groups, so that it is not just formal accountability, although this happens too. We have formal reports of the working groups to governors, formal reports of staff meetings and formal reports for the parents to see. There is also a formal complaint route for parents but that is rarely used. We make it very clear that no worry, or no delight, is too small to not share it. We share concerns and delights as often as we can. Of course we also have each child's records or 'Profiles', including examples of work and written reports. That's a sort of accountability too. During self-evaluation we sent out a series of question-naires to parents to ask how they thought we were doing as well as carry-ing out some interviews. It may well be time for more questionnaires. In general I think that our openness is a great method of accountability, enabling communication to flow – inviting my parents and others in the community to share views and together for us to work out ways of improv-ing our service.

CP: What about your own professional well-being and development? Where do you find support?

SM: One of the important support groups is our local partnership. It's got a wonderful name, AESOP, which stands for An East and South Oxford Partnership. It's a lovely group of nine heads and I think we are lucky because we are a very like-minded group, working very hard for the chil-dren, helping each other as well and not competitive. Oxfordshire is keen on partnership, both with the LEA and the schools, and it gives a lot of support, and financial support, through the Partnership Development Fund that Richard Howard and others have created to let us do innovative work. It's been wonderful and through them we are working on developing European links and on developing shared schemes of work. We have also shared INSET on lunchtime supervisors' training and other issues. The support also works on an individual basis. If you meet up and you think 'Gosh she's looking tired', you can provide some personal support. One of the heads in the AESOP partnership was also on my initial new heads' training and he's been a real support ever since. He's been a 'critical' friend throughout the seven years and I have relied a lot on him. I think critical friends are impor-tant and it is also important to have a mentor or an older, experienced head to go to for advice. Courses are all-important for ongoing development but a personal, almost a pastoral relationship, is very necessary.

CP: Is this hard in a competitive climate?

SM: Oh no! But we're lucky. I am also on various other groups which provide me with good support. I have still kept up with the Equal Opportunities Network and there are the obvious ones. The teachers I work with are such a support, and so are our governors, our parish churches, friends and a most wonderful family. People laugh at me and say 'How do you do everything you do' and I say 'Well, because we share things at home too, we are a very equal opportunities household. That means on Monday it's Lucy's turn to cook, on Tuesday it's mine and so on', and they say 'But there are only five of you' and I say 'Well, on Friday nobody eats or we have take-aways!' But I am sure it would be difficult to have such a happy balanced family if they didn't care about what I was doing. Fortunately they do care, and I have a husband who's been supportive throughout my career and has shared in raising all our children. Other supports? Yoga, theatres, films, books, walking, listening to music!

CP: Do you think that headship is a job that is still manageable and do you enjoy it more or less than you used to?

SM: I absolutely enjoy it, but I do say that if you feel you have wonderful people to share the job with, then it is manageable. But, don't do it if you feel you have got to do it all yourself, because then it becomes an impossible job. If you do have lovely teachers and governors and children to share it, every single day is different and that is wonderful. To work with young children is an absolute joy. Talk about the 'gift of each day'. I think the children are giving to you as much as you give out. In fact, they give you three times back and they are such tolerant, wise little people. It is a privilege that the parents trust you with their child and I care about them all. When you think that there is hardly any other profession like that, where parents give you the most precious thing to them in their lives and we've got them from 9.00 am till 3.00 pm. Talk about trust! We were talking about heads trusting others to do jobs with you and for you or whatever, but this is a different thing again. In a way I know it's a legal thing but the parents don't do it because it's legal they trust you with their most precious people. I think it's a wonderful job. There are ways that people could make it easier for me but I can't believe that there is a more important job. I remember at a friend's house talking about various jobs and someone said, 'Isn't he lucky, he's a GP, saving lives.' Then somebody turned to me and said, 'Sue's doing a much more important job than that!' and it was so good to hear somebody else saying that. To help a child learn and develop and thrive is about the most important thing that we can do. It's a frightening sort of power though too, when you realize there are little faces looking to you and the trust that's there, and we don't succeed all the time. It's a great responsibility we have but I love it.

CP: Do you think that you have to be a 'nutter' to take on the job nowadays?

SM: You've seen the people in this school. We have a caretaker in a million, we've got a secretary that would work until midnight, people that care so much about looking after children. They are a dedicated and excellent teaching staff. With such support you don't have to be a 'nutter'. Not to say there aren't challenges. As I said before, the pace of change in the curriculum and the way they rushed into financial management without proper training and just sort of said 'Get on with it, and learn!' was wrong, and my goodness we had to learn! They could have done that much better. I'm still not convinced that some aspects of financial management couldn't be done better by the LEA who have the expertise rather than us who are good at other things. We have had to struggle, we managed it but it meant time away from looking after teachers and looking after children and that we could do without. I think some of the other changes have been negative, including, I am sorry to have to say, the nursery vouchers scheme. This is as ill-thought-out a scheme as ever was thought possible. They did not look properly at the evidence. It is a scheme that is not going to help anyone.

CP: What is your vision for the future of your school and primary education as a whole?

SM: If anything my vision would be about providing more support, more resources and more recognition for the work of early years education. It is such a privilege to be a part of British primary education, which always had a real belief in children learning by doing. I never understand the view that somehow learning through topics, or experiential learning, is not rigorous. I don't know who to blame exactly, but maybe it was partly because the National Curriculum was developed in subject areas, without taking advice from the people who had done much to develop learning in an integrated way. That is how young children experience the world. I just feel that British primary education had earned so much admiration, particularly from American colleagues who had come over. They would say, 'Aren't you lucky to have this time to let children develop.' My goodness, we were leading the world. So, if you are looking for vision at the end it is about being inclusive not exclusive, and seeing our job as being about setting children up for a whole lifetime of learning.

CHAPTER 7

Leading an 'excellent primary school'

JOAN McCONNELL WITH PETER RIBBINS

Joan McConnell is head of St Mary's RC Primary, a voluntary aided school in Bromley. It is listed in the Chief Inspector's second annual report as an excellent primary school. Joan was born and educated in a small village in Eire. She came to England when she married. Her husband was a primary school head, they have three children. After some years as a full-time mother she joined the first intake of mature students undertaking teacher training at Rachel McMillan. Her first post was at Gloucester Infants in Southwark where she spent 13 years, latterly as acting deputy. She has been at St Mary's since 1989. During these years, the school has become grant maintained and is in the process of becoming two-form entry.

PR: Could we begin with your personal background. Who and what made you the kind of person you are? How has this shaped your view of teaching and of headship?

JM: I'm Irish, that is very important to say first of all. I was born and educated in Ireland and didn't come to this country until I was about to marry. My primary school education took place in a small village in Kilkenny called Johnstown. It was formal, prescriptive, kindly and pleasurable. I thoroughly enjoyed my school time.

I then went to a boarding school, there was no facility within the village for secondary education. My father wouldn't hear of me travelling on a bus. He knew the sort of character I was and that I would either lead others astray or be lead astray myself. I found boarding traumatic at first. I was very young and very small and it seemed fearsome, but I loved it. The school was an Irish school. Everything took place through the medium of Irish, which added extra pressure but was something I enjoyed. Wonderful friendships formed throughout my school years and I am still in touch with many from those days. I've always kept in touch with the nuns who ran the school. It was a very formal and basic education but very thorough. I appreciated that very much. Many of the nuns were excellent characters. They were good fun as well as good educators.

PR: What attitude to education did your family take? Who were the key influences on you?

JM: My family were very positive. On my mother's side there were many teachers. I didn't know them, they were grand-aunts, but knew education was important. From my first years my father supervised my homework. If I got anything wrong it would be gone over and over and I would be taught the proper way. He had great insight into children and learning. He wasn't involved in teaching, but felt very strongly that each of us should have a good 'education'. It was a very supportive background.

PR: What was his occupation?

JM: He was an electrician. In a small village he was the man everybody went to and he knew how to sort things out. He also had a background of accountancy and did a lot of work for the local shopkeepers on their accounts. I was used to seeing my father sitting with figures and with books and I think that's very important for a child, especially for a female child, it certainly made an impression on me.

PR: You sound like you have come from quite a large family.

JM: There are five of us in the family. I was on my own for seven years and my brother and I were together for a further seven before the next lot started coming along. It was a very split family in terms of age groupings, but a very close family and that's still true.

PR: Presumably the schools were catholic with catholic values?

JM: They were catholic schools. I received very clear catholic values, very clear moral values. It's difficult to explain exactly what this meant. Basically when I got up in the morning I knew my parents were there for me. I can remember once coming home from school, I had absented myself. I can't explain to this day why. But it did not lead to chaos and confusion and my being worried. I was sat down, I was talked to. My mother was baking at the time, I enjoyed the fruits of her morning's work and was then taken back to school. That support was there always. We were important people in our family, all five of us and things were just done for us and with us. When we went out we went out as a family, it was a very supportive atmosphere.

PR: And the wider family?

JM: The extended family was simply across the road. My maternal grandparents lived across a narrow country road in the main farmhouse. My uncle and aunt lived about 200 yards away on the other side of this narrow road. My other uncles lived in the farmhouse with grandma and grandpa and as a young child I would be allowed as a treat to go and play cards with them, it was a perfect way to spend an evening. There was no television in those days. The radio would be turned off and the concentration would be on the game and conversation. My aunt had only boys. She was a tailor by trade and always made all my clothes. I always had the best of everything because it was cheap and easy to do, not because we were wealthy. I had lovely dresses. That meant a great deal to me – I was a very girlie girl. Once a week we ate at grandmother's house and I can still remember the conversations around the table. Everybody had a turn. As the youngest I would have my turn to say my bit about how my day went. I would listen in turn as others explained what had happened in their lives during the week since we'd been there. These things leave a great impression on you.

PR: And the Church – how influential was it?

JM: The Church was always there. We went to church regularly. We were encouraged to pop in, not for a set service but to acquaint ourselves with God again. All my relatives were buried in the churchyard. We would often take flowers to the graves or go for a Sunday walk and return via the church and pop in for a prayer. Church was important in our lives but not over-intrusive. There were a lot of social functions around the church and we were involved in all of those. My uncle was the local CYMS leader and my mother was on the catering committee of the local Townswomen's Guild. Everything she was involved in I was involved in. The net was embracing but not restricting.

PR: It seems there was consistency in the values you encountered from those who mattered?

JM: I was very fortunate. The entire village went to that school and the only people at the school were from that particular village. Many would come into our house because of the nature of my father's work and so we were well known. The teachers, when they took a walk in the afternoons or evenings, went by my house. They would pop in to say hello and we would be expected to go and greet them. School was a terrific experience. It meant having to come to terms with other people's values when you only knew your own and thought they were shared by everybody else in the community. They weren't. I was exposed to children who would do things I knew instinctively were wrong but to whom I was very attracted. I suppose it's my personality. I liked to be a bit deviant at times and it was nice to get involved with a group who were up to something. So a good bit of character formation took place. The teachers were all local people so there was always a very close network. If things were going wrong at school, your home would know about it very quickly. During their evening walk, one of the teachers would pop in and things would be sorted straight away. There was always utter respect for the teachers. If they were going by we would stand in the road and say good evening in Irish to them, and they would respond in kind and walk on.

PR: Was there any particular teacher in your primary or secondary school who influenced you? Did you have any contacts with your headteachers?

JM: The head was a teacher. They still didn't seem bothered with the administrative burden we have today and still don't. I must go and see how they avoid it. They were good schools. The headteacher was very lady-like.

I admired her tremendously. She would use the tongs, for instance, to pick up a sod of turf. At home nobody would dream of using tongs. I would ape this, putting the turf on the fire with the tongs, much to everybody's amusement. She was a highly principled woman – just and fair in all her dealings. If she was cross with you she would say to you, 'I'm bitterly disappointed in you Siobhan. Now go away and don't disgrace your family.' Those words had tremendous impact upon me because it brought home to me that how you behaved was crucially important in determining how other people viewed you. In my own dealings with children I find myself trying to act as she did.

PR: What of the nuns? What do you remember of them?

JM: The nuns were a different kettle of fish altogether. I remember two in particular – one has just died. I feared her. I had no reason to. She looked fearsome but was kindly. Even so one did as one was told. We were devils in the convent – we got up to all manner of pranks. The nuns, by and large, were very kindly, especially towards the boarders. They knew we were away from home. I was a puny child. One of them would make me hot milk with carrageen mould and moss. I adored the ground she walked on. She was full of fun and good humour – a lovely person. She is still alive and corresponds with me. We both loved Irish and so we got on very well together. She would put her trust in me and knew I would come up to scratch.

PR: It sounds like an ideal school. Was it good on the learning as well?

JM: Very formal, no frills but an excellent education. It was a place of work. There was no doubt of that in our minds, even the workshy. We knew we had to work there and we did.

PR: Were you a successful student?

JM: I think so. I got honours in my Leaving Certificate and could have gone to training college in Ireland or into the Civil Service. None were appealing at that time, mainly because in my last year at school I met my husband to be. He was a teacher in England and came over most holidays and met my family. I came to England after my Certificate initially just for a holiday with my husband to be and his family in Bromley. We realized we were going to get married as soon as possible and I decided to stay. We got married the next year in Ireland. I was very young, only 19.

Once we returned to England we had three children in quick succession. Then I decided it was about time I did something other than just being a mum. I got a place at Rachel McMillan, which was then taking its first intake of mature students. I cannot describe adequately the influence the college had on me. I loved every minute of it. I suppose having been at home for so long and having brought up the children, I was raring to go. At the time my youngest was six and settled in school. Her sisters were doing well. I had no reason to suppose the last one wouldn't either.

PR: Why teaching?

JM: It was something I had always wanted to do – from my fifth birthday. I remember lining up on a tiny wall around my grandma's garden patch all my dolls and calling the register. That's my earliest memory of what school was about. It was always something I wanted to do. When I had my own I read a great deal on children's learning. When the opportunity arose to go to college it seemed natural to work hard and do well.

PR: One hears criticisms of teacher training. What made your experience such a good one?

JM: It was not good, it was superb. We were worked hard and I like that. For the first time I had an opportunity to work in a larger group with people who had the same sort of ideas on life. We had excellent lecturers. They had a real commitment to their subject. They were determined this group of mature students would do well. They were on a mission to prove it would work and were utterly generous in their time for us. If you had a problem they were there, somebody who would unscramble it for you. That was typical of the generosity we met. They taught me an awful lot about man management and about give and take: simple things but utterly fundamental to the job I do nowadays.

PR: How did you come to the decision to take up teacher training?

JM: My husband was a headteacher at that time and having tremendous problems. He had a member of staff due to go in for surgery. The governors were cutting up rough wanting him to do something about this person's absence. But he believed this person needed his support, so he said, 'Joan why don't you come in and settle this class down for a few days and then their proper teacher will be back.' That's how I started back, I loved it and it gave me confidence. It was only a small step to move on. My husband was supportive and knowledgeable. My children were supportive and my mother-in-law was always there for me. But it wasn't easy. We were worked very hard at college.

PR: Did you ever consider specializing in secondary education?

JM: I taught briefly in a secondary school. I was anxious about attitudes in secondary schools in those days, in the 1960s. There seemed a 'them and us' scene in which the pupils were very much regarded as lesser beings. It was a natural thing to go into primary. I loved the lower age groups of children. I started teaching in a school in a large housing estate, North Peckham, which had huge problems socially. In addition, the job situation in those days was horrific – it had one of the highest unemployment rates in Europe. It also had wonderful people. Once you got them on your side and they understood what you were trying to do for their children you couldn't get nicer people.

PR: What kind of a school was it?

JM: Very mixed ethnically, a huge school in those days, 400 infants. Behaviour could be very difficult. There was a tremendous turnover of teachers. But we built a lovely team. We had a good head with high principles. He was keen on fairness and very appreciative of children. It was a happy experience if a tough one. I did many jobs at the school. It was always changing. You returned every September and did something different. Although you were in the same school you felt you were getting lots of experience. I was there for 13 years in all. A wonderful experience.

Then we had a new head. The ethos of the school changed in terms of its work orientation. Many of us already believed this necessary but she led us beautifully through it. We battened down the hatches. Behaviour wasn't our key concern any more – learning and teaching became our dominant themes. Gradually we turned things around and ended up doing very well. I enjoyed that experience. It was very formative for me.

PR: How was this achieved?

JM: Parents were brought along. That was the key to our success. Nothing was sprung on them. We constantly had meetings where they could come and look at things. There was good staff discussion going on although high turnover was always a problem. In those days the numbers in classes weren't anything like what we have in my school today. I remember an inspector asking me if I would be prepared to take a class of twenty-one 5-year-olds? I could have this provided I had them all reading by Easter. That was just glorious. I did that for a couple of years until we had spread the expertise throughout the school. It was slow building all this up but it worked. Then the school was amalgamated. I was very against this because it would mean it ceased to be an infant school for 370 and became a junior and infant school for 700. This was to take place at a time when things, in any case, were getting even more difficult on the estate. The authorities decided to split up the estate and to make the walkways safer. Yet in the school they were planning to do the opposite. They were making it into a huge conglomerate. I warned the inspectorate that if this happened I would go because I felt it was the wrong thing to do to those people at that time. I still believe this even though the amalgamation has been successful. I still believe it was done for political and not educational reasons.

So I decided that I would leave my lovely world of Peckham. My husband said, 'What on earth are you going to do?' I said, 'Well I don't care, I'd rather be a cleaner than work in something I haven't got my heart in.' I pulled out the *Times Educational Supplement* and there were a couple of jobs advertised and I applied. I was short listed for a headship.

PR: What were you at the time you left Peckham?

JM: I was acting deputy. I never liked deputy headship. It is the most difficult role in the school. You've got to have a class in a small school. You've got to know something about this, that and everything. You are a jack of all trades and a master of none. Many of the deputies I saw didn't seem to have a role with any responsibility.

I applied for the post here and one other. The other one came up first. I was interviewed and short listed. Then this one came along, I was interviewed and got the job on the same day. It was a very different school from anything I had experienced. First, it was a catholic school. Second, it was in an affluent area. Third, it had very high expectations.

PR: At what point did you decide headship was for you? How did you prepare yourself?

JM: From the beginning. When I graduated a lecturer said to me, 'You'll be a head within five years.' I loved teaching and with things always changing at Peckham I felt no urgency to move out or up but always knew headship was what I wanted. There are things you can't do as a classroom teacher, or a team leader or even as a deputy. You have to be the head.

During my time at Peckham I went on a very good series of management courses and enjoyed them enormously. Apart from that I always had headship at home with me. My husband was a head. We are complementary in character and I learned a great deal from him. This has been a good influence on my character and on my ideas of headship.

PR: I often ask headteachers what they have learned about headship from the heads they have worked for. It seems that you learned most from your husband.

JM: I did but have been influenced by both my heads. The first was different from me. He was dedicated to children and forced us to look at things from their point of view. This could cause problems even in those heady days when one could be child-centred. His attitude was not one I instinctively shared but he did make me think. There were good things about his approach. The ethic of work emphasized by my second head has also influenced my thinking. She had tremendous energy and drive. Both of my heads had enormous limitations. So have I. But these are not the things I'd highlight.

PR: Were you surprised when they offered you the post here?

JM: I was shocked. I asked them if they were sure. I can remember that quite clearly. We were all sitting round in the usual way and somebody asked me to come back and I thought they were going to let me down kindly. The local Education Officer was on the panel, and he and I had an argument about amalgamation. It was a very sore point with me and I thought I will put him right if I do nothing else today. I forgot about being in an interview and became much more interested in getting him sorted out. We became good friends, he has been a great support to me here.

I think the parents swung it. They saw me for some reason as somebody they could work with. I think they felt they had somebody who would take the school forward. Remember a whole raft of recent reforms were upon us. We discussed these at great length during the interview. When the question on LMS came up I thought what on earth is this? I was able to dredge up some memory or other and cobbled together enough of an answer to show them I knew what it could be. But really I was very uncomfortable. The parents were probing. The catholic authorities seemed against me. I had no background in catholic schools. That was a sticky point for me. I was asked to do the Catholic Teachers' Certificate and my appointment was subject to that, which I did and that was fine. I should say by that time I did want a catholic school.

PR: Why?

JM: I strongly believe children progress better when their parents are supportive of the school. I felt catholic parents might give me such support. Having got it, I felt panic and self-doubt. I resigned from my previous post and was hoping to have a term off. I love decorating and gardening. I was planning to spend a good deal of this three months just reading, trying to prepare myself for my new post. Then I had a phone call from the head here. She wanted to retire earlier than planned. Her husband's health had deteriorated. Could I start a term earlier? I arrived in a state of nerves of a kind I had never suffered before or since. I sat here for two days and wondered what on earth I was doing.

PR: Others have said much the same. What did you do?

JM: I clean and tidy when I'm under pressure and that is what I did. I had a bonfire at the back, I'd start it every evening when the children were going home and they'd gather round and I'd get to know names. It was a non-stressful situation for us all. The parents would come along and one Irish parent said to me, 'Ah sure, you know, you're always at it Mrs McConnell, you want to slow down and take your time ...'. That was what I needed to hear, but really all I wanted to do was to get going. Then there's the dilemma – you're in a good school: what do you do? You think why do they need me, this is a waste of time. It was a big learning process for me. But things did need to be done. The National Curriculum was looming and we had to get a move on and get that sorted out. That was wonderful. It gave me a job to do, a reason to be there. We got on with it and we've had a lovely six years. We've had our ups and our downs, our disagreements, all manner of problems and joys but we're together. The staff are very much a cohesive force.

PR: Do you think things like Headlamp and the National Headteachers Qualification will help to ensure that the next generation of headteachers is better prepared than your own?

JM: I suppose anything must be better than nothing. I soon realized Bromley is very different from the ILEA. You were talking about a totally different culture really. I had to learn all manner of things very quickly. I had some very good support from local heads – they were lovely. You'd get a call asking, 'How are things going? If you've got any problems don't hesitate to pop in.' I was invited to a cluster group straight away. Conversely, at the level of LEA, I wasn't even introduced to a group of heads with whom I attended an authority meeting. I found that very difficult. I'm a courteous person by nature and I think courtesy is an important if old fashioned idea which must be preserved. But Bromley did have a wonderful inspection system in those days. I saw this as a useful tool. I wanted to do the best for the school. I wanted to make sure that we were progressing as well as we should. But I was beginning to feel vulnerable. I knew I needed outside help and that came through the BIR inspections in Bromley. This has worked well for me and for the school. It was always a good school but we have made dramatic improvements in its ethos, work ethic and in planning, organization and managerial skills.

PR: As Michael Fullan puts it you don't have to be bad to get better.

JM: Exactly. We have done a great deal but there's much more to be done. The first big problem was the National Curriculum. I thoroughly agree with the idea of a National Curriculum and believe this country desperately needed one, but I disagree strongly with the way it was implemented. We did three separate schemes for maths, science and English before we arrived at the present one. Schools were re-inventing the wheel for the hell of it. There was little outside guidance and help at early and important stages. It came subsequently but not soon enough.

PR: How would you describe yourself as a head and what are your key values?

JM: I'm a mixture of a manager and a leader. You've got to have your systems, therein lies the management role. But the leadership role is very important, you have to be aware of the issues. The key issues where schools are concerned are the quality of teaching and learning that goes on within them. Most of us can teach but to sustain real and developing quality into that teaching across the school we need to rely on appropriate and robust systems.

It is not enough for the head to be a good teacher. I'd hate to be regarded as the worst teacher in the school but I don't think this is as important as lacking a clear understanding of the issues relevant to quality in education and a clear knowledge of how to implement effective systems. I also think that in schools too many go on and on about the leadership of the head. This is important but so, too, is that of the management team as a whole. It is only when my deputy head, my leaders in the curriculum areas and I are together on things that we can be at our most effective.

PR: Quite a lot of the literature suggests teams need leadership.

JM: I think they do. And leadership entails a lot of things like energy, drive, caring about the place, liking the children (daft though that may seem) and being able to get on with people. I'm not looking for clever, esoteric things. When I think of leadership I think about those sort of things and their importance in getting people to work with you. If you get those things right the other kind of things come along on the back of them. On my staff I get people who come to me and say, 'Joan, I'd like to have a go at technology. I know it's been shunned for years but I'd like to have a go at it.' I reply, 'If you want to have a go at it, feel free. How do you want me to support you?' And we sit down and plan what's needed. When people feel ownership for something, that becomes important to them and things move. But if you need to involve people you also need to be outward looking.

Being inward looking is the death of education. We are involved in the wider community here. We may be a grant-maintained school, and we may be one of the few grant-maintained primary schools in Bromley, but we belong to everything that Bromley has to offer in terms of sport, music, in choirs – everything you can think of. We're little, we're only a small cog in the wheel but we are outward looking. We want to learn from the larger environment and from the people out there. We've a lot of parents who come in with expertise. All this makes us look outwards.

PR: Why did St Mary's go grant maintained and how far was that at your instigation?

JM: It was my governors. We were one of the first schools on LMS. I valued the Local Authority because I recognized they could be very helpful to me. We were one of the first schools to be given a cheque book in the primary sector, so we were moving along quite nicely on many fronts at the same time. But when the issue of grant-maintained status came up, my governors latched on to it. I was keen to retain the good I found within the Authority. I have found a lot that was positive in Bromley. For instance, when we were going grant maintained a few schools asked the local Heads' Group if we could stay within our cluster group – and we can. So we are still drawing from, and hopefully contributing to, these schools. I don't see GM as an isolationist or an elitist idea. Both are a long way away from my thinking.

PR: Would you rather have stayed with the Local Authority?

JM: No I like the autonomy. When the governors suggested it I was quite pleased. Things were different to what had made me leave Peckham. The impact of GM would be felt on the management structure of the school and not by the children. I was happy with that.

PR: Who led on the process of going GM?

JM: I took most of the meetings. We tried to present parents with a balanced view, so we invited people from the Authority and people who were very pro-grant maintained so that parents had a good idea of the case from both sides. The ballot was very tight. A lot of secondaries but not many primaries – about six – have gone so far and there are several more in the pipeline I believe. I voted in favour. The governors who were interested in it came and discussed it with me. I had done plenty of reading and so was prepared to take the lead, but with reservations.

PR: Initially the Church took an equivocal position didn't it?

JM: It did. They still feel rather unhappy about it. The thinking then, or at least what we got back from the Church leaders, was that if some went GM this would diminish the pot for others. I can see how that could be a principled stand, but I don't believe it is correct.

PR: It is often suggested that many of those who go GM do so for the extra money?

JM: Absolutely. There's not much money in it – I can assure you of that. There may have been in the early days but not by 1994. It had all gone, and mostly on secondary schools. The funding arrangements from the FAS still favour secondary schools. Small primaries are having a tough time of it economically. It matters little whether you're GM or not – the pot is very small and the demands are very great.

It worked for us. For example, as our OFSTED report notes, we had a very inadequate library. I feel strongly about libraries, books and reading. If a child can't read and doesn't love reading you can put the National Curriculum documents on a bonfire. They must read to access other areas of the curriculum. When I came I felt our children had very poor facilities for reading. Not for class reading – but for extended reading, for research. I wanted to do something about this. I scrimped and saved but we could never get anything like the money we needed for a capital project. We now have a new library and achieved this over two years from capital funding. I wouldn't be able to do anything like that again because I haven't got enough money in my main funding now. My capital funding will have to go towards major things wrong with the school.

PR: Did you tell me the LEA's decision not to support school meals has cost you £15,000?

JM: I did. Also last year Bromley refused to fund the pay rise, after promising they would. We still carry the effects of this. These things make it much more difficult to manage. In due course they will rob headteachers of the ability to manage because we will have nothing left to manage. If you look at the papers they are full of stories of how difficult it is to recruit heads. I think the government must do something about this.

PR: What difference does being voluntary aided make to you?

JM: There is a great degree of autonomy within the voluntary aided sector which suites my personality. You do have another layer of management called the Catholic Commission to cope with. They can help in various ways but you lose this when you go GM. You don't benefit from their schemes for capital projects. You are dependent for funding on FAS.

PR: Your Chairman of Governors is a priest? How does that work?

JM: Extraordinarily well. He is a thoughtful man and is very interested in education and the school. He knows a lot of the families. He has been in the parish for years. There's a good infrastructure in our governing body. Its members are helpful towards the school.

PR: Can you describe St Mary's to me? What is your vision for it?

JM: St Mary's as a school is first of all a place of work. Anybody who comes here knows that's what the place is about. We are very conscious of the society we live in and its shortcomings. We work very hard to try and preserve some of the good things we see around us. We try to keep out the things that are less than helpful to children in their learning or in their social life. These things are very close when you are young. They mix and mingle all the time. We firmly believe here that children have to respect each other and that they learn that because we in our turn respect them. We constantly work towards that aim. The children are encouraged to belong in the wider world. We don't see St Mary's as the be all and the end all: it's only one small part of the jigsaw of their lives. We respect utterly the homes they've come from, and understand the problems faced in many of these homes. We try to do the best we can to make the learning experience a good one for the children. We're very, very keen to enable the children to move towards greater autonomy in their learning. This has been a difficult and slow route but we're getting there. I think the key to a child's mind is when he or she wants to do something, and the minute that you've got there you're half-way home.

Our children are encouraged to think about other people and to take on issues from the outside world. I might get a couple of children from Year 2 ask if they can have a fund raising event. If I agree, they will have to give me a plan and a list of suggested dates and we will sit down together and put that into the diary. Everybody will support it on that day. Every teacher in the building, every child in the school. We have school initiatives at key points: Lent and Advent. We also have one other major fund raising idea in which the parents become totally involved and that is for the Lourdes Association. So we are always looking outwards and in doing so recognizing there's a big wide world out there and one day we will all be part of that world and we must be able to influence it.

We encourage our children if they have a problem to share it. They know I'm here for them and if all else fails they can ask the secretary if they can see me in order to spend time together and try to sort things out. We work extremely hard to get the children involved in issues such as the environment. Recently we had new desks from a very good company. But the design was poor and the teacher said to me after a few weeks, 'You'll be appalled when you see what's happened.' There were gouge marks on the desk. 'The little devils,' I said. 'No, no, it's not them' and she explained how it had happened. She took the problem back to the class and each individual member wrote to the company. It was a wonderful learning exercise for them and it brought an interesting response. The company have taken on their ideas and will incorporate them in their new design for these desks. Those are the people we want to turn out – who care, who feel they have a voice and who know how to use their voice. The academic is important and we want good results at St Mary's but more than that I want rounded persons.

PR: Is there anything special about St Mary's which relates specifically to its catholicity?

JM: Being catholic is important, but catholics only form a part of society. As such I don't think the fact that we are catholic should be intrusive. I don't think we should be religious fanatics because we are at St Mary's. We are a very ordinary school. I feel there is nothing elitist about this school. We work with a wide variety of children and staff who come to us with all their inhibitions and baggage every day. We are catholic and proud of it but it's not something that I'd wish to ... I can't put it into words really ... This is a place of education, a place of catholic education – that's the way I would put it rather than 'This is a catholic school, a place of education.' The difference may seem small but I think it is important.

PR: You have had a very good OFSTED report. What has been your contribution?

JM: My contribution to the place is a willingness to listen, a desire to do well and a dedication to the children and the parents. I hope if you met one of them out there that they wouldn't say anything different. Perhaps some would, come to think of it, but there you go ... It would be very easy for me to say that everything good that has happened here is because of me – but I couldn't have done anything without the co-operation of the people I've got here. Whatever your vision, it is finite: it's clouded by the baggage we all bring to it, by our characters, our ideas, the lot.

PR: How far have good schools got good heads and less good schools got less good heads?

JM: I think that there's something in this, but it's not the full picture. Heads are in great danger if they feel they are the alpha and omega – they're not, they're a cog in the wheel of a big machine. Of course, they may be a very important cog at certain times and in certain ways. One time it might be in the exercise of leadership, another time in management, another time just going around the school doing a little monitoring role or something. The job in hand isn't the important thing, it's the way it's done and the lessons learned from it. Here we know each other very well as a team. I try to involve all of the staff in the school, teachers and others are important. We work well together because we know each other well and have worked together over a number of years. We don't have to start at base every time. An example of this can be seen in the way we tackled our policy and practice on records recently. We had a meeting in which we asked ourselves what records should we send out? This is a big, thorny problem. I then sat down at a table and started working out a policy for the infants because that's my field. Meanwhile on another corner of the table one of the junior teachers was working out one for the juniors. Before we left we both had something credible for both parts of the schools – we had a draft. By the time I came back the next morning I had refined mine and she had refined hers. At the meeting a teacher had said something I didn't quite understand. I followed this up on the next day and as a result refined my draft a second time. By the time we met again at lunch both of us had a working document for both parts of the school. Now that kind of thing can go on for weeks if the people involved haven't got the kind of closeness of working which we have here. Furthermore, since we trust each other, we don't mind being wrong. There have been times when my newest recruit has said to me, 'I think we're looking at this incorrectly. We've got it wrong here.' Nobody takes offence. That's a statement of fact; in the case I am thinking about we looked at it again and found she was quite right. This young member of staff could pull us back and make us look again. That's very much encouraged. We have no secrets from each other. There's no such thing as a closed door. They applaud each other's work; they improve each other's work. The children are all well known and ideas about them are swapped on a regular basis. All this cuts out an awful lot of the dross. If a job needs to be done we all pitch in; everybody can have their two pennyworth and we sort things out.

PR: Could they do it without you? Or, rather, without a head?

JM: I would refute that completely, wouldn't I? Unless somebody in the organization has an overview, schools can get bogged down. You need the vision the work ethic. These two are almost inseparable – and you've got somebody who can keep those together. I also think headship is very important from the child's point of view.

Parents too. Supposing Mrs X had a problem with John in class and he then goes home and complains bitterly. Who on earth is his parent, let's say it's his mother, going to relate to? There might be a poor relationship between her and the class teacher. The child returns reluctantly to school the next morning and the mother disappears into the background in great frustration because she doesn't know what else to do or who to go to. You can't run things like that – headteachers are necessary.

PR: How do you know about the quality of teaching and learning taking place at St Mary's?

JM: You need to be God to really know. I have an idea about what happens. I monitor and evaluate systematically. We couldn't exist without this. Teachers are honourable: most want to do a good job of work. They like to be told when they are doing job a good of work and that doesn't happen too often in schools.

PR: Even fewer tell heads?

JM: Nobody tells a head. You are just expected to do the job. Some time ago we came up against a problem which decided me finally that I must have systematic monitoring. We now have a term when we're monitoring maths, a term when we're monitoring science and a term when we're monitoring English. I am involved in this along with the curriculum leaders. Everyone here carries some kind of curriculum responsibility and most carry two and three. Teachers in small primary schools are the most hard worked people in this world. Take my deputy head. She does maths and music. She was instrumental in the technology breakthrough. Some workload for a young woman. She and I monitor together for one term and that means on a given day once a week we turn up in a given classroom. We have a schedule we work to. A process for deciding on effectiveness. A kind of mini-inspection. There is feedback to the teacher to the children. Children like to know how they are doing. We observe the lesson and watch the follow up. Then the deputy head and I sit down and discuss that session. If everything was fine we have a brief meeting with the teacher to say 'That was great. What you need to watch is ...' and that's it. Very short, very pithy, very to the point, no big deal.

PR: About 10 per cent of the lessons observed by OFSTED were rated not satisfactory. This is very low but it seems that even very good schools have that kind of residual percentage.

JM: I can't see how you can annihilate it. And you're not talking about a bad teacher or bad teachers. You're talking of quite an effective teacher or teachers who, in comparison with their peers in that school, are rated less effective. If, in our observations, we find something radically wrong, either in the teaching or in the learning, then that is pointed out to the teacher and we would expect to see an improvement. We would also expect to see this reflected in the planning for the next term.

PR: You don't tolerate unsatisfactory work?

JM: We can't afford to. We'll survive into the next lot of children but these particular children only get the one go and we must make it as near perfect as we can for them. We'll never be perfect – but we can at least cut out some of the anomalies that creep in for all sorts of reasons. You might have one child who is disruptive, he might be screwing the whole thing up for the teacher and the other children in the class. Now that's a very important thing to point out, to notice and to build in strategies for the children's sake. You can't let it drift on. Equally it might be something simple like the teacher did a great lesson, the children did a great piece of work, but nobody pulled the whole thing together. A couple of minutes of evaluation at the end of the lesson around the blackboard may be all that is necessary. I was very struck by a report a few years ago which said that children sometimes didn't really know what they were doing in school. They didn't know what subject they were doing and I found that sad. I thought that's something I must watch at St Mary's – I must make sure history is history and geography is geography. There are times when there are planned overlaps between different subjects. Properly organized integration is one thing but I'm dead against fuzziness. You must not have it in the classroom. You've got to be clear, you've got to be precise.

PR: To whom are you accountable? What do you see is the role of the governing body?

JM: I am accountable to the governing body. I think it's good. It keeps me on my toes. They ask interesting questions and some awkward – I don't mean the governors, although some governors can be – questions. I worry about those more than I do about the awkward governors. They're no problem at all. I think it's important to be accountable to people. They expect me to run this place as efficiently as I possibly can and to continue to make it an even better school. They don't want hassle from it.

PR: They don't want to take over as the managers of the school. They let you get on with it.

JM: They're marvellous. They let me get on with it. They do want to know what I'm doing though, and rightly so. The way we achieve this is mainly through the governing body and its committees. We have a Curriculum Committee who would look at the latest in curriculum development at St Mary's. Usually the teacher or teachers involved in that development and I would be present at the meeting along with a few governors. We would explain in detail what we did, we would show them the planning that went into that development and how we would expect to plan in future, and we would show them some outcomes. The governors then report this back to the governing body. That's brilliant because the governing body are happy that this area has been looked at as thoroughly as possible. They would ask me about resourcing implications, about time management and they would come back to me on various related things. That's all good stuff.

PR: Do they ever overstep the mark?

JM: I've never known one of them to overstep the mark. They're very interested in the school and determined that we continue to improve as much as we possibly can. For other areas of management – say building maintenance – I have a little committee for that and they would come in similarly. The difficulty with governing bodies nowadays is that they take up a tremendous amount of the head's time. I don't think that's appreciated out in the big world. I don't think it is fully appreciated even by my governing body. There are many of them and only one of me and when it's a small school it's very difficult to delegate, very difficult to withdraw yourself from it. If you do, it can look as though you're not interested in that aspect of development and you can find yourself being asked pertinent questions about it like 'Why weren't you there?' This has not happened to me now but it could. You can spend a great of time in meetings with various committees of the governing body – an awful lot.

PR: What do you see as the role of parents within the school?

JM: We wouldn't function without parents. Why would we be needed if we didn't have children in the school? They are the first educators of their children and they've got to be respected for the role that they have played for four solid years before we ever see the child. If they are with you they can be a wonderful force in the school. Here, they are involved in every single aspect of the school: practical things like preparing the food and decorating the hall for the first holy communion children – all that adds to the ethos of

the school. They're there for you at every step of the way. I had a very difficult period a few years ago and I remember parents coming in and telling
me they were in support. That was all I needed to know. I didn't want them
to take sides – it wasn't a sides issue. They were there for me when I needed
them. They're there in the fund raising capacity ...

PR: They raise a lot of money don't they?

JM: They've just equipped my new library for £15,000. They're wonderful
people. They put on many events and are involved in various fund raising
activities. They are extremely interested in their own children's education.
If they weren't, I'd be worried. As such they have a right to know what is
going on in school because this is the place where this education is supposed
to be taking place. In fact only a quite small part happens in school but the
perceived wisdom is that this is where most of it happens. If they have a
worry they're entitled to a hearing. When they want to come in and say
'Thank you' they are entitled to do that. When I need help in school, they're
here. They support all areas of the curriculum in this school. There's rarely
a day you could walk around and not find at least six to eight parents within
the school working with groups of children.

PR: How do you plan this?

JM: Our parents, when they come in, know the job of work they're coming
to do. They have a briefing from the teacher. The teacher knows exactly
what to expect of them and they take their group of children and do just
that. Of course, we have quite a skilled parent input. Many are ex-teachers.
A few of them have good experience with computers. Many have very good
parenting skills and we can draw on all of these at various times in our
school. They enhance what we do in all kinds of ways.

Let me give you two particular cases. First, last year I mentioned to
them that I was worried about the comprehension skills of children. Their
reading skills are good but their comprehension skills not so marvellous. We
suggested how this could be improved and asked for help to carry out an
experiment in one class with the help of the parents – we got our volunteers
within minutes. It's this kind of support you need. Second, I remember the
case of a child coming to school who was non-English speaking. Immediately
the parents rallied around to help the mother, who was also non-English
speaking, with her English: they befriended her. They're totally integrated
into the school. That's the sort of help individual parents can give at every
level. Then, of course, there is the PTA. It is a very powerful force in itself.
It meets regularly – I'm on that committee along with one of my teachers.
It's hard working and very dedicated to the school. It has a very good class
representative system in the school. Everybody knows their place and that
there's a job to be done. Everyone gets on and does the job and there's a
minimum of interference. They don't pester you every five minutes. They
make decision within the body and it's done. It's self-regulatory, self-
controlled, very good indeed.

PR: What do you think about OFSTED and your experience of an inspection?

JM: I still think it was a sad day when the LEA lost the right to inspect. We had a very good system in Bromley. It was finely tuned and rigorous but its biggest advantage was that the teams knew each other and had often worked well together. They had learnt a lot in the process of their work – they were the first to admit that. They knew the schools and so could feed back appropriately, they could recommend people who could help. There was much useful spin-off for schools when they had their BIR inspections. We didn't have a good word to say for them when it was about to happen or during the process but like everything else the wounds healed and by and large whether you come out well or not so well on the spectrum the learning process was great.

Then OFSTED took over. A number of things struck us. First, that we received so little information or explanation about how the process was to be organized. Second, that these people weren't used to working together. Third, that the inspection was in no sense developmental. That was an awful shock. Now you might be surprised to think I'd be shocked about something like that but everything that I've ever done in my life has had some sort of developmental pattern. There's a lot of money, energy and expertise going into these inspections and yet at the end of the day you wonder about what value it can have for individual schools. We came out of the inspection very well and I believe the country as a whole needed an inspection system. But what I think it needed was a rigorous local inspection procedure. I use the word rigorous deliberately, I am not frightened of it. The OFSTED team were on a hiding to nothing. Individually they are nice people, by and large. I've heard others have had negative experiences but that's not what it was like for us. But they weren't as objective as I thought they should be. For example, an issue that kept coming up was the presence of parents in schools. One inspector had a huge problem with this and she, and they, kept bringing it up.

PR: Do you mean that she felt that parents were in school too much?

JM: She felt this wasn't advisable. Now I can see there are times and circumstances in some schools where this might not be advisable. But at other times and in other circumstances in certain other schools it can be a very good idea. It is for us. The inspector I am talking about was not open to the evidence. She came with her own fixed views. I don't want to exaggerate this and I do not claim it was the norm. But it did happen, and not just on this issue. I really did feel inspection teams should leave their personal baggage at the school gate when they come in. I know it's difficult but as professionals they really must learn to do this.

PR: Did they tell you anything about yourself or the school that was new to you? For example, they suggest that your developmental planning wasn't fully thought through.

JM: I don't think at that stage many schools had good development plans. We've improved but my development planning is still weak, even after

OFSTED. It's not something I spend a great deal of time on. I think the problem with primary headteachers is that we carry an awful lot around with us in our heads, we know a lot about our schools. I can see the value of a development plan and I do plan for development: I now link this to the budget and budget cycle. This is something I wasn't doing then. It came as no great surprise to me. On teaching and learning in the school, I learned nothing I didn't know before.

PR: Did you find the inspection a useful experience, a learning experience?

JM: It was harrowing, it was interesting, it was exhausting, but it didn't teach me anything about the school that I didn't already know. The children were desperately tired and stressed at the end of it. The teachers were totally demoralized even though we were well prepared and confident in what we were doing. It didn't feel good while it was happening. It was a horrendous process, horrifically stressful. You worked long, long hours. I'm used to this but felt terribly frustrated because I had to set aside all the things I had hoped to do for a whole half term because of it. I resented that bitterly. Getting everything ready takes quite a great deal of time, and where you have a very small staff in a small school office it can take over, and not much money was left to spend anything on any more. We had five OFSTED inspectors and two religious education inspectors in the same week. This, in a seven-classroom school, takes some managing. They were very accommodating. I asked them not to flood classrooms – to avoid having two of them in one classroom at the same time.

PR: Did they conduct the inspection efficiently and sensibly?

JM: I asked to meet them on the first morning they came in. I don't think that had happened to them before and I briefed them on their behaviour in and around school during the week. We have expectations of our visitors at St Mary's. They have to be clearly identified as visitors. They were very good on that. What they tended to do was to retreat to the spare classroom that had been set aside for them.

PR: You seem to be describing an expensive, stressful and not very helpful experience.

JM: Exactly. It was a very stressful, very expensive and not particularly helpful experience. I can't think of one really positive thing, which is unusual for me because I tend towards the positive – I really can't.

PR: Primary education has been coming in for criticism recently. Unflattering comparisons are being made between our schools and those of Taiwan, Korea and elsewhere.

JM: I wrote a letter to my son recently. He lives in Spain. I was trying to explain the vagaries of life in education here at this time. A number of issues have been raised. One is the supposed dichotomy between class teaching and group teaching. Another is on methods of teaching reading. I said much of this is a smoke-screen designed to draw attention away from the main issue which is funding. The government know they are on borrowed time, and are not interested in putting new money into education. Many of them have no experience of state education or what it is like to operate on the levels of funding allocated to state schools. I don't know what the Labour Party response is. That's being made up on the back of a cigarette packet as they go along. I have great fears for education in this country over the next ten years, whoever is in power, particularly for the small school.

PR: What would you like to see happen?

JM: First, new moneys must be found. Second, it is grossly unfair to compare a school in Beckenham with a school in Peckham. I have no problems with inspections or tests. But they are pertinent only to that year's intake in that particular school. Let's not kid ourselves they are more than that. To do so is to create further lies about education.

PR: How would you respond to those who claim that chucking money at the problems of education has not been very successful in the past? They might also argue that a number of countries who spend a great deal less per capita than we do appear to enjoy much higher levels of pupil achievement.

JM: I would ask them if they would like to live in Taiwan. I would ask if the political regimes of these countries would be suitable to the temperament of the English person. You cannot make such comparisons. You are not talking about the same curriculum. Many have a narrow and restrictive curriculum. Maths in these countries is usually one area of achievement, computation. Here it is five or six different areas. People are blinded by these broad brush strokes. One would expect better of them and one would expect them to look behind the statistics and see what it is exactly they are comparing.

Nor am I claiming that chucking money at problems is the best way to solve them. I do believe, however, that you need a reasonable level of funding to be able to manage. The analogy of a school being a business is all very well but we haven't got a sweat-shop here and I can't turn out 1000 sweat-shirts at the end of the week to improve my productivity. Having said that, I am dead against pouring money into schools which are failing. What they need is help and support to tackle the problems they face. That's the way to do it, not just by chucking money at them.

PR: Who should define what a reasonable level of funding would look like? Major variations in the unit of resource as between different parts of the country and different local authorities long pre-dated the introduction of LMS.

JM: I am not trying to defend what happened in the past. Just because we had these variations then does not mean that we should allow them to continue in this sophisticated day and age. Surely we have statisticians in this country capable of working out proper levels of funding? This does not mean that everybody must get the same. They could take local circumstances into consideration. If my school were popped into Lambeth I would have the best part of a £1,000,000 extra funding. This is wrong. If I was popped into Dudley I would probably have less. Patently this is wrong. A child in Beckenham must be worth the same as a child in Dudley and in Lambeth. We've got to move towards a common national formula even if this means building in appropriate local variations.

PR: It would take a brave government to introduce this.

JM: Bravery is not a bad thing in government. I don't think we see very much of it. But perhaps the dangers of not doing it can be raised. Inequalities and inequities of funding are creating a growing body of discontent within the country, particularly amongst headteachers. Headteachers are a bad crowd to start having problems with. We are vociferous, we are capable of getting together, we are capable of organizing ourselves and because we care passionately about our children we will do it, and we will mobilize parents and parents are voters – they can hit politicians where it hurts most.

PR: How do you cope with stress? How do you keep up to date?

JM: I genuinely believe that I'm not paid enough to get stressed. If I were a top executive in Shell or ICI and was rolling around in lots and lots of money I would probably feel I needed an analyst and would indulge myself in one. But I can't afford it. I get stressed but I can work it off. I love my garden. I work very hard in my garden. I like decorating. I don't do nearly the same amount of decorating. I enjoy reading.

PR: And you've got a family too.

JM: I've got a family. I've got a husband. I've got a good social life with lots of friends. When things are going badly they make things happen for me. I do get worried – worry is my worst enemy and then I eat badly and sleep badly. You can only do that for a few weeks at which point the safeguards you've built must kick in.

PR: How do you keep up?

JM: I don't believe you ever do. We are always a step behind. I read quite a bit and have favourite people to turn to on educational issues. I enjoy reading Robin Alexander. Ted Wragg I enjoy because he has the devil in him. I always read the *Times Ed* because I feel if there's anything going down I can at least pick up on it quickly in there. We discuss education a lot at home. My husband has retired, but we still discuss education a lot. And then I have various networks of colleagues. I am a member of the NAHT. That is useful. I also have a very good close network of friends within the grant-maintained sector and within the old LEA cluster. I enjoy those meetings and I miss them very rarely because I regard it as a perk almost to meet with these colleagues. If you have a worry you can discuss it with them and get it sorted out.

PR: You mentioned Ted Wragg. He suggests you have to be barmy to want to be a head?

JM: He's right up to a point. It's still very fulfilling to be a head though. The bureaucracy is there and it has taken up more and more time and this is very irksome. You can feel that everything is crowding in. I do it because I feel strongly that schools deserve good heads. They need the leadership. You need to know where you are going. You need to be able to build in the series of little steps along the way which makes for excellence. At the end of every year you have a cohort of children moving from your school to the next schools and eventually from school into the next phase of society. There's potentially a great fulfilment in the way they turn out and the part you have played in this. When they have left, it is good to hear about them, about how they've managed and organized their lives, about the trials and tribulations they have faced – it's all important.

PR: You seem to enjoy headship still?

JM: I enjoy it very much. I love it very much indeed. I enjoyed the article but you mustn't take Ted too seriously. He often writes tongue in cheek. If he does mean it then he is wrong. I think it is still a very rewarding job. In fact I don't see it as a job. When I get up in the morning, I don't think, 'I've got to go into work today.' I am much more likely to be thinking, 'When I get in this morning I want to ... I must remember to.'

PR: What do you say to people who come and say to you, 'I'm thinking about headship'?

JM: I warn them of the difficulties. I don't think you should lead people along a blind alley. I share my difficulties with the staff. When things are really on top of me here I go and unwind to them in the staffroom. I end up saying, 'Well it's not your worry anyway.' And they say, 'Joan, can we do anything to help?' There is a nice atmosphere. I so feel that we've got to do something about easing the burden on heads, otherwise they will not come forward in the future. Last week I left here at 9.30, 10.30 and 11.30 pm. I will be late again tonight because there is a meeting of the governing body. I start most mornings at about 7.30. That is a long day. I try and make a point of being in the staffroom at midday at some stage or other with the staff. On a Friday I have a quick staff meeting but on the other days of the week I try to get in there for a short period of time. I'm very aware it's their room, but I like to be there – we chat about various issues. If they've got something to tell me about a child we can sort it out in there. It's an informal but often very effective way of getting work done. But it is a long day, and in the course of the day you are not just doing one job. I remember going home when I was early in headship and saying to Bill, 'Well I don't know whether I'm going to stick this or not because the problem is I can never get anything done.' He would laugh and say, 'Well didn't you realize it was like this?' and I would reply, 'No, I didn't.'

CHAPTER 8

Well, what does a headteacher do?

LIZ PAVER WITH PETER RIBBINS

Liz Paver is Head of Intake First School in Doncaster, South Yorkshire. She was born in South Wales but has spent most of her life in Doncaster. Her teacher training, however, took place at St Mary's College in Cheltenham. After that she returned to Doncaster, being appointed to Kingfisher Infants. Subsequently, she was offered the post of deputy at Waverley Infants. She spent almost eight years there, during which time her son was born, before being appointed in 1976 as head of Denaby Main and subsequently of Askern First. She has been a member of the OFSTED Task Group charged with the revision of the Inspection Framework for Primary Schools. She is about to become National President of the NAHT in its centenary year of 1997.

PR: Can you tell me something about your background and the way in which this may have shaped your values and made you the sort of person you are?

LP: To the best of my knowledge we've had no teachers in the family. My parents met in South Wales and I was born in Pembroke Dock towards the end of the war. My father was in the RAF at Milford Haven. Before the war he worked for the Co-operative Society as a driver so his job was assured back in Yorkshire. When he was demobbed we moved up here. At first we lived with my grandparents and then were allocated a council house in Doncaster. My mother never worked till I gained a place at teacher training college where she supported me by becoming caretaker of the local community centre. I'm the eldest of three and she was a home-maker and could and did do everything mothers were traditionally expected to do and so we had a very comfortable home. My father was the bread-winner but my mother was the spender of the money! He worked very hard for a very low pay, and yet he kept us immaculately. There was a tradition of sitting down and having meals together. We had lots of things I wish more of the children at Intake could have, including a mother who would read with you and a father who would do sums with you. In my home, education was held in high esteem.

I wanted to go to school. I remember going to pre-nursery and there was a lovely new school to go to which had a nursery. I stood with my nose through the railings wanting to go. I was admitted early to nursery and I can never remember not enjoying primary school life. Very early on I was attracted by the idea of being a teacher. I remember having an old air raid shelter in our garden which I turned into a classroom and having my desk out there. My earliest recollections of teachers and people who have cared for me are good ones. I struggle to remember problems – perhaps one. My name is Elizabeth Caroline and once when my mother went to collect me the nursery nurse said, 'Liz has had a good day' and mum was highly affronted. She said, 'She's Elizabeth' and from that moment I got Elizabeth Caroline throughout my nursery life!

PR: You decided so early that you wanted to be a teacher?

LP: I remember my headteacher, Miss Shearstone. She was statuesque: a five foot ten inches lady in an immaculate blue suit, steel grey hair and an imperious manner. But really she was a gentle soul. I remember her taking me to read stories to the reception class when I was only seven. My mother says, 'Miss Shearstone said to me "She'll teach".' That was where the rest of my life was formed as far as work is concerned. But I suppose the gene was always there.

PR: How would you describe your family and the local community?

LP: Very much working class in a working-class community. When we moved here my mother found herself in an industrial town, something she had never known before. Her own home circumstances were much more middle class. Her grandfather had owned a fleet of fishing vessels which plied in and out of Milford Haven and her aunts were the shopkeepers of the town. I think within her own community she would have always been felt to have had a little more than the average working-class lass and I think she brought a lot of those standards to her home-making. When, for example, new families came to our road, if their children were allowed to rampage around and create noise this wasn't acceptable to my mother. She wouldn't have come to the front garden and shout at us to come in, she would have expected us to come home at an appropriate time. Being the good cook she always was, she would make a stew on Monday which would go to another family later in the week. She realized we had more than some, even though in monetary terms I don't suppose we really did. But we had more of a culture of home than many of the families around us did and she wanted us to make our friends amongst children of similar homes. I think she was a little bit fearful for us. I don't think she ever really got used to being in Yorkshire and she still speaks with a very strong Welsh accent. She had been brought up with high standards herself.

PR: She valued order?

LP: And cleanliness next to godliness – she scrubbed us away, never mind the house. You would have to take your shoes off before you came into the kitchen. It became a natural process. Her career was being a home-maker. I appreciate now all she gave me in the way of standards. It held me in good stead when, as one of only four girls from my primary school to do so, I went to grammar school. I suddenly mixed with girls from professional homes. I understood the standards they were talking about, that wasn't a culture shock. Although many of their fathers did professional jobs and many of their mothers were teachers, I could fit in very comfortably with them. We shopped at the same shops for our school uniforms because I'd always been used to having Sunday best. I don't suppose I realized then, but I realize now, that for some girls who went to grammar school it was a very difficult transition into another culture. It had a very public school ethos, it was very much the ladies of the town who wore the green uniform. I got a really good primary education which stood me in good stead.

PR: Your mother seems a dominant influence on you. What of the wider family?

LP: We are a matriarchal society in our family, no doubt about it. My maternal grandmother was a lady of great standing in her own community although she never had a career as such. She was Aunt Rose to everybody I ever knew. They overlooked the sea, the front doors were never closed and an elephant tooth held the front door open. The whole of these 20 to 30 houses overlooked the sea, and people would simply knock and go in. That was how life was. For the children it must have been wonderful. We went every summer holiday until I was in secondary school. My father's joy was to own a new car when few others did. My father's side was very much paternal. My grandfather was a police sergeant in Doncaster in the days when folk who needed it were clipped around the ear. I remember him taking me to the old Guild Hall in Doncaster to see the cells. One of my first pictures was in grandfather's police uniform jacket standing on the table holding my Easter egg. It was a family who had a real understanding of standards.

PR: Can you say a bit more about these standards?

LP: School was very important. If you brought anything home it had priority. I can remember our first television. There was a different feeling about childhood then. You didn't come home and just switch on the box and sit there. You'd talk to your mother or go out and play, you would make your own entertainment. I remember playing cards with my father in the evening. He loved mathematics and wanted us to have instant recall of all the tables. As soon as you could do your tables you were rewarded. School mattered. There was a mothers' club at my primary school, but mine wouldn't join, she thought they were elitist. She's not confident in herself. My father, working for a bakery, could get sugar and butter. I used to take brown paper parcels for the head. But mother would never become part of the mothers' club. Miss Shearstone, I can still hear her, would often say, 'Ask your mum to come and see me', but she wouldn't. Home was her scene. She was fulfilled in a way I could not be. I'm not a home-maker – housework isn't my scene!

I've always been surrounded by quite dominant women, within their households and the school: Miss Shearstone the head teacher, Mrs Kilhourey, the reception teacher. They were there, they were my mentors, they were strong and colourful people who made you want to achieve. They made you responsible. What we could do easily as 7-year-olds then does not seem possible until 9 or even 11 now. We were very autonomous little 7-year-olds, I suppose I was a proper little madam. That's how I see school then, I see us surrounded by very firm discipline – you wouldn't have dared to have spoken back to anyone in those days. School was much more regimented. When I came into teaching in the mid-1960s, teachers were much more respected. I don't think you would have parents, mothers even, rushing in and swearing at the head, which is quite common these days.

PR: What do you remember of life in your secondary school?

LP: I wasn't academic in their terms. I passed my 11-plus, but I was conscious right from the beginning that I needed to work very hard if I was going to keep up. I remember coming away with a good set of examination results at the end of the first year, but I knew I'd worked very hard to get those and to establish friendship groups. I was fortunate to become friendly with a group of girls, most of whose mothers were teachers. We joined the tennis club at the other end of Doncaster. So I immediately got into a social group I would not have got into had I gone to the local secondary modern. I enjoyed that and they did different things socially than I did. We went to the theatre and that sort of thing but they all loved coming to our house. I feel privileged to have had the bridge made for me. I was allowed to do everything, for example, to go on school visits. It must have been a struggle, but the money was always found.

PR: Did you enjoy your secondary schooling as much as your primary?

LP: I don't think I did. In one way I became class conscious and wondered if I was making the grade, not only academically but also socially. Yet it was a school where if you put in the effort, you were rewarded. I could become a prefect and all the regular things. I felt it was a privilege to be there. It was somewhere to be and want to be. The headmistress had great standing in the town and would truck nothing but the best. We all took Latin. It was only at the end of the school when there was any division made as to how many GCEs you took. Somehow teaching as a career had just always been there for me. I don't think I ever aspired to university, but teaching was acceptable. You went off to training college. That was acceptable.

PR: How do you remember your teachers from the secondary school?

LP: There was a divide between the subjects you were good at and the teachers were lovely and the subjects you struggled at and they were harridans. I still look back at all of them with respect because I think that was just how we were.

I went down the track of humanities rather than the sciences. I got a hang-up about science from the word go. I was never ever going to be good at it. I talk myself into not being good at things. I think the worst experience perhaps was with the languages and with Latin. I didn't get on with Latin and thought, 'Dear, dear I shall never be any good at this at all.' The problem tended to be with subjects in which I couldn't get any help at home in the way some of the other girls could. I remember being helped by another girl's parents. The father of one of my good friends, we've just met up again after 30 years, was vice-principal of the Tech. If I struggled I could take it to Mr Pearson, he would always help. This must have been frustrating for my parents. They became less and less able to help me as I grew up to later teens. Not that there was ever any question of my not being able to stay on. A good friend wasn't allowed to stay on and she got much, much better O-levels than I did. I remember sitting and feeling Ann had been let down and she was saying, 'Oh no I want to go and work at the railway.' But I thought she is so bright, she could do anything, she is a true academic. Everything just fell into place for her but she couldn't do anything with her right hand. So she did my maths homework and I knitted her socks. That was how things were. I went on to sixth form and enjoyed that and then applied for teacher training college.

PR: What were the core values at your grammar school?

LP: Respect for people, property and the school. To have pride in the school was very important and to do your best because it was clear where you came from. That was where the importance of school uniform came home to me. Miss Mellor's philosophy was if you were in the green blazer and green skirt you were an ambassador for the school no matter where you were. The boys' grammar school was along the way. When we became interested in boys, woe betide you if you were seen in the road with a boy. There was pride in achievement, a school where lots of things went on. The house system was important. It gave us a feeling of belonging and doing your best by the school.

PR: You then went on to training college?

LP: Cheltenham, St Mary's. We hadn't had a girl there and I remember being told 'You will do well at your interview and you will get a place because we haven't had a girl there before.' Another girl went with me and my father took us down. I was fortunate to be offered a place. What rang in my ears for three years was the demand that you will do well because we need an opening for those to come after you.

I can perhaps best describe the school using an example from my life there. It happened in lower sixth. We went on a school visit to Switzerland. A ski-lift caught my spine and dislodged a disk. I had to be brought back by the Red Cross. A member of staff stayed with me. I was hospitalized in

Dover for a week when I got back. The head or deputies visited my parents every day. They were taken to the head's home to telephone. When I returned I was on my bed for weeks. Every week the head and the senior teachers came. That was the type of school it was, and to this day I can hear my mother saying, 'Miss Mellor's coming this afternoon' and the scones would be baked. I'd be scrubbed to within an inch of my life so that everything would be wonderful for Miss Mellor. That made a great impact on mother, that the head herself would come from the grammar school to visit and spend an hour and have tea, just to make sure I was all right. I could not say anything which better told you about the values of that school.

Eventually I went to Cheltenham. I remember a drama teacher there who prided himself on being able to place us in the country to within ten miles of our home. We sat around in a semi-circle and he pitched me at about Sheffield, which was about right. I became conscious for the first time of the north/south divide. I remember being very conscious of the girls from the south, they spoke so differently. I was sure they must be aristocrats.

PR: Can you describe your career as a teacher up to the point to which you became a head?

LP: In those days they did blanket interviews. Doncaster was still the Borough of Doncaster with the West Riding surrounding it and the West Riding interviews for this area were held in Doncaster. There must have been 50 of us. The first person who came through the door said, 'If you've got an interview with the West Riding this afternoon please leave now.' That cut the numbers down. I can't remember anything about my interview. We were told they were taking on six in the primary sector and we had to wait. Then we were allocated a school. I got Kingfisher Infants School. This was interesting because it was a school at the opposite end of Doncaster from where I had been brought up but with a similar catchment area. The head, Miss Auckland, was one of three sisters; another was head at Intake Infants and the third lectured at Ripon Training College. Their father had been councillor of the town and a past mayor. She was another Miss Shearstone. When she walked down the corridors of power I trembled more as a student teacher than as a child at my infant school. She was a wonderful person. The first time we met she said, 'I haven't had a probationer for 15 years Miss Taylor, I hope you are going to measure up. Here is your register, have you got a fountain pen?' I had my best Parker. 'Go to the staff room and fill in your children's names and bring it back to me.' In my very best, I did this and took it back, and must have passed muster. However, the next time I was summoned to her hallowed office I had put a red ring in felt tip pen instead of fountain pen. I'd defaced an archive and would I kindly not do such things in future. She was very interested in mathematics, so we were a Nuffield Show School. She would march visitors down the corridor and say, 'My probationer is in there.' They never visited, until the fateful day when she said, 'We're having visitors and they will be coming to you tomorrow morning.' I got my reception class set up in our groups and told them a story until I heard the steps coming down and I said, 'Right, you all know what you're going to do, so as soon as I say "go" you go.'

That was my probationary year. I loved it. I was there for two years and then somebody came to the next classroom. She had no infant experience and so we shared a stockroom and ideas. She became a friend. Two terms later the school I attended as a child, Waverley Infants, wanted a deputy. I had no more thought of it than the man in the moon. But, after it had been advertised three times, Graham White, the adviser, came to see me and said, 'You will apply.' I was just two years and two terms into teaching. So not knowing what the reaction might be, as a bumptious, newly qualified, I decided to apply. I had my Associate of College of Preceptors so had an additional qualification and that was all. At college we were the last students who didn't get degrees. Those who had got distinctions in theory and practice of education could have gone back and done a further year and qualified for a degree. I had just got married so didn't want to do that. I have regretted all my life not having a degree. I applied for Waverley and got an interview, but my head wouldn't give me a reference. She said, 'It's not that you are not a good teacher but do you think you can do Mrs Pearson-Jones's [the deputy] job after just two years? No, ten years and I will give you a reference.' That was it. So with the day of the interview looming I said to Graham, 'What is going to happen? I have no reference.' He said, 'You will have a reference.' Anyway, the Director of Education came and had a quiet word and I had my reference. I remember him telling me 'Wear a hat, it will make you look ten years older.' I said to my mum I must look ten years older and she sorted me out. I went for the interview and I got it. But it was too soon.

PR: Your head was right?

LP: She was. I would give the same advice. Unbeknown to me my new school needed somebody prepared to kill themselves. At the interview the head said, 'I want someone to be my arms and legs!' and meant it. She did no teaching and didn't come out of her office if she did not have to. I virtually took on a headship without the ultimate say so which is death. It was a great challenge and had I not been an overconfident person I would have given up. We got going and eventually it came right, but I had to work tremendously hard. I had been there three years when I became pregnant and was devastated. That I might have my own children had not entered into my thinking at all. I was going to be a head when I was 30 and that was it. Anyway Philip came along and I took maternity leave. Fortunately, my mother lived in the next road to the school where I was deputy. So although we lived five miles away this made it possible for me to continue my career. She adopted her grandson. He had two mums from the word go. If anyone did, I suffered. We gave him everything when he was at home and she gave him her whole attention all day, every day. I did not have the joy of bringing him up.

The headteacher held the post open for me. She had a strange attitude. She had had a great tragedy. Her daughter, only 18, was killed in a road accident while I was her deputy. Then her husband died. I might have got out of there in five years, I had already begun to apply for headships, but I couldn't leave her then and certainly the LEA needed me there. I became increasingly frustrated. I could see people getting headships who didn't have my experience. I eventually got my first headship after seven and a half years in Denaby Main and didn't feel it was any too soon. I had missed my deadline, I was 31 when I got my first headship, but had a son and that was a bonus.

Denaby Main had just come into the Doncaster LEA because the Metropolitan areas were being formed. Sir Alec Clegg described it in his book as the worst village in England. At that time they were spending lots of money on it and building new housing. It was a modern little school and I loved it. I can remember that first day of headship as if it were yesterday. Rushing into school, loving everything. Chatting to the staff of four teachers and the nursery staff. Nine o'clock arrived and they went about their business and I went to my office and found myself standing there thinking, 'Well, what does a head do?' I was no longer a deputy with a full class of children. I didn't really have to do anything. I felt totally unprepared. How do you get from that to spending seven and a half days a week in school as I did in that first year? I was there proving everything to everybody. I warn people against this, you are not everything to everybody. But I tried to be and my home life must have suffered terribly because my son spent as much time in our school as he did at his own. I had very good staff, my first deputy was a lady about to retire who had made it known that if she didn't get on with new 'young thing' that she would go immediately, but she was lovely. She was so traditional but could teach a houseplant to read. She was so committed and good and we complimented each other. She was so calm and knew the area so well that everybody trusted her. At first I was this new and unknown 'thing' but the team became very strong. I was there four years.

PR: How had you prepared for headship?

LP: The LEA had a scheme by which after you were appointed you had a long weekend at Wooley Hall in Wakefield. We had things like the school and the law, discipline, school policy and that was the only preparation I got. There was nothing previous and certainly no audit of your own skills like there is now. I was fortunate when I got to Denaby that one of the first people to ring me was someone I had never met in my life but who was head of the nearest infant school. She was a great character and we became firm friends and still are. I had a mentor, even if she was only two years ahead of me in headship. I joined NAHT. I got pulled into the centre of things, and therefore had a group of heads who I could always talk to. Two or three mentor heads kept me on the straight and narrow. I also had a community which, if they saw you were a worker and loved children, were 100 per cent behind you. So headship didn't hold any great fears for me.

PR: What did you learn about headship from your previous heads?

LP: As a pupil, my primary and both my infant heads were fine and my secondary head was superb. My first head as a teacher was someone I wanted to be like, she was lord of all she surveyed. This is my interpretation of headship. When I first became a deputy head and realized you could bring your newspaper in and your electric fire and your toast and sit and be a head, this was foreign to me. I had no respect for that person as a person and none as a head. In retrospect I can forgive her a lot but I can't forgive her for not being the leader. A head has to be fair. I don't think you should make friends with some groups of staff and not others. This head was familiar with some and marginalized other teachers. I learnt more from her than others because she taught me how I should never allow myself to be. Her lack of appreciation of other people was a great lesson, and the fact that if we ever had irate parents she wouldn't tackle them and she wouldn't defend her staff. Furthermore, whilst you don't have to be first on site and last off to prove you are a good head, it does help to be there at the end of the day. No one is out of school more than I am now, but you have to prioritize the times that you are here. I didn't want to have that kind of reputation. I didn't want to be somebody who people felt was not in control and committed.

PR: You seem to have come to terms with your first year of headship unusually quickly?

LP: After the first morning I went out to find out what there was to do. I found I could take every class in the school for music and give every member of staff an hour. They thought that was wonderful, I thought it was wonderful. I was doing a thing I was reasonably good at, the children loved it and the staff got free time to develop other things. I soon realized it was a great privilege to be there as the person who can make things happen for other people. I was very committed to school meals and to working with kitchen staff. I was having staff meetings for everybody, the cleaners, the caretaker, everybody. We had a wonderful rapport and everybody was part of the team. I really enjoyed being the head.

PR: Did you get your first application for a headship?

LP: It was my first interview, I had applied for two other schools. That's when I became disillusioned. As is my wont, I telephoned the Chief. He said, 'I'll send somebody to talk to you.' He sent an inspector who said, 'You will be a head.' I said, 'Yes, but I want to choose where I am a head. Why couldn't I be interviewed?' He answered, 'You will be.' I was arrogant enough to think that if I had been interviewed for one of the others I might have got it. It wasn't in their great plan. I became a bit difficult to live with. I had outgrown deputy headship. What finished me was preparing the children's school orchestra to go to a festival. I did everything: brought them to a festival the school had never attended, got the mums to make uniforms of gingham dresses for the girls and white shirts for the boys. We looked wonderful, played beautifully, everything was fine. But the head, who had

had nothing to do with this, on the final rehearsal came to the hall and listened. After the children had performed brilliantly, she said, 'We better have the music stands painted next year' and left. I thought that's it I must go, our philosophies are just too far apart.

PR: What did you feel when they offered you the post?

LP: Totally elated. My mother has been through some awful traumas in my life because I always assume I will get things. Take my election as vice-president of NAHT. My husband said, 'Your mum's ever so worried.'

'Why is she worried?'

'Because are you going to live with not getting it?'

'Yes of course I am'. She tends to worry but I have an optimistic attitude to life. Four years later I had a major put down. I applied for a headship in another mining community, and went round the school. It hadn't moved from Dickensian days and I looked at it and thought 'I've got to come here.' I was short listed with the current deputy of 22 years in that school, and the deputy head of the middle school attached to it. We went to be interviewed, and as we were sitting waiting to go in the adviser came out and said, 'You haven't met Councillor X have you?' I said, 'No.' He said, 'Be careful.' I thought what on earth does he mean. I went in and sat at the end of a long table surrounded by people with the councillor at its head. He said, 'Is it Elizabeth, is it Caroline or is it Liz?' and I said, 'It is Mrs Paver to you councillor.' End of interview! It was going very well, all the vibes were right, then he walked down and he blew his nose very loudly. I though what a dreadful man and he walked back and sat down. So we came out and I went back to my little school and thought fine, I haven't got it, the current deputy had got it. When I got back one of my nursery nurses came and said, 'Sorry about the interview Mrs Paver.' I asked, 'How did you know I didn't get it?' She said, 'I went to the party last Saturday in the local working men's club for Mrs X, it was a celebration of her getting the headship.' That was the Saturday before the interview. It was a salutary experience. The same adviser came to see me the following day. He stuck his head round the door and said, 'Have I got to throw my cap in?'

'Don't ever set me up again to make everything look kosher because I am not on that lark.'

'The Chief sent me out to say, super interview, no problem, do you want a first school?'

'Yes, I want a first school, but I want it on merit.'

A year later two came up and I applied for both. At the interview I was asked which I would prefer. My second headship was a school of 250. It had a lovely setting, a brand new building and a beautiful field. Five years later the area in which my present school is located was being reorganized and Intake was to become a first school. An inspector came and asked, 'Would you apply for Intake?'

'No.'

'The Head wants to retire, he does not want a first school.'

'No. You can't promise it to me, it is up for interview and there can be no guarantee'.

A year later he came back and said, 'The Chief thinks you are ready for a move.' I said, 'You want me to go and see Intake don't you?' So I came, saw Intake and thought I'll apply. There were five deputies and me on this short list. They looked at me. I had run courses some of them had been on. I said, 'This is not a foregone conclusion if I was sitting on any of your seats I would be saying to myself, I'll show that Liz Paver, I'll get this headship! She might have been a head for ten years but I'll show her! You get yourselves in there and show them.' I got it in the end and have never really regretted it. I had about 580 children on site when I came, 24 classes and a nursery. You had to deal with it as if it were a secondary school whilst retaining the ethos of a primary school. It has given me insight into managing schools which has helped in working with secondary colleagues. It made me look at headship in a different way, much more as a senior management team, building and making sure that lots of delegation went on and valuing other people as leaders. I'm only the managing director of a well-oiled company. It makes you prioritize your time differently. It is the first time I did not have a teaching time table. I can't because you let people down by being pulled into meetings, etc. I regret having to be 80 per cent social worker but if I don't do it the school isn't what we want it to be. In any school, a small group of families take up an enormous amount of your time. If you don't sort them out it can have knock-on effects on the rest of the school family.

PR: You have had 20 years as a head. Has it changed, for better or for worse?

LP: I still feel privileged to be a head. My work for NAHT tells me, Headship is a very stressful occupation. Heads are answerable on so many fronts – financially, pupil performance, all the rest of it. Despite this, I say to my deputies and my staff 'We still have children to educate, teachers to develop, a curriculum to deliver.' We have always had a high expectation of what the children should be able to do and the standards they should achieve. We have always wanted to have an environment that is well resourced, happy to work in and well presented. Children feel welcome here. Our ethos is unchanged. But some things have changed for the worse. The stress on paper accountability, for example, has changed out of all proportion. I am not good on paper. We should have a minimalist approach. When the National Curriculum came in we said, 'OK, what is new that we are not doing now that we must do?' We did the musts, we did not say we must do everything new. We have not chased bandwagons. We have said sometimes you must class teach, sometimes group teach, sometimes individual teach. This has not changed.

In one way the experience I had prior to the National Curriculum, prior to testing and assessment, prior to OFSTED, prior to LMS, made me able to look at it all pragmatically and say I can turn this school into a bunch of neurotics overnight if I want to but what good would that do? They were already giving me detailed accounts of what they were planning, of how they were assessing, of how they were evaluating. Responding to the changes has fine-tuned our thinking but has not required us to re-invent anything. When people say 'It's changed out of all proportion, it is not the job it was' I agree. It is very demanding, but you can make it more so than it need be. If you go into 90 per cent of primary headteachers' offices nowadays you will find a computer terminal in a prominent position. It tells you something about how we are allowing the outside world to change our culture. I don't have a terminal on my desk. I have people who understand it and can run it much better than I can. I do the managing, they do the hands on. Headship has changed but it is still possible to adapt to the change and make it work for you instead of the reverse. We have not had our brown envelope from OFSTED. When we do, we will panic and go into hypertension because we will want to be at our best. On the other hand I said to the staff we are the school and they are visiting, and they will do their inspection. I will make sure they are professional and work within the bounds of the framework but we will go about our business. They will judge us as we are. This might be more difficult for a new head. But it is no use demanding just because the inspectors are coming that we have got to be 200 per cent right, nobody can be. What I don't have now is many of my own generation of heads or experienced people in the LEA. Where can I go for help? Perhaps more to the point, where, as an experienced head, can I find the time to support other and, especially, newer heads?

PR: How do you regard the educational reforms of the last decade and their implementation?

LP: The National Curriculum was long overdue. What has happened has been to focus class teacher attention and debate on curriculum development in a way that could not have been achieved by any other method. The whole country looked and saw this is what they say we must do. We got it wrong because they went about it in the wrong way. It was too big and too broad. The teaching profession had to come to this realization themselves so they had to have all the discussion that went behind it. This discussion focused thinking on what is appropriate at what age group. Take the science document as a case. There were things at Key Stage 1 which were terribly inappropriate, but teachers tried to teach it. We did to some extent find that children are able to take in far more than sometimes we give them credit for. So it did focus us on what we were teaching, how we were teaching and the ways in which children were learning. In retrospect we must welcome that and I think we are getting towards a new curriculum that is deliverable. I think we still have got an overload in Key Stage 2 but we are getting towards it. In addition, I have no problem with testing children. I have always wanted to know what levels they are at. You have to have some comparators to do so and these cannot be just in terms of your own achievements but also more generally. It does cause me a problem when they compare my school with every other school in country, without taking into account that quite a few of our children come from very linguistically impoverished backgrounds. What we now have is based on a simple market model and I think that is wrong. I see little advantage in a system which puts us in opposition to surrounding schools and vying for pupils. The local management of schools can only work if it is based on a needs-driven budget. If a school puts up a philosophy and a policy for delivering education to a specified number of children there should be the money to supply that. A formulae approach which cuts out the recommendations of teachers can't be the way forward. That upsets me because it is taking our professionalism away.

PR: To what extent do you see this as a formula problem or a funding problem?

LP: Both. You have a party in power who are not going to allow local government to succeed so it starves it of resources. Our LEA has been rate capped for three years. It may not have used all its money as well as we might wish but capping has a knock-on effect in schools and other public services. Children have an entitlement to education, that means an entitlement to proper resourcing. I would go for a national formula.

PR: Can you see it happening?

LP: If we have a national curriculum and a national testing system we ought to have a national funding system. I did not believe this two years ago but the more I see of the anomalies in what are going on, not just here but all over the country, the more persuaded I become. Take heads and deputy salaries spines. If you are in a school like this how can you go to your governors and say pay me a little more? I have not had a pay rise since LMS, other than the yearly percentage. I am still at my assimilation point. I am £4,500 behind the top of my spine with 20 years experience. There is no way I am ever going to get to the top of the spine and therefore my pension will not be what I should have but the pension my school can allow me to have. There is something wrong in a set-up in which if I happened to be in a school where the teacher profile age-wise gives a surplus, I can have a pay rise, and if I am not, I cannot.

PR: Do you continue to have reservations about LMS as a whole?

LP: I think it is a good principle. It gives proper flexibility to governing bodies and schools to prioritize. If the budget were right LMS would give you the flexibility to decide how you spend what is available and to do so on the best possible information. I am sure schools are in the best position to know whether they should spend more or less on staffing, or the buildings and grounds, or on learning resources. We should be able to make those decisions, but the crock of gold has to be such that it is worth worrying about.

PR: Some have suggested that recent developments have made heads into accountants and/or administrators and have prevented them being significant educative leaders?

LP: It would be untruthful to say it hasn't. Capitation is all we were really responsible for many years and now there is so much more. I think as a headteacher much of this has been put on our desks. You have to deal with it, the deputies have to deal with it, the governors have to deal with it. I don't believe every class teacher should be going home worrying about the budget and its management. I think there is a way of handling that. In part we devolve parts of the budget. This year we decided it is going to be spent in year group packages. You are going to have £300 for your year group. How are you going to spend this? Or this year is going to be subject based. Will each curriculum subject group look how they would spend a £200? The staff go away, make their plans and spend the money. However, they don't expect to run out of pencils, paper, etc. and it is still my job and that of the deputies to organize that and the secretary keeps me informed of what is happening. If you deflect the attention of teachers from planning lessons and working with the children in order to get their minds around LMS, then LMS is a nonsense. But somebody has to spend the time on it and that is me. Even so, I think we spend minimal time here. I don't on a week by week basis worry about what is happening. There are certain budget heads and they are running along during the year at the end of which you might get a February panic. In February and March I do spend a lot of my time discussing how the budget is looking with the chairman of governors. For that short period it does become predominant, apart from that it isn't. But of course we have to monitor the budget and I appointed a financial secretary three years ago to do just that.

PR: I have also heard from heads that it was hard for a year or two while they got used to managing the budget but once they have done so it was only hard if they wanted it to be.

LP: We have a budget of about £700,000 annually but I have hardly any flexibility. The largest item is staffing, once that is established there is little more you can do. The next item is keeping the site open and in the best possible condition by lighting, heating, maintaining, paying the rates, paying the insurance. Once we have decided how much that is going to cost us, that is it. You are right, at first it looked horrendous, but once you have understood it and see it in the way I have described above, it is manageable.

PR: What do you see as the role of the governors? What of the role of the chairman?

LP: Our chairman is a local councillor who has been on the education committee. He is the regional officer for NUT, so he understands education completely. He knows the paperwork inside out, and his idea of a meeting is that if it goes on for longer than two hours then you are not chairing it very well or people are having far too much flexibility in the discussion. I am very fortunate in that many governing bodies have made headteachers' lives a misery in wanting to be too much involved in detail and on a day by day basis. I don't think that is what governing bodies are for.

The conflict that you are beginning to get between chairman and heads all over the country is horrendous. It happens where people are told they have power and feel they have to use it. Some parents will say something bad about the school to the chairman of governors who will then burst in and say to the head you are suspended. Nearly 30 heads have been suspended nationally and over half of those because of a conflict between the governors and the head. It is something I can't really appreciate because I have always had governing bodies who have been challenging on occasions but respect the fact that you are there on a day by day basis to lead the school and develop it. We have had mutual respect. I think the governing body should be a good place for heads to go and say 'Well I think this is your problem and what shall I do about it?' Unfortunately some heads try to steer the governing body far too much, and then wonder why it all backfires. Having a good governing body is important and a good governing body can be one of many factors that make for a successful school. My people turn up for the governors meetings but I have very little hands-on management support from them. I know some large schools have governing bodies which are involved much more fully and closely. I wonder how it works.

We have all the sub-committees we are supposed to have but they tend really to be quite dormant groups. So the site management group will walk the site prior to each meeting but one of the deputies does the day to day hands-on work. They don't have the kind of active role some claim they should have. I'm sure Gillian Shephard believes they are running every school in the land for us so that as heads we are almost a redundant profession. In practice, it does not work like that.

PR: In a conversation I once had with John MacGregor, he talked of heads having all these new and exciting powers. He didn't mention the governing body until I reminded him that the 1988 Act had given them almost all these powers. Was this appropriate?

LP: What they didn't get correct was the allocation of powers. The NAHT, along with other teacher unions and associations, have produced a code of practice for governing bodies which, we hope, will be adopted nationally. It will attempt to clarify what the remit of the governors is and what the remit of the head is. This needs to be laid down much more carefully than it was in 1988. I have no problem with governors having powers. What cannot work is a situation in which the chairman of governors expects to see the head every Monday morning for three hours and go through the work pattern for the week and to make decisions. That is happening now in some schools. What we need are much more clearly defined understandings about the leadership of the school in terms of its day by day management by the head and its governance by the governors. It is this that the NAHT is putting together with the other unions. We have had it on an agenda with Gillian Shephard and she said 'Go away and do it and we will support it, but we won't do it for you.' The department doesn't see it as their remit to write a code of conduct but if there is one they will be happy to support it.

PR: Do you see yourself as competing with other schools and heads?

LP: We fool ourselves if we think we can be a head these days and not be competitive. I don't think that I have ever been anything other than competitive in some sense of the term. I have always felt my ducklings were swans, any head worth her salt will always try to see their school as being something to be proud of. If you are proud of something then you tend to go into the market-place and sell it. I have sold my schools for the last 20 years as being something special but never to the detriment of other schools in terms of trying to take children from them. I have always been very committed to the idea of the catchment area school. It isn't the same as in the secondary sector, in primary schools in 99 per cent of cases you get your catchment area children. You do with that catchment area what you can and the best you can. I have always been in areas where we have had children who have not been as privileged as others but I don't want any quarter given. I think there is a sort of competition in such a view. But there is a new kind of competition now. Children come with crocks of gold, that can make a great difference with what you can do in the school. It never occurred to me I would approach a marketing consultant but I was interviewing one here the other day with regard to our new brochure for September. I need to know that when my new parents take it out that it stands against the others in the community. I can't let us be less well publicized than the others. In that sense we are in a sort of market-place and you can't opt out of it. I do not want to grab new pupils but I do want people to say 'Our school is Intake, this is our school brochure' and feel proud. On this, our thoughts have been sharply focused by the fact that every parent in the school last September received a letter saying whether their child should be coming to us this September or going to the other site. They had to make a choice, that was salutary. Would everyone accept that a new line had been drawn and accept it? In fact 70 to 80 per cent of our parents have decided to leave their children here right through. I am not saying I haven't been far more attentive to parents coming around the school who have told me 'Well, we are a bit undecided Mrs Paver.' I'll tell them that I have got five minutes and will show you around and talk to you. Am I marketing? If people say they are not conscious of it and the rest of the world is doing it they fool themselves. You are bound to be involved in some way or another.

Even so, I think it would be wrong for a primary school to try and change the profile of its pupils by marketing. I would never ever want to go down that route. But there are problems ahead. This year it will be possible to select 20 per cent by ability. Nowhere in the White Paper does it say that is only for secondary. Can you imagine us giving a based assessment to 5-year-olds as they come in to see if they were bright enough to come here? If we are not careful we are going to be in a situation where we select by parents and select by test. We will loose so much of what has been our inheritance as far as education for all is concerned. It might not happen in this end of the country but there are areas where it will. Especially if at the end of Key Stage 2 there are going to be national league tables of performance. If this happens, what are heads to do? You are going to want to have the highest profile you can in achievement. That worries me. I cannot see myself fitting into such a situation.

PR: How do you know about what is going on in the classrooms of your school?

LP: There is only one way and that is actually to visit, not necessarily to sit for long periods observing what is going on but you have to walk the site regularly and be informed about the quality of work taking place. I walk round here before the staff arrive in the morning or after the last person has left and the caretaker's gone home and look at what is on the walls. I can do it during the day and so can get a feel about whether or not we are stretching the pupils and whether the environment is being looked after. There is a great deal you can see and hear by just being around and talking to the children. Then you need to talk with the senior people in the school, the people who have responsibilities for how things are going. I have to have very good deputies who can say 'I don't think that Mrs X is really on top of things, something may be wrong?' So you have to have a dialogue about individuals, and then you have to have an opportunity to meet groups of teachers to talk about different things like the progress being made in the Key Stage 1 group and the Key Stage 2 group. You don't have to actually teach children to get to know about these things. The current trend, if I read things rightly, is that headteachers must teach more. That begs the question that while I am teaching a group of children what is happening in my other 14 classes? I can't teach all these classes. As head I must be able to glean that information in other ways. I often say to newly qualified heads you have got to remember now that the buzz you got when you taught you must now get by having a teacher come in and say, 'What do you think about so-and-so?' You are now a developer of professionals not pupils, you can't be both. I know we have many small schools where heads do have to teach most of the time but I don't believe they can be heads in the same way as you must be in a large school. The head of a small school has an almost unmanageable job – no wonder it is so difficult to recruit them.

My teaching is mainly cover now. The secretaries will say to me, 'You enjoyed that didn't you?' and it can be wonderful, it is so refreshing. I think heads often miss opportunities to be teachers, particularly of large groups. They exist in assemblies, acts of collective worship, etc. where you are up front as a teacher and what you are doing is teaching children and training staff at the same time. That is why I love taking assembly. It is a time when I still feel I am a teacher. If a child comes in with work to see me I get an opportunity to be a one on one teacher but I don't think I have to justify my existence by a teaching timetable. If OFSTED or anybody else are going down that line they are going to make headteachers less effective in schools not more effective.

PR: Can I ask you what you think the role of the LEA is and should be?

LP: One change is regrettable – the move from LEA advisers to LEA inspectors, who, in many LEAs, are in fact OFSTED inspectors who spend only a proportion of their time in the LEA. What schools have lost is the guidance, the mentoring we used to have in the past. We have our pyramid inspector who visits once a term, but really and truly he hasn't got the time to get to know the staff. Teachers feel much more remote from the LEA now than they did when I was a teacher or even when I was first a head. At that time we had a great bunch of people at the centre who were developing education. Now the LEA can be an administrative bureaucracy which schools don't feel part of. This is sad. It is an us and them situation rather than all being a team. It will get worse as less and less of the money can be retained at the centre. They, like schools, are strapped for cash and are wondering what to prioritize. Heads do need the kind of supportive structure they used to have. In many cases they don't feel they have it now. How can you be an OFSTED inspector one day with a clipboard and an adviser and mentor the next day? It is asking the impossible. I was very grateful as a new head 20 years ago to be able to pick up the phone and speak to an officer and say 'X, Y and Z has happened and I am going to do this, this and this, is that OK?' Always knowing that the advice would be sound and it would be to the best advantage of your school and your situation. Now I don't feel we have that same confidence any longer.

PR: Might this change with a Labour government?
LP: It might. We have said for many years that if you got rid of LEAs you would have to reinvent them. You can't have a national structure with 30,000 schools and one state centre. You have to have a local or regional structure. That was what the LEAs were. But in a situation in which they are so starved of cash that they are reduced to having to beg our money back from us to keep the services going is useless. Either abolish them or allow them to have sufficient resources to perform the function they were intended for.

PR: What kind of a leader are you?
LP: I have seen *Les Miserables* five times and see myself on the cart with the big flag, and out in front. I like making decisions, I sometimes get things wrong, but can't do it any other way. It is either come follow me or it's nothing. After 20 years I realize I know so little and can do so little. I hope I am approachable. I try to be an open-door head, if it is closed then I am speaking in private. People wander in and out. I can only lead from the front, I can only be positive. Even on the greyest days, I would say, 'Oh yes, that's possible.' I try to be positive even if in the end I have to give a negative response. I try to encourage from the front, by letting people have their head and going with it. I don't want clones here. Everybody has their own character and must do things in their own way. The staff might say I am too willing to find a compromise and perhaps don't often enough just say 'That simply will not do.' I do get to that point but it takes a lot to drive me there. The staff think I am a bit of a whirlwind and my work with the NAHT doesn't help as I am only in school an average of three days a week. I have to pack into those days a five-day week because I do need to know every-

thing that is going on. Perhaps that is not a good thing. I do need to be a hands-on head. I don't like things to be happening I don't know of. I would be upset if I felt I was being marginalized. In the end I think we have got something here at Intake that is worth being part of.

PR: Ted Wragg suggests that to be a head today you must be barmy. Some have said much the same of those who want to be teachers. Do you agree? What do you say to people when they say they are thinking about teaching or about headship?

LP: I take him to task on that. I think the worst thing happening to our profession is that we are becoming too cynical. We take students from three institutions and when they come I always say, 'Thank you for considering becoming a teacher. We need new enthusiastic teachers. Thirty years ago I was where you are now and don't regret a single day of it. If you want to do it and can keep positive, it is a great profession to join.' I would say the same to heads. We need heads to be young, enthusiastic, energetic, positive. You will get things wrong but you will be a leader and you will be very autonomous. It is good to be a head. In my presidential year these thoughts will be my flagship. I will say if we don't have a positive profession who are encouraging others to follow on then we might as well give up. There is nothing that has happened in my life as a head that has made me think I really shouldn't have come into this line at all. It is so diverse and you can be successful as almost any character type. You don't have to be like me. You can be a quiet contemplative and still be an excellent head. I have a loony team here. We are always doing mad and crazy things, taking nursery children on barges and on trains and taking 7-year-olds camping. Next week we are going youth hostelling with 9-year-olds. Things can happen around you all the time and everything is changing – you never know what the day is going to bring. I say to Ted Wragg, 'How loony do you have to be to be a dean of education?' You will be fortunate to get through 20 years without at least one great conflict. I have been accused of doing all sorts of things by parents. In the end I have always had people around me who have supported me through it.

PR: How do you cope when things go wrong and with the pressure?

LP: I have always had a superbly supportive home. My husband has been my mainstay. He is not in education and never has been. He worked for ICI and is semi-retired, but he has always been able to soak up all of the emotion. I can go home and kick the cat and scream and shout and take the gin and swear and he just listens, and I come back refreshed. I have always been terribly lucky in people like secretarial staff, who see you at your worst. They see you stamp through the door when somebody upsets you. I have always had people who when I have had a really bad morning will walk in with a strong black coffee and say, 'You have had enough, you are having five minutes before you see anybody else.' Only they really know. That is the only way to survive. You can't be a recluse in headship.

One thing we have not discussed is my religion. I was baptized Welsh Wesleyan, came to Doncaster and was sent to Sunday school at the Methodist chapel with our neighbour's daughters who taught Sunday school there. I went there until I joined brownies and then guides in the local Church of England. I was confirmed in the Church of England, a very high Anglican church, and taught Sunday school there. I became president of the Anglican Young Peoples Association, met my husband on a church outing and went to a Church of England training college. I have always worked for and in the Church. About ten years ago we joined a new parish because we moved house and met a very charismatic, very go-getting Anglican priest who, within five years, had me on the PCC, the Deanery Synod, the Diocesan Synod and finally, in 1990, the General Synod. Within the first year I happened to say to someone, 'I find standing orders quite fascinating' and was invited to become one of the panel of chairmen of the General Synod. I have done that for three years and have just come to the end of my term. I have just got a letter this week asking would I go onto the Board for Education. I was terrified when asked to join the panel, I had chaired everything, but to go into Synod and to get into the throne and chair that just terrified me completely. I work at it, you try to get everything right, all the bishops are sitting there in their pink and there are all hands up and they all want to speak at the same time. I thought I would never cope. I did so by thinking of them as if they were my reception class on a bad day. That and my NAHT work has given me access to different groups of people and an enriching perspective on the job. I have been very lucky, the LEA has always supported my NAHT work. It does have benefits for the school. When I am working on new government initiatives I bring papers into school and the staff can read them. They feel they are being kept abreast of what's going on.

I know I have got quite a high profile now with the media through one thing or another and people from all over come and say, 'I saw you on so and so and fancy you saying such and such.' I get letters from people I have never met saying 'I read this in the *Yorkshire Post* and I agreed with you.' I got a letter from a reformed drug addict working with youth clubs in Bradford saying 'Thank you for your article.' All this sustains you in the mundanity of the same job. Now I shall be on Synod until the year 2000. I have just been elected National Vice-President of the NAHT. But I shall stay in school and do extra days out here and there and undertake a lot of weekend and evening work for the Association. In the following year I become the National President and will spend a year out of school, working from home and from our headquarters. Call it a sabbatical. The deputies will have the extra budget to run the school for that year. They will take six months each because they have parallel job descriptions and I am out so often that one or other of them is always here and the parents relate to whoever that is. It will work for this school. The teaching, non-teaching staff and parents hold them in mutual respect.

So I am sustained by a very strong faith. When things get very sticky, I know I am never on my own. I went onto the Synod because I opposed the ordination of women. People simply couldn't come to terms with this high profile, union activist woman who was always out there with her flag saying 'No' to women priests. I don't believe that this is right at this time and went very firmly to vote against it and hoped to get it defeated. I know some devoted women priests, but I have not changed my theology. Time will tell. I had an interesting couple of years running up to that vote. I am active because I think that whatever your opinion, things must be held together. I am working at the moment trying to make sure there is a place for the Anglo-Catholics within the Anglican church. Let us see if the ministry of women as priests will develop to any great extent. It hasn't yet. Mostly they are still chaplains of hospitals and universities. Even parishes who said we have no objection seem reluctant to take a woman priest. It is a real problem.

PR: Will primary schools be different in the future? Have they changed much in your time?

LP: I don't think primary schools have really altered very significantly. We may with the infant schools see a change to a more regimented order for delivering the curriculum. In one way I want to scream against that and say that the methodology should be left to the school. But in another way I want the most literate society we can make. If we allow the pendulum to swing too far one way then I think we have to draw it back. If we are going to have children who respect themselves, and there are many who don't any more, we are going to have to give them back their innocence. I don't know how we can do this. We have now got a much more open access to all sorts of knowledge but they are not mature enough to take some of this on board and that really worries me. If only we could allow children to be children for longer.

Information technology is going to be important. Let us put a computer into every home and every classroom in the land. But that on its own is not enough. What people do with such technology is what matters. Ninety per cent of my children will have a computer in their home no matter what socio-economic background they come from. Some parents come and say to me, 'We are thinking of buying him/her a computer for Christmas, now what does he/she need, what will help with his/her work?' You tell them not to get the top of the range. They need to be able to use the type of programs they use at school, and some fun games, let them have that. Another will go and buy the most sophisticated thing they can and discover that all the children are doing is playing games. It was 15 years ago we got the first computers into primary schools and it was going to change the education, but really the changes have been marginal. For ten years we have been trying to buy enough hardware to get it into every classroom so that it can be treated like an easel or a library book. It has to become a tool pupils can go to or not as appropriate and not have to line up for half a week to get half an hour of word processing. In my view, well into the next decade the average primary child will continue to have much more than 50 per cent of their education through nothing else but teachers.

PR: So things will not change all that much over the next decade?

LP: I hope the world will become smaller for them. It has in terms of travel for most adults now, they don't perceive Africa as a great deal further than a 12-hour flight away and they can bring everything into their homes with good documentary programmes. I just hope the children will start to feel that they are part of the world. I think racism, even in a school here where we have 99 per cent white children, still exists. We still have racist remarks. We are going back not forward in some areas of accepting people for what they are and learning more about other cultures rather that just learning people are different. We don't really celebrate, even with the new require-ments for RE, other people's culture as we should. Things like the Internet and e-mail should be used for encouraging this. If we can get our school linked with other schools on other continents this would help. The change in the children that I have seen over the last 20 years is the extent to which they now come in as aggressors and challengers rather than wide-eyed and eager. So many by the age of 3 and 4 are aggressive, depressive, non-recep-tive and with chips on their shoulders. How can 4-year-olds have chips on their shoulders? But they do. What saddens me is that change in the chil-dren.

PR: I am still in shock from the Dunblane disaster.

LP: I was in Falkirk when it happened. We were there visiting two primary schools at the time and were all saying we mustn't turn it into fortress education. We must maintain an open aspect. A primary school must be a place where people can come and talk about their children and feel comfort-able. It must be part of the community. It would be so easy to step back 20 years by changing the locks and keeping everybody outside the gate.

CHAPTER 9

Bridging different cultures

USHA SAHNI WITH CHRISTINE PASCAL

Usha Sahni is Head of Argyle Primary School in Camden, London. She was born and raised in Northern India, one of seven children. She completed her first degree, and master's degree in psychology, at an Indian university and then obtained sponsorship for a doctoral scholarship in the United States. However, an arranged marriage prevented her from taking this up and she came to the UK with her new husband in the 1970s. She worked in a number of primary schools in various London Boroughs, and was head of a Learning Resource Service and voluntary community worker before she got the headship of Argyle. She, and her nursery staff, were formative participants in the implementation of the Effective Early Learning Project, a national research and development project in the UK.

CP: Could you tell me about your background and the people who have shaped the kind of person you are and who have had a significant influence on your life?

US: I was born in India and grew up in Northern India. I came to this country when I was 18. I was one of seven children, we were a large family. My father worked and my mother was a full-time housewife. We had a very large house with a few acres of land at the back. I went to school when I was two and a half. We all started school very early. I started, and was schooled throughout, in a convent. That shaped me, well and proper. It was a very loving atmosphere, a very caring environment but very demanding academically. I was the third of seven children, four sisters and three brothers, and my father was perhaps ahead of his time. He was very ambitious for his daughters and wanted us all to be independent and able to look after ourselves. It was the way people thought about us in our family. I was 11 when our father would drive us to the bank, and teach us how you open an account. He really wanted us to take care of ourselves, to grow up to be independent, autonomous people.

In India, take up of free, state education is very low. It is very expensive to send children to good schools and that is all that my parents spent their money on, sending us all to first-class schools, and paying for us. In the evenings it was a very structured situation, like an academy. Any child in our extended family who was not doing well, or was at risk of going astray, would be sent off to our home. It was seen as the place where children just flourished and did well. The expectations were very clear and we were very well supported. I think for my parents it was a full-time occupation just to make sure that all of us got the support we needed. My mother would sit with us in the evening to supervise our study, and my father would sit with us in the mornings. They spent a lot of time with us. My father would keep in touch with the school. In fact all of us were doing very well in school. The convent was very good for us all except for my eldest sister. I think the other three of us didn't pay any school fees, our places were reserved on concessionary fees because we were doing so well.

Throughout my childhood we felt extremely well cared for. We had masses of space to ourselves. We had a very big farm on site and we lived in a sort of farmhouse. We had a very secure and very loved childhood. There were very high expectations and my brothers and sisters would worry if they were just going to 'pass'. We would worry about the grades and what percentage we got and it was quite challenging. At the time, I didn't feel it, but in retrospect I can see that we generated the pressure on ourselves. You had very high aspirations for yourself, but I am sure in the end it paid off because it becomes second nature to you, you want to excel from what you did the last time. I think the parental support certainly worked for me and for my family. I am sure the seven of us weren't all born with the kind of calibre and very high standards that we have achieved. A lot of it was to do with the environment we were growing up in and our parents. If things are going well at home with nothing to worry about, and the relationship between your parents is good and general living conditions are comfortable, everything is there for you. I feel that secure home circumstances contribute enormously to children becoming secure adults. It's not because my parents were terribly wealthy, not at all. It was just that those were their values. It was not as if they had been left with masses of inheritance, it was what your life was, what you made of it. Seeing my father work very, very hard and seeing that it was a struggle but that it was possible with a large family made an impression on us. But I think the support that we had amongst ourselves was also very important. We never needed people from outside, just our brothers and sisters, we were very self-sufficient. I believe family support is terribly important, and that is where children sometimes miss out nowadays. Very many times when things go wrong there isn't anybody to pick things up. If a parent is not there then the children haven't got the support. Whereas, in our environment, there was the feeling that you could be playing anywhere and everybody would look after you. It think it is the same in India even now, I was there last week and even now, everybody takes responsibility for all the children. It is not just that you won't tell a child off or you won't take care of them, it is very much an extension of the responsibility undertaken by everybody in the neighbourhood. But for my childhood it was the security, the happiness, the care, coupled with the very high expectations, and the support of our parents, that I remember. Also we became very motivated ourselves to do well and we took responsibility for things we could do and achieve.

I think my own self-image was raised to a level that I wanted to live up to it for myself because it felt good, so I did well. So much attention and praise was showered on us children that we wanted to keep it that way. I suppose this is why I believe children need a lot of praise because I know how motivating praise can be for children. We are often very mean with praise, being forever ready to pounce on children when they do something wrong. We don't exactly acknowledge enough what they are able to do. This attitude is becoming more and more institutionalized now with the way things are in the curriculum. We label children, looking for things they can't do. They get very little reward and acknowledgement for things they can do. I feel it is extremely damaging for young children particularly, because you need to have a place to build them up from. It is only by telling them that they have done well that they know what next to do well. I still remember that in school we would very often have public performances. We would have recitation days, and declamation contests and speech days and public speaking days. Of course we wouldn't get it right the very first time, but your parents were always there in the audience, always giving you some feedback, not always saying that it was brilliant, but giving you constructive suggestions and helping you get it right. That was how you gained your confidence and I think it is the right way.

CP: Can you identify any particular individuals that were strong models for you or influenced you?

US: One teacher, Miss Sherry she was called, an Irish nun, is particularly memorable. My first memory of school is of getting a pop-up book of Cinderella at a whole school presentation when I started to read at three. I still remember climbing the white marble stairs to go up to Miss Sherry to receive my present. It gave me the feeling that people doted on you, all the teachers praised you and thought you were a star.

I think it was a great feeling of warmth that the school gave out. It rewarded success and cared for individuals. My school was selective, it didn't take anybody and everybody and this meant they were pushing for a certain standard. They were able to because they were catering for a very limited range of pupils and a selected intake. Now how that affects my views about things nowadays, I don't know, I don't think it does. I really cannot relate my own way of thinking about ability grouping to my own experience because I think it is one of the less good things about the school. You worked very much as an individual and I found that hard when I went to college. I wasn't used to working with people, I very much did my own thing.

My close friends who I grew up with had a great influence on me. They were older than me and seemed more worldly wise. In India you do your school certificate, then you go to college to do your first degree. You then go to university for your postgraduate study. In a convent, if you were doing very well, you would jump classes. Twice I jumped classes so I went to college and joined my first degree course at 14. I was very young in comparison to other girls. It was a girls college. I was very used to doing my own thing, doing my individual work and rushing through it. Literally speeding through the work single mindedly. It was very one track. I was 16 when I finished my first degree and went to university, so I was 18 when I got my master's. I was very young. I think emotionally I hadn't caught up. Academically I might have been competent but it left certain gaps. I had a real problem because my friends used to treat me differently. Even now my friends who I have been very close to for 26 years treat me differently and are quite protective of me. I think it is the nature of friendships and relationships in a place like India where emotionally, you are in a close-knit society. Generally, your circle is small but it is very close. You get a lot from it, you grow up very secure knowing there are not many uncertainties, insecurities, not in my environment anyway. I feel comfortable, competent and 'together' in my personal relationships and I don't find it difficult to relate to people. I wonder if it has something to do with the skills you develop in that sort of environment.

CP: What led you towards teaching?

US: I did my master's in a university which is quite highly regarded in India. It was in a brand new city, a very new university, very innovative, attracting a lot of high calibre people because it was well funded and very well equipped. I did my master's in psychology and my major was educational psychology. My dissertation for my research was on learning patterns among young children. For my field work I went into two schools quite regularly and that was, in a sense, my first contact with young children. It was a two-year, full-time degree and a lot of this time I spent on learning about young children's thinking patterns. That is how I became interested in young children. After that the university sponsored me for a doctorate and they got me a scholarship for study in the United States from the US embassy. My parents had other plans! They found a husband and arranged a marriage for me. So within four weeks I was married. The families knew each other. My father was quite keen that I should go off and study but my mother was very reluctant, and didn't really want to send me abroad on my own at all. She said, 'Look he's a good man, and we know the family well. You want to study abroad so here you are, go for it, go with him and he can take care of you and your study!' Since I have been here, I have been studying off and on and teaching all at the same time.

CP: Can we explore the culture conflict? You had been brought up to be independent, autonomous and to make your own choices, was this change difficult for you?

US: There was conflict between my mum and dad as well. When it came to marrying the daughters off it was my mother who made decisions, not my father. Although we were given independence and autonomy, there were also very strictly drilled-in values of conformity, which is very interesting. You conform and I think there are certain values you don't question. I would not question that my parents had made a decision. You believed that what they did was in your best interest and somehow you go on believing that. I didn't question it even though I wasn't happy with it. It wasn't the fact that I didn't want to marry this particular man, I just didn't want to marry as yet. I wanted to study a bit longer and wanted to be allowed to do that. I had only met him once and I didn't know him. But when one is 18 one is not very sure of oneself. In the long term it became more difficult. I am very much my own person, and I find it very difficult because my husband's expectations are very different. I say to him, 'Look I have been brought up to pursue my career, to do things the way I want to do them' and it's very difficult to reconcile the two. I didn't have a problem about the reconciliation with my parents' expectations of me but I do of my husband's expectations of me. You have to work hard at it, it's a struggle, and it is quite strange. In one bit of your life you very much operate as a traditional person who just tolerates the rules. It is very difficult because you have these different sets of rules for different situations. At times you compromise, and if you compromise willingly you are not too unhappy. But again I think growing up the way I did gives you skills to resolve these situations, because I am very clear about what the values are that I was brought up to believe in and I respect these, the principles that guide your life are quite clear. Yet within that, I must be able to pursue my career and to achieve things personally for my own fulfilment. To do otherwise, I would be no good for anybody. The social obligations are equally important and to pursue my role and responsibilities as a wife, mother, daughter-in-law, etc. I have to find an equal place for these. Potentially, this is full of contradictions and conflicts. One has to resolve the tensions.

So I married and came to Britain. I thought I would work, but I didn't know how to or where or what to do. I thought I would continue my work with young children. We lived in Ealing so I went to the Ealing Education Department. My husband would go off to work, and I looked through the directory and found the Ministry of Education, Honeypot Lane it used to be in. So I remember I made the journey there. It took me till 3 o'clock to get there, and I got some forms, and I found out the procedures and applied for my qualifications to be validated. Then I started making applications for a teaching job.

CP: You hadn't had professional training at that point?

US: They had said to me, if you had a post-graduate in psychology and you had worked with children then they would accept your qualifications and experience. You would be on two years' probation. I thought that was OK. It took me six months to get an interview. It was really, really hard. I couldn't get any other job. I applied for clerical jobs in the meantime but I was just going crazy sitting in the house. They said to me I was over-qualified so I wouldn't get a job. I went to Brent Education Offices as well as Ealing.

CP: Were you determined to work with younger children?

US: Yes. They had said to me that I was going wrong and should apply to secondary schools. In my first degree I majored in English and they asked me if I would like to teach English, but I said I would really like to work with younger children. But getting a job was very hard. I remember that in Brent, the education officer for schools, whom I got to know very well later on, said to me, 'You know children are very different here.'

'How do you mean?'

'They are very difficult to discipline. Would you be able to deal with them?'

'Yes, I can't see why I would have a problem.'

'For a start (I used to wear saris) you would have to dress differently.' I remember having a long discussion with him as to why would I have to dress differently. He said, 'They would not really respect you if you go in wearing a sari like you are.' We had a long chat about why that would be so. He didn't give me an interview and he didn't give me a job. He said I would have to dress differently, to integrate more, and I said, 'Integrate into what?' I know later on when I worked in Brent we used to rehearse that conversation because I have never worn Western clothes. It is not that I have anything against them, it's just that it's not me.

So even though they had verified my qualifications and accepted them, I found it very hard to get a job. Then I got a break through by getting some supply work in a special school and that was the starting point. They must have thought I was such a pest. I kept on, I was very persistent, and I used to end up at the office door every second day, and say, 'Any work going?' and they would say, 'You have no experience' and I would say, 'I am never going to get experience if you don't give me a job. I am just out of college and I need a job.' But one day they sent me to a job. I think they were very desperate for teachers in the early 1970s. I got a supply job in a special school and once I got into that school, the head then asked me to come back the next day, and then the next day. She then offered me half a term maternity leave cover. Once I got into a school I was OK. She gave me half a term's work and then another head phoned her and I was never out of work after that term. The break through was actually being able to get into a school, but you couldn't do that unless you went through the local authority office. It was getting through the bureaucracy and breaking that initial prejudice. It doesn't take you six months to get a supply job. I know that now, but I thought, well maybe that is how it is, maybe it takes time. For a term they gave me long-term cover. And then, the second school I was in, was a primary school and the head had a vacancy from September and offered me the post. So I was thrilled. It was very quick progress once I was in school.

This second job was in a main stream primary school in Brent and I was to be on two years' probation, but to be honest, nobody ever came to see me. I think they relied on the headteacher's reports. The adviser just came in one day, I think it was in the beginning of the fourth term, and said, 'By the way, your probation has finished, you have passed it.' I was so thrilled but I think I was managing OK. I worked very, very hard. In those days there was no such thing as support for newly qualified teachers, there was no induction, there was no mentoring. All of what we have now for our newly qualified teachers seems like luxury to me. I just went to different college libraries, did a lot of reading, used my own initiative and trained myself as I went along.

CP: Were there people in the schools you worked that also influenced you?

US: The head of the primary school that I went to impressed me in that it was a very difficult school. The area had tremendous pressure on it. It was one of the first high-rise types of estate that was being developed. There was a lot of demolition work, a transitory community, a lot of coming and going and a very mixed community. I think the main problem was the teacher turnover, and a lot of children living in very poor housing accommodation with a lot of drugs and violence on the estate. Even at that time, there was a lot of drug dealing and a lot of social deprivation. We also had a lot of very young, Afro-Caribbean families on the estate who were very unsupported. I suppose the young parents as well were not having the support of the extended families that they must have been used to when they were brought up. So, it was a very difficult place but the head had a great deal of empathy with the children, he knew them really well. He knew the kids and he made it his business to get to know them. He took an interest in them and knew all their names. I didn't see him very much about the school. I don't think he knew what the teachers were doing but I gather he used to look at classrooms when we had all gone home, and look in children's books. In his own way he was monitoring what we were doing. What I liked about him was that he knew the children and the children had a lot of time for him, he was warm with them. In fact, I think he liked being with the children better than the staffroom. He was an experienced head and I think that he was managing a very difficult situation, because the staff were coming and going all the time. But to be honest with you, in terms of professional skills, I am really not sure what he gave me except that I watched him interact with the children and learnt a great deal from that.

As time went on of course you met people. Those were the days when the Teacher Centre was a big part of your life, a real community. I was just very interested in what I was doing. I was desperate to learn. A lot of it was very new and I just wanted to learn a lot myself. I think I get on with children well, I don't feel intimidated or affronted when questioned by the children. I think I have that respect for children and it's because I respect them that I am able to get on with them. I found this approach worked from very early on. I talked with the children and explained what I needed them to do and why, and they responded to it. It was a very difficult school but in time I found that I was able to establish my relationships with the children. In school we would never talk down to them. I would not shout at them and they were very gentle with me. I took a lot of time explaining things, and telling them why a particular task needed to go that way. This doesn't feel like a strange thing to do and even now I spend a lot of time with my school children. I like to talk with them like they were my equal. It really does work with them and I say that to teachers when they are in difficulty or something happens between an adult and a child. You can't just tell children to do anything, you've also got to believe in what you are wanting them to do, otherwise, it just doesn't work. I have never found a child who was rude to me, because I try not to warrant it. I suppose I do get angry and upset sometimes and when I do, I say so, but I try very hard not to blame them for it.

CP: Can you describe your route to headship and what experiences you had on the way that prepared you for this?

US: I went into headship through a fairly unconventional route. My experiences as a classroom teacher were an extremely important preparation for headship, because it is there that you develop an insight into the management of learning. As you widen your network and management responsibilities you adapt to different situations but fundamentally you are expanding on your repertoire of 'class teacher' skills and strengths. In the various roles as a class teacher with responsibilities, middle management positions, Head of a Learning Resources Service and a voluntary community worker, I learnt from all the people I worked with, especially the very many children. The wider the range of people you work with, the more it sharpens your understanding of different perspectives. You learn that there is no one way of getting it right.

CP: Can you tell me what kind of head you are as a leader and a manager?

US: The people who I lead will be in the best position to tell you that. I can only talk about what I think I do which is not always what you really do. You can be thinking one thing and doing another. I am quite a systems person. I like to have structures in place. The thing that has proved to be most effective is having a really strong team of people in the middle of your system. They are the ones who make it happen, because they are the people who are on the chalk edge as well. You need more than one of you to be able to make a difference. That has been most important. Having people in the middle who are first-class teachers so they have a very clear credibility, and are very conscientious, very capable, competent teachers. I also ensure people have very clear responsibilities for the curriculum, so they are curriculum co-ordinators as well but we avoid people becoming too obsessed with their own subject. So you have a very strong team of middle managers who come together regularly. They are looking at the whole curriculum and how the same principles, the same teaching methods, organization, assessment and planning apply, cross-curricular. I try to blur the boundaries between the divides of one sort or another, be it subjects, status or personalities. Children need a seamless experience as they go through different adults and different areas of knowledge. It all needs to fit together for them. Supporting the professionalism of these people is my key role.

I think in primary schools you can create structures and systems but a lot of it is face to face work. It really comes down to talking to people. You can't run a school on the basis of relationships of course, but you can't run it on the basis of systems and structures either. I also write notes and memos, and when I write a memo people know talking is not working. They know it is something I am not happy just saying, because I don't normally write notes. When I worked in the education department it was quite common to just write a memo, but in school, I get up and talk to people first. When I have spoken to them three times and the same things are still outstanding, then I write a note. I just give that as an example. I would much rather go and talk to staff than write letters and notes. I try to be very visible for my parents, the teachers and children. I hadn't been in school for three days last week and this morning it was so lovely, because children are so used to seeing me about. They said, 'Where have you been? It's so nice to have you back.' It feels good because you think, 'Thank God, they notice you are not here.' Relationships are so important. You can say the hardest thing if you have the relationship to carry it off, otherwise, you can get into terrible conflicts. I am forever trying my best to avoid conflicts as far as possible and to find a way around things. I am not afraid to compromise if someone has a better idea and I don't get too hung up on my own ideas. However, there are times when I do say I don't want to do it that way. But more often than not, I am quite open to suggestions, and I would normally say to people in staff meetings, this is the way I think we should do it and if you have a better way tell me and we will go for that.

Primary school management is unique in my experience. What puts a lot of pressure on primary heads is that everybody who walks through the door wants to see you. No matter what systems you have in place and how well trained your secretary is in helping you manage your time, people want to talk to you and very often no one else will do. If you don't respond, parents can think you don't care. Things will come back to you, and that's only right, they should, because you are the person who, at the end of the day, is responsible. At the same time you have to make room for your staff to grow through delegated responsibility. Yet, there comes a time when, for example, I am away and my deputy head is here, that he has to make a decision. I try to work in a way whereby people who will be responsible know how decisions are made and what the boundaries are within which we operate. So, more often than not, I am pretty confident that the decision he takes would be the right one. Not because we think alike but because we know what the school prescribes to. If it happened that the decision he took is not the decision I would have taken, I have to find a way of supporting it. The only hope is, that we would be able to talk it through and next time round you are not put in that position. The job is not to undermine staff. If something's happening in my absence that I'm not happy with, then there is something wrong in the way we have set the place up. They have to know I have confidence in them. In a sense it is the same with parents. It is all right to be tolerant on procedural matters but when it comes to children, I cannot compromise. If a child has been wrongly treated then I will say to a teacher, I cannot support that, I am sorry, it is wrong, it shouldn't have happened. Then the support for staff is ensuring that it gets put right.

CP: Who do you feel accountable to?

US: To my children first and foremost. I have to be able to look them in the eye and say that it was in their best interest. They are the people I have got to feel comfortable with and know that I am not cheating them. The children are the ones who I am probably most responsible to but in terms of explicit accountability, it is probably my school's parents next. So, it is my parents, my teachers and the other staff and then the governors. I have got to be able to justify what I do to these people in that order. The children, the parents, the staff and then people who are outside of your immediate school environment. I do my own testing in my head. When I make a decision I think how does it affect the children? Does it do anything for them? Is it going to make it better for them in any way? If it isn't then it is not worth considering. And this is quite difficult, especially nowadays, to be able to establish those links. I think that is where the job becomes very difficult because you end up doing things half-heartedly. You know you are only doing it because it is put upon you as another thing to do. So, you try and find a way round it. It is like when the National Curriculum first came, we were not only implementing the National Curriculum, we were trying desperately to see how we could fit what we were doing to the National Curriculum. It was a case of trying to find matches between what we were doing and the National Curriculum rather than saying, 'Look, let us stop what we are doing, let's implement this.' It's that kind of a thing. It really doesn't make sense. I suppose it's the system we have to work in. I talk to the children quite openly about this. Take SATs, for example, for Year 6. We have had long chats with the children and I say to them, 'This is the system and you have got to learn to play it. This is how everyone will make out how well you have done, so you have to beat them at it.' They all know they have got SATs, what value is placed upon these and what will happen to the scores. They also know that their secondary school will look at their report, see their scores and make judgements about them. I just say to the children, 'You have got to really try hard and work at it and do your best. This does not show everything you have achieved but you know this is an important part of showing your achievements, because this is what people want to see.' I suppose children have got to learn because this is the reality that they will have to live with.

It's the same with racism or prejudices. I say to the children there is no point pretending it doesn't happen. Of course the world will treat you badly at times, and of course they will look at you and think all sorts of things about you and make judgements about you because of the way you look or the clothes you are wearing. You've just got to know that is what they are doing. In a sense by knowing that gives you a measure of control over it. And I say to the girls, 'Of course your mum and dad would rather that you do not go to university, you've just got to work at it and work your way around it and you'll see that they will come round and won't stop you doing the things you really want to do and are good at.'

CP: Being the head of the school is a very pressured job. What strategies do you have for managing that stress?

US: There are a number of ways. One is attitudinal and that has got better as time has gone on. It is something I have learned only after 26 years. Whereas I used to get terribly upset and terribly hurt, I don't. I take things much more as they come. I am able to see things in perspective and that only comes with experience and age. I am able to distance myself, I don't take things personally. I think I've been pretty good at that for quite a while now. I am able to remove things from myself and not see them as personal insults. For the first headship I did, I used to get very upset and was terribly hurt about things which I don't any more. I just feel I am able to see people and put their behaviour in their context and see their motives for the way they behave. You are able to distance yourself from it and know it is not you. It is human nature and due to a variety of reasons. That helps a lot, but it should not mean that you give up easily or accept any and everything. I believe I am more resolute than ever, I persist and I pursue things, I don't let go easily. I am able to give it longer and I think my own repertoire of skills and my own approach to understanding what motivates the staff has developed. You learn that as you go along. The same thing is not going to appeal to everybody. I try and make judgements about how different people work and I try and work on those particular accents of their own personality. So I work very differently with different people and my own approach changes depending on who it is I am talking to and who I am working with. This takes the tension out of your day to day work and helps you manage your time better and stress better. You deal with sources of stress rather than symptoms.

It is also about getting to know people and that takes time. I spend a lot of time talking to people and getting to know how teacher A and teacher B works, what their particular hang-ups and obsessions are, and what their particular needs are, and I try to meet those in a way that is possible. Usually, this is something that helps. It does mean that you take longer but that does not mean I am less demanding, it's that I'm more patient and am prepared to give it longer, but I am not prepared to give up. I think fundamentally I believe in people as well as myself. I am instinctively optimistic and I am not very easily defeated. I also have a sense of humour and it helps enormously in dealing with stress. You could almost laugh at everything. Each story has its funny side most of the time.

CP: Do you think the job of headship has become harder? Do you still enjoy the job?

US: I don't think it's become harder but the nature of the job has changed. I think what has also happened is that you cannot just walk into a headship. Young people used to be able to do that and get away with it. You cannot do that now and that's what has become different. It requires a range of well developed skills and a real desire and ability to work with people in a positive frame of mind.

CP: And what has caused that change?

US: I think it is something to do with the changed nature of the job itself. It is multi-faceted. You really need to be a person who has got a wide range of skills, who is quite knowledgeable, who is quite experienced at very different sorts of levels and can enter into different kinds of negotiations. You also need to be pretty skilled at curriculum. The job is about leading people who have got a wider range of experience. You can't be a class teacher one day and a head the next. I really think that has changed. Carefully planned succession training is more important than ever for headship.

CP: Do you think that has changed for the better?

US: I think it has changed for the better. I would still like to believe that it would always be people who come from the classroom who end up as heads. That is absolutely essential. You have really got to have that insight otherwise you might as well not have headteachers, you could just have administrators who administer the school and then have a professional leader in the school as well.

CP: Do you think it is possible to have that blend of professional leadership and administrative competence?

US: Something is going to have to change for deputy heads for this to happen. My deputy head will need to have had experience and he already is a very capable person. But I think deputy heads need to have structured opportunities for a lot of preparatory experience and work before they take on a headship. It is not that you can't do it, but it is very much harder. I now do mentoring for newly appointed heads. Talking to the new heads who I mentor, I see the difficulties which you learn to resolve only with experience. There are things that you really must have because mistakes can prove expensive in a headship, both professionally and personally.

CP: Do you think courses could help?

US: It is making judgements on the spot, making the decisions, the day to day, the immediate that you need to have the confidence for. You must have quite an insight into all the implications of what you are doing in those five minutes, when the crisis comes. You need the kind of ability and confidence which comes with experience, which brings a knowledge of what there is, and what the options are. You also have to be able to weigh them up very quickly. You don't get those things on courses. I just think there needs to be something like a period of either deputy heads having a period of acting headships, or some sort of hands-on experience before people can take over with confidence. I think that has changed. I can remember when I went into my school on my first headship there was a lot of learning but also a lot of support. But the whole structure has changed. There aren't the advisers and inspectors at the end of the phone. There isn't an educational officer that you can talk to. You don't have the same systems and structures for headship groups that we used to have. We always had very well run head support groups and mentoring groups and self-styled help groups. With the way things are at the moment, it is terribly competitive and there isn't that kind of support available. Generally, heads, as well as teachers, are very much more on their own than they ever used to be because the infrastructure has gone. It is all pretty depressing really unless you, as professionals, are prepared to put things into place yourself.

CP: What is your perspective on the changes in the system that have occurred?

US: I think what has been for the better is now there is a basic entitlement for all the children and that is a good thing. That in itself has raised expectations, or at least articulated an expectation for all the children. I think the whole thing to do with teacher support and the GEST programme has been very useful. Emphasizing the need for professional support for teachers is a positive move. When you look at the way the schools are funded and local management, while the principles of giving decision-making to organizations where the activity and the learning is actually happening is sound, all the detail to do with funding, the pupil numbers, the level of prescription from which the curriculum is defined, has great limitations. To say you'll fund every school on the numbers of pupils in the school is a fallacy. That is really not how schools are, that is not how they will work effectively and not what they need. To have league tables based on the curriculum which is defined on a notional 'average' somewhere in the country is completely ridiculous without value added measures.

Also, the way the curriculum has been defined for primary schools with a subject basis was a mistake. I am not saying that it should not have been broad and it should not have been balanced but we did not need to go to the lengths of the last eight years or so. We did not need to have all those documents. It was such a foolish waste of money. There has been such lack of vision and thought and such apparent ignorance about how young children learn, what basic learning is about and what teachers are doing in schools. Having said that, I can see that some of the breadth was not there, and some of what was happening in a small number of places was pretty awful, pre-National Curriculum. I wouldn't want to go back to the beginning. If only they had talked to teachers more about what they were doing rather than setting up all these subject working parties to begin with. I think some of the thinking has done a great deal of disservice to schools like mine and other schools where children are multilingual. It does not recognize their presence if you look at the National Curriculum, or even if you look at the English curriculum. I think it is such a retrograde step for some of us, we have gone back in time. Prior to this the curriculum was more innovative, more exciting and teachers had a lot more at stake, and more interest in what they were doing because they had thought through the needs and relevance for the children. A lot of the excitement has gone. The relevance has weakened, and it is an important dimension in the way one defines curriculum.

I think it just became too politicized and that is where it has gone wrong. All the emphasis on specific bodies of knowledge for primary children, for example, in history, literature and standard English, is depressing because it stopped the curriculum being a professional issue and it became a party political manifesto. I think this is where the mistakes are being made and I believe we will live to pay for these mistakes. The narrowness is inappropriate when young children should be grasping the basic concepts and developing the tools to pursue their learning and interests in the long term.

CP: Given that context, what are your visions for this school and how you might take it forward into the twenty-first century?

US: I think, in our school, what we are really striving for, first and foremost, is to work in a way where children will leave having become confident, competent people. We want them to be able to hold their own, to have succeeded and to have developed the core life skills of co-operation, communication, numeracy and literacy. These are very conventional values, but they are the fundamentals. We aim to give the children the skills to learn, to ensure they are ready for learning, they are motivated, enthusiastic and not going to go to secondary school and think, how can I bunk the next lesson? We want children who are actually interested in learning, who are inquisitive, who enjoy learning and have developed the skills to be with other people and adjust and adapt to a whole range of demands and situations. We hope they will have a rounded development as a person and are well balanced. I think it is about attitude and disposition but also skills. They need to know how to go to the library and look up what they need and, having found it, be able to read it and so learn themselves what they want and for however long they want.

CP: Will the school have to change in order to develop that or will the system have to change?

US: In our school what we find difficult is the pressure to cover the content because you know that come Year 6, the children are going to be tested on SATs and their score will matter. We find it difficult. We try really hard to define our core skills and the core competence for our children, so that through the content they are developing knowledge as well as social skills and are able to collaborate and co-operate. The pressure on content coverage has got to change to give a little more time for children's physical and social development. In our school we put a lot of premium on performing skills, performing arts and drama. The children are participating in lot of community activities and to us it is about educating our children so they are learning with their communities. We have a lot of projects that the children work on with parents and local groups as well. But all that is time taken out. The community involvement through our work is terribly important to us because they live in this community and the relationships between the children and the folk who live in the local area have been pretty appalling.

We have really worked hard at building up links and positive relationships. All that takes time and for primary schools, ensuring that the children learn how to learn is probably the most important thing to do. Developing those desires and very positive attitudes to learning, as well as believing that they are capable and competent people, able to speak for themselves, stand up for what they have done and take responsibility, are central to our work. Those are the important things but there is a lot of pressure on time. In that sense some things have got to give in schools. I think what we are finding most difficult is trying to get the balance right. We find that we want to strike the right balance between subject knowledge in the curriculum, and the skills, attitudes and concepts which apply right across their learning. In practice we find we are spending more time on content and the other bit is not quite getting the same time emphasis, and that worries me.

I would like a slight shift in the other direction because I think the knowledge and the content will come easy if children have developed the concepts, skills and attitudes. For me, I would like a slimming of the content. In my own experience I don't think we covered an awful lot of content when we were in fifth grade, which is when we must have been 9 years old. Whereas here, the pressure is on come Year 2, especially with my children here, all of whom are coming in not speaking very much English. Access to content is an issue. They learn pretty fast given the time and effort, the energy and the right environment and the opportunities. They are pretty quick. But then, the time it takes is no joke. Last year we could not cover science sufficiently. We took a decision that we just couldn't. My SATs result in science reflected that decision. We weren't surprised, we knew. We had focused on literacy and numeracy and the outcomes in terms of pupils achievements in these areas were impressive.

If we were able to change anything, I would like to take a bit of pressure off, so you can talk to children more. You are not forced to just drill, drill, drill, rush, rush, rush. There is so much of that, especially with older children. Pastoral care is equally important when children are living in very pressured circumstances. I believe that a certain amount of rigour is necessary and good, but I think the emphasis should be upon helping children to grow as wholesome people during the most impressionable years of their life. If we get it wrong now with too much pressure we risk putting them off for life. To be able to have time to work on building confidence with children who are lacking that and preparing them for the massive big, and sometimes bad, world out there should not be too much to ask for.

CHAPTER 10

Working with the angry

M ARGY W HALLEY WITH C HRISTINE P ASCAL

Margy Whalley is founding Head of Pen Green Centre for Under 5s and their Families, and Director of its Research, Development and Training Base. She has managed multi-disciplinary early years services in Brazil, New Guinea and England. She was seconded to the Open University writing course materials for parents wanting to increase their knowledge and understanding of child development. Margy is part of the Labour Party enquiry team into Under 5s' education and care and was the Association of County Councils representative on the National Audit Commission concerned with children under 5. She is involved in research in this country and in Europe. She has been running a training and consultancy service throughout the United Kingdom for the last eight years.

CP: The first question is about your childhood, your family and your school experience. Can you tell me how you think that's shaped the kind of person you are and your philosophy?

MW: I was brought up in the north of England and that's very important for me. I always think of the north of England as home. I have a twin, and I come from a family of four. My parents' attitude to education was very positive. They wanted us to be high achievers and they encouraged and supported us. They didn't know much about the university system. My mum was very bright academically and had been a nurse and my dad had been in private school and then gone to the war. He wanted us all to have the experiences that he hadn't had. He viewed private education with a real antipathy and that was quite significant because we were the only children in his extended family not to go to private school. He sent us to the local primary and the local grammar school. From when I was a very young child I enjoyed learning. I think I was a high achiever at primary school and my twin and I competed like mad, although I wasn't aware of it at the time.

CP: Were you identical twins?

MW: No, fraternal twins. We were very different temperamentally and we played the extrovert/introvert game. I was supposed to be the extrovert and she was supposed to be the introvert, which actually wasn't true but it was the front we put on for people. I think grammar school was very problematic, we had the nightmare 11-plus and our parents were very scared about whether we would both get through. We were coming top of the form so I don't see why we wouldn't have. Anyway, we both got through and went to grammar school. I was going through a difficult time at that point and my way of responding to grammar school was to go wild really. My sister went on achieving very highly and I didn't. I kind of under achieved at everything in the first year except English and art, which I loved and found easy. Having been terribly good through primary school and doing what everybody wanted me to, I suddenly just kicked out. I loved the drama, the band and all the extra-curricular activities but I wasn't at all stimulated by the academic bit. Then suddenly at the end of that first year we were streamed.

Nobody had let me into this secret of streaming and then suddenly we were sitting in assembly and apparently the teachers had all made this decision that it would be very good for us to be split up as twins. I think they thought it might spur me on to work harder. I will never forget sitting in assembly and being told I was going to a different form. We'd been inseparable and I found that simply an outrage. I found out afterwards that they had all planned this for our own good. When I asked my parents about it years later I found out that there hadn't really been any reason to separate us. They just thought it would be a good thing to do to twins. My anger was enormous when I found out that this was a planned thing. Nobody had even told me this might happen. Sometimes I talk to colleagues about the trauma they experienced failing the 11-plus, which left people with terrible self-esteem for the rest of their lives, but actually being streamed at the end of the first year of grammar school was also very scarring. I had always believed in myself until then, I'd always thought I was very academic, and suddenly the A-stream/B-stream thing hit me. I had never been very aware at grammar school that there was A, B, C, D and then there was S and T. The S and T were for Secretarial and Technical. In our village there was a grammar school and a secondary school and I hated the fact that when you walked past the secondary school they called you grammar grubs. I hated seeing people I'd been at primary school with treated in a different way because they went to secondary school. I think because that happened to me very quickly at grammar school I had a lot of anger about being labelled. Along with this was my own sense of injustice from when I was very little, from sometimes feeling 'not heard' about important things. I think those feelings are very strong in me. I came from a family where the lively debate and argument was wonderful. My family life was very rich but maybe we weren't so strong on listening to each other. I'd grown up believing that you could challenge anything and it gave me a real sense of my own power.

CP: What happened when you challenged what was happening in school?
MW: Well I got into the most terrible trouble. The first day in grammar

school I was made to stand on a chair with my hands on my head because I talked too much. We were always being punished for things. I'd been a goody-two-shoes at primary school so I don't know what was going on, but obviously something was and my sense of injustice was very strong. I also used to play practical jokes on teachers and imitate them and this wasn't appreciated.

CP: How have these experiences shaped you? What are the things you've taken into your philosophy?

MW: The more I look back I think that I was very committed to teaching. I knew I always wanted to be a teacher. My father's godmother was one of the first women HMIs, and she used to stay with us. She was working in Liverpool and places like that, and would talk about what classrooms were like in the 1950s. She was an enormous influence on me, her sense of what was right. She was one of the most principled women I've ever known and she really listened to children. So I always had this incredible respect for HMI after that! She was just a quality person, an artist and a writer in her spare time. I didn't think that positively of my own school teachers. I felt that teachers only dealt with what they saw on the surface and did not look any deeper. It was like this with me, people not looking behind my behaviour. I was wild for all sorts of reasons when I started school and nobody was looking, and nobody was thinking, why is she like this? I feel we have an obligation to children to look behind their behaviour, to look at patterns in their behaviour and to think about why. I'm very committed to working with the angry children. I always thought as a teenager I would work with autistic children and I used to read books like *The Wild Boy of Avignon*, about non-communicating children, even in the fifth and sixth form. I remember being fascinated by children who couldn't say what they wanted to say.

CP: But you were quite articulate?

MW: But not about the deep things, not about the things that I needed to say, so I was identifying with that. I was very active in the debating society, I was very good at talking but not necessarily very good at getting heard. And I was also getting slammed by teachers. I remember in science the teacher taught us that the atom was the smallest particle or whatever. Then she said, 'But that's not actually true', because this was post-Hiroshima and she knew that you could actually split the atom. When she said that she was teaching something that wasn't true, I really resented it. I also remember being taught 'facts' about Richard III in history. I passionately loved history. My old gran had always been a storyteller and she used to tell us stories about the olden days and I loved it. We used to sit in bed brushing our hair and she used to tell us these stories and it made me really interested in history. Then the teacher told us that 'Richard III was an evil man' and I happened to have read the novel *Daughter of Time*, and I wanted to enter a debate with her. I said, 'I've just been reading this book' and she said, 'Well, this is what I'm teaching you, this is what you're learning for O-level.' It was that narrowness that I found so awful.

So I believe that teaching is about listening and about encouraging children to challenge and question and to have a disposition to learn. I mean, I loved to read, I read everything, and to have that denied by that history teacher was awful. I really don't believe there are a lot of facts that are worth teaching. I found some little notebooks that I took to Brazil when I left this country in the mid-1970s and went to teach out there, and it was full of ideas from the 'de-schoolers' like Illich and Holt. I loved all that kind of writing because it seemed to be all about the learning process and my own experience was of that learning process being denied. I remember we were sent to a private school for the last two years of secondary education because we moved back to the town where my dad was having to close a factory. He didn't think we'd be very popular with the rest of the community, so we went to this private school. This was a big mistake in many ways for my sister because it gave a lousy science education, but it was fine for me because I was doing history, art and English, and you just got on and ignored the teachers. You just read and read and read. My memory of the sixth form is of teachers dictating notes, and not listening at all, and actually learning hugely from reading.

CP: So what do you do with that now in your work within the Centre?

MW: I think I'm very committed to children having a voice and to early childhood educators learning to listen better. I'm very uncomfortable when I feel I don't listen to children. I also want the staff to be able to listen to children. I want them to be very empathetic with children and not stereotype children. One of the things that makes me most angry is when people underestimate children because of stereotypes, class or gender or whatever. Educators mustn't think that because a child's parents aren't educated, they don't have expectations. Parents' aspirations are incredibly high for their children but they may not be very confident to come out and express them. My belief about working with parents came more from my experience working overseas. I had never worked with parents in this country, so until I worked overseas I didn't have the right kind of experience or understanding of community education.

CP: Can you tell me now about your career line and how the experiences on the way have shaped you?

MW: Well I knew I wanted to be a teacher in the sixth form. I managed to get three A grades at A-level, just to show people basically that I was academic and I was a high achiever. Then I was told 'You shouldn't go to teacher training college, you would be wasted now.' Suddenly all these universities wrote back and said 'Yes, we would like you after all.' There was an irony in that. I think my parents had been thinking she's a 'doer' as I'd always done drama and drama courses, so the idea was that I'd go off to drama school and my sister would go to medical school, both going down to London, or whatever. I had applied for drama school and I'd also applied to Bretton Hall because I'd always heard that was good. Then people said 'try university', so I started looking at universities that had drama courses and

Birmingham, Manchester and Bristol had. I applied for Birmingham and Manchester, and I went to Birmingham. Birmingham was at that time the only completely single honours course, with the others you had to do another subject. I knew since then I was going to be a teacher.

CP: A teacher of young children?

MW: No, I thought I was going to work probably in secondary, but with disturbed children, so all my placements were in theatre in education, or drama in education placements. I had a placement in an autistic clinic in Birmingham and then I had a placement in a psychiatric hospital and in a secondary school. I'll never forget that secondary school placement, it was a nightmare because I couldn't see how all these subject specialists could work so separately. It didn't make sense even then, because drama is so integrated. That experience made it clear to me that I couldn't teach in secondary schools. I worked with a remedial drama group up in London and went up to the Edinburgh Festival a couple of times. I really thought I would work with those children, but actually the regime in the psychiatric settings with adolescents was awful. They used the drama session I ran as a reward for the children, so if they'd behaved well, they could come to the drama session. I couldn't accept that sort of regime. I felt the autistic clinic was very much about behaviour management and I didn't enjoy that either, so I decided I would do my teacher training. I looked at the list and Goldsmiths was top of the list at that time and I wanted London, so I did my PGCE at Goldsmiths for the junior age phase. All the time I was doing the junior course I kept looking at the students who were doing infant/early years and thinking that it looked so much more interesting and relevant. Although the Goldsmiths course was hardly a course anyway, you were out on teaching practice almost all the time. They prided themselves then that you did more teaching practice than the three-year course, so we only had about 36 weeks and we seemed to be on teaching practice all the time. I did my teaching practice with 4-year-olds in a wonderful school. The thing about Goldsmiths was not the quality of the course at all, because the input was not particularly memorable. I think the early years input was probably a lot better than the junior input from what I saw, in terms of helping you to be a better teacher. I don't feel that the input helped me to be a more effective teacher but we visited some of the best schools in Britain and I'll never forget those schools, We saw Ted Tatersall's school, we saw the Oxford schools, and because I was prepared to commute I had a placement in Essex and went to this tiny little village school, which was brilliant and I worked with forty-three 4-year-olds and will never forget it.

CP: What did you bring from that experience?

MW: The dedication and the commitment of the staff, the sense of teamwork in a little country school. I'll never forget the head who used to protect us from our tutors; he'd give us sherry and little cheese biscuits, and look after and nurture us. And the joy of the children; it was one of those schools where children were really happy about coming to school. It was a school where children walked into the hall and found their places, they weren't drilled, they weren't made to do things, they did it because it was a very loving school. They were very privileged, it was a rural community and I don't know what the socioeconomic factors would be but when I go back it still looks pretty privileged. The relationships among the staff were very creative, very flexible and very responsive to the children. It used the reading scheme ITA and things like that, but it didn't seem to matter. It was the relationship and the trust that I remember, and the staff were very good with students. I was allowed to make a lot of mistakes and take a lot of risks and I will never forget those first children. William, the first child who told me that he didn't want to be grouped and herded, because I had 43 infants and my tutor was putting pressure on me to take them all. I remember working alongside the deputy head, she was so supportive, and we were team teaching. My tutor didn't want this, she wanted me to take over the whole of the 43 and do it to prove I could, which you didn't need to do in that school because we worked together as a team. So I had to put them into groups and I remember them all sitting on a mat and I had got them grouped, skylarks and snowdrops and such like, and William saying to me, 'I'm not a skylark, I'm a person.' I wrote it down and thought 'I'll never forget that' because he isn't a skylark, he is a person. And I remember also the first time I really failed to listen to a child. I remember a child bringing in a dog rose, and saying, 'I want to paint this dog rose.' I said, 'Bring your dog rose to show me,' and I didn't have time to look, so I said, 'Go away and paint it.' When she came back she'd painted the actual rose black. I thought 'You didn't listen to her, and you didn't give her the time she needed, so she did what you said!' But that was a brilliant school.

I was externally examined by Christian Schiller and I remember the whole school was trembling when all the external examiners arrived from Goldsmiths. It was the most beautiful hot and sunny day, and I was terrified, but I'd gone out on the playground and was playing with the children. The gravel was melting and William was very vocal, and had got his truck stuck. I was trying to be very helpful, and I remember thinking, 'They're going to arrive any minute and I've got to be in control' and William's truck was stuck fast. Then I remember seeing these spats, because Schiller wore kind of 'spat shoes', and thinking, 'My God, the external examiners are seeing this!' and looking up, and there they all were, surrounding me on this playground. But it was good experience, I mean it was a very loving school, it taught me a lot about teamwork, caring, compassion and giving permission to children and trusting children. I've never seen children just walking into an assembly since then. They're still all lined up and regimented, but they can do it if you trust them. These 140 children would just walk in and do it, no bells, no lining up, no external discipline.

CP: So what happened after that?

MW: Then I went to a school in Deptford High Street and had a teaching practice in Orpington where the teacher wanted to test the children on what I'd taught them on my teaching practice and was very punitive. I wanted to teach in Brighton, because my partner was at Sussex University and we wanted to be together. Brighton did a board interview, and I went for an interview with this head who taped the interview. He was only interested in reading scores, and he had them mapped out on the wall chart. He offered me the job and I said 'No'. You were not 'allowed' to do that, the Board doesn't offer you any more if you refuse them once. So then I was put in touch with a head in Tunbridge Wells who was one of the 'Plowden Heads'. The 'Plowden Heads' used to meet, and I was put in touch with him. He was an outstanding head.

CP: When you say 'Plowden Heads', what do you mean?

MW: Well there was a Plowden group. Christian Schiller was working at Goldsmiths and he had a group of heads every year who were seconded to work with him. Then they formed themselves into a group that later ran Plowden Conferences. They were all outstanding heads and a lot of them had been Len Marsh's colleagues. Geoff was one of those, he was a bit anarchic though, not a conventional head. He was very unusual, and I was his first appointment. I wanted the job, and he wanted me for the post. Now he's my child's godfather and we still keep in touch. He's a very important influence. He was trying to turn that school around, painfully, to be a very different school. It was on a housing estate in the only grotty bit of Tunbridge Wells at the time, with a children's home backing onto it. I think that taught me a lot, because, unusually, a lot of the children in my class were from the children's home and my class had got through three teachers the year before. I met one of the teachers at a party and she described the class to me, so I was really intimidated when I got them. They were the youngest juniors and pretty wild, the head let me have them for two years.

CP: Can you tell me a bit more about the head? What did he give you and how did he do it?

MW: He trusted me, he rewarded my commitment. I mean, I worked so hard I slept in the classroom. I'd also slept in the classroom on teaching practice in Essex, I'll never forget that. We used to go to a night club one night in London and then sleep in the classroom the next night. We worked such long hours, I had never worked so hard in my life. Then at my first school in my first job I felt that I had something to prove. He gave me a chance and each year he gave me more responsibility. In the first year he gave me a scale point for language and literacy, and the next year he gave me a scale 3 for managing a team of four staff. He always gave me opportunities, he knew I was hungry for opportunities and he wasn't frightened to support that. He let me take enormous risks. I remember he let me organize this amazing residential trip with children, and the place we were taking the children cancelled about a week before. I remember fainting in the stock cupboard. His first remark was, 'Was I pregnant?' and the next remark was terribly supportive, and we found somewhere else to take these children. We always took children away and for him to allow a very young probationary teacher to take children away was very trusting. He didn't say, 'She's a probationary teacher therefore she better just stick to her classroom.'

I found working in that class was a huge challenge, but I was hungry for other stuff as well. I wanted to manage a team, I wanted to experiment. He gave me a big budget which I was allowed to spend on books, but he knew that I was very committed, that I would research what the school needed and that I would do it responsibly. Before anybody had had writers in schools, we had an incredible Read-In (this is 1972, probably), and we invited about five authors and had children in charge of cameras and videos. We just had this wonderful event and I'll never forget, he knew how to say thank you too. He wrote me a beautiful letter on elegant paper saying he'd never seen a school work like this. He wrote that he'd never seen or felt that atmosphere in a school before. I kept this letter and carried it around with me for years. It was just wonderful to be part of it, but he'd let me take it on and he'd been there to support me in every possible way. The school secretary in that school is a very close friend of mine still, and she went on to become a teacher. There was also a lot of parental involvement, not in the way we talk about it now, but parents were encouraged to come in.

CP: Were you carrying from him the model of a leader giving people responsibility and room, and also that personal touch?

MW: Yes, and the ability to learn from mistakes. If I made a mess of things, which I did frequently, he wasn't afraid to allow this to happen. He was not afraid of emotion, which is unusual for a male head, you could just go and blub and wail. He was capable of showing his feelings too, and if you messed something up, you could really wail about it, and he would always be there for you. I would be in my classroom until 6.00 pm, or whatever, but he would also still be there, and that was a very important lesson for me. You cannot afford not to be there if your staff are prepared to do it. It wasn't a competition about who would stay latest, but he was there to support you, and when you had problems he was responsive. I made relationships with those children and their families, and that was before teachers really did home visiting, but I always used to home visit them before we took them away residentially. We camped out in a Georgian manor house before the county established a residential centre. The head allowed us to camp on the floor in this house, and the top juniors did all the cooking, because they knew more about cooking than I did. He'd also allow you to bring your friends in to help. He encouraged lots of risk-taking.

As a head he was a learner, he never pretended to know it all, he was an incredibly knowledgeable man, but he was still learning. I think he's still learning now. He's a reader and a thinker, a deep-thinker. He also taught me some of the things about what not to do, because he was impatient at times. He was a new head in that school, and wanted to push things through. In hindsight, it's either revolution or evolution, and I think evolution is the only way. But he was a trusting man.

CP: Let's leave him and go on through your route to headship.

MW: At the end of that school I had a scale 3 and was feeling very confident, but I hadn't thought about headship. In order to encourage me not to leave and go to South America the head said he would let me not have a class, and have some autonomy and take a lead curriculum role. This was very tempting, and I was very interested in staying, but my partner and I decided to go to South America. I ended up in Manaus, which is the last city on the Amazon, and didn't speak a word of Portuguese, because you couldn't get Portuguese classes in England at that time even though I knew I ought to speak it. I looked at the system there and worked in an American mission school for about eight weeks with American children, but I hated it. I hated the fact that the school was not part of any community and that it was private, so I just used that experience to ground myself there. I learnt Portuguese, and then started to look at what was around. The state system in Manaus didn't start until 7, and what they did with 7-year-olds was very formal. It was like a Victorian classroom and I didn't want to be part of that, I just couldn't have worked that way.

There was a philanthropist scientist at the place where my husband worked and he wanted to support provision for the early years. In northern Brazil, out of all the 7-year-olds who start schooling, 50 per cent fail and never go back. Then the next year they fail again. It's like the American system where you repeat, but they don't repeat, they just go off and become street kids. The Director of the Science Research Centre wanted to do something to support young children's learning, so I wrote a project which suggested he worked with the Ministry of Education, and the Prefeitura for Social Welfare. The Project suggested that he fund a school in a squatter settlement near the National Institute for Science in the Amazon, so it would support his staff, and it would also support local people. He allowed us to buy some wooden buildings that had been houses in the squatters settlement, and we turned them into a school. The toilet was a hole in the ground outside initially.

CP: When you say 'we', who was that?

MW: Well me, and an American woman colleague and Graça, who was an Amazonian woman, a local teacher, who still went on teaching at the local primary school, but became the local community representative on the project. So we applied for funding from the governor, the State of Amazonas and everywhere, and we got support. Northern Brazil is very different from the south of Brazil. In Southern Brazil they've even got OMEP, they've got early years provision, much of it private, but there was a lot of it, whereas in the Amazon there wasn't really anything.

CP: So who was the driving force behind setting up this project?

MW: Me really. I went to the head of the Science Institute and wrote the papers and made suggestions about who could help. He was a committed philanthropist, and he really cared about education. He had written this alphabet book because he could see why Brazilian children weren't learning to read. This was because they were having to use textbooks from America so he had written this Amazonian alphabet book. Although I didn't like this narrow way of teaching children to read, I appreciated his ideology, which was trying to get the people into literacy and empower them using local images rather than imported ones.

The other inspirational force for me was Paulo Freire. You couldn't mention that name really in Brazil because he'd been banned at that time. I was taking his books through customs with the covers ripped off, but it was right in that area that Freire's adult literacy programme originated. I learnt a lot from the adult literacy campaign about making what we were offering relevant to the local community, and I found all that material extremely useful in setting up the school, because I think I was set in a British model. I was even sending for my powder paint by ship from England, because if you try mixing berries in order to make enough paint for 160 children to use, you actually get very tired. So I used to have it all shipped out. We got Oxfam to fund the project in the last year I was there. Writing up projects was interesting for me because the funding had to be based on nutritional need. The most money we got was for health, because the children were severely malnourished. That was the first time I had seen the need to include health, education and social welfare together in one service, so that was a very marked influence. Also having to set up something and to appoint all the staff, which I had never done before, was formative for me. The decision to use local teachers and local women educators was crucial.

CP: Do you feel that this was your first headship? How did you implement your philosophy during this period?

MW: I just carried all those concepts of teamwork with me from working with Geoff, that is, that I must let people go at their own pace, and I must respect people's differences, and I must build on their strengths, because for the local teachers their training had been very narrow. We always saw the teacher training as a basic training and had to build on it. It was a very untraditional first headship but I was just like a teaching head though. I had to go in and open up in the morning, and relate to caretakers and appoint people. It paralleled an English headship. I had to deal with the local authority as I do here, but the issues were different. For example, fish coming out of your water tap and no water in the barrio for two weeks!

I became very political. I learnt there are some things that heads have to be very careful about and one of these is never not to be there when somebody significant comes. I'd been nagging the Governor of the State to come, and then the day he came I'd taken all my teachers on an away day. We'd flown them down to Belo Horizonte to an OMEP conference, and he came and visited our school and we weren't there! So in the papers that night it said 'The Governor visits, and the Head's not there!' Then we had no water for two weeks and I took a gang of children in a bus to his house. They had become very dusty children by that time, and we took the local film crew with us and we got the water back on very quickly. All the children jumped into his swimming pool and he used it as a publicity campaign. From then on I realized the power of local government and that if you actually need anything for your school, you go to your local politicians and learn to use the media. I had to learn Portuguese as I became a teacher, so I would go home and practise at night and write down all the things I thought I'd need to know and then speak it and learn it. In a way when you are learning the language of your community you learn the words that are really important and these words tell you a lot about the culture of that community.

CP: Is this true of any community?

MW: Yes. When I came to Corby I had to learn all sorts of words, 'Wain', 'hen', 'Going up the road'. All these expressions are the language of this community. I think in Brazil the experience of not being able to speak the language was very humbling and not being able to communicate easily was very good for me. I was very culturally arrogant initially, and I think probably most of us are, as new Heads. I did have a philosophy which was very child centred and was all about learning from observation. But I was very mono-cultural, I thought you could give a piece of paper and paints to any child and they would love it, but in the barrio they were actually frightened of blank paper. These children were very intimidated by what we were offering them and actually that's probably true of children in this country too. Some of what we offer is very scary and when I look at the curriculum I was offering to these children in Brazil, some of it was very inappropriate.

But there were parallels with an English headship. I had to appoint staff and I had to engage parents. I blew that completely because I was white and colonial and thought that what we were offering was 'a good thing', which is probably how a lot of heads see what they are offering in schools in this country. I couldn't understand why parents wouldn't come to parents' evenings but the day after the parents' evening it was like a harvest festival because they brought in all these presents to say 'We're really sorry we couldn't come'. Basically this was because they didn't want you to throw their kid out or not like them, but they didn't actually want to come to the meeting: to them it felt irrelevant. So the first year of the children coming to school, I never hooked the parents in. The second year I listened to Graça who was a local parent. I asked her, 'What gets parents in?' There was no electricity and she said what would get parents in at night was to have lamps and candles and run bingo. At least, this was how the priests did it. So we ran bingo sessions and then talked about the curriculum and their children afterwards. I actually think that's constructive and we always got all the parents in after that. Parents became parent helpers in the classroom, parents ran the kitchen, parents did all sorts of things after that.

We also often do not see children as whole people. In the barrio, children would sometimes come to school having been beaten. It was all very tangible, you fed a child, they had terrible worms and terrible health problems and they couldn't cope with school a lot of the time because they were malnourished, it was very stark. But there are children in this country who are in the same situation. I think I was aware at my first school in Tunbridge Wells of the children who came into school with sleep in their eyes, who looked troubled. I was aware of it but I didn't understand that it was my job as a teacher to do anything about it. I think in Brazil I learnt that that had to be my first priority. How can a child possibly do anything if they've just been hit on their way to school or if they're hungry or whatever? You've got to start with where they are. So we had breakfast at school, and then we had a very healthy lunch and some of the children went home; then we had another lot of children in the afternoon. Food became very important and was part of children's sense of well-being. This experience shook me up. When I came back to England I was hugely interested in social work suddenly and I hadn't been before.

CP: How long were you in Brazil?

MW: I was there for three and a half years. I came back in between a couple of times and used to go to Plowden Conferences. The hilarity of working in tropical heat under a tin roof with no water, no road and no paint, but trying to offer very experiential, child-centred learning struck me at these times. In the south of Brazil in the 1970s, everything in pre-school was done through colouring books and crayons and was very clean and tidy. Our project was completely different from anything else. I'd left the country just as Bennett's Report had come out and teachers were feeling very wounded. For the whole of the three years I was away I kept up a correspondence with my old head. We wrote every week. He sent me all the letters the other day, hundreds of them. We kept this dialogue going about what was happening in school in England, and I used to come back and see. I was very angry with what had happened in England. Teachers were respected in Brazil, they were very badly paid, but they were respected. Education was respected and valued by everyone.

Then I came back, had my baby, and went straight out to Papua New Guinea with my husband and my little girl. I managed an early years team who went out and worked in all the different village communities, so it was like running a rural pre-school in all these different villages. It was called 'Scoolnabout' and it was a mobile pre-school. We had to work in Neo-Melanesian, and in the local language groups of the villages. Again I think it was that sense of community and working with women's groups that attracted me. You had to find ways into each community that were completely different, and they were all very individual and I believe it was very challenging in that way. I don't know whether you'd call that headship, but it was certainly management. I had to manage a very different kind of team, working with local parents again. In each community you went into, you had to negotiate a new contract and you had to work through the fathers. You couldn't go straight to work with the women and children, you had to negotiate an agreement. In some of the villages the men would build you a hut to work in, and in some you worked in old shacks, and they didn't bother to build you one. It was valued in different ways in different communities, so that was a lesson. This was the first time I brought parents on to residential courses to train as parent helpers because the idea was that we would set up in each of these communities an early years base and that they would run it themselves and we would only come for one session a week to support them. So we brought in all those women who were setting up centres to train. I think what I learnt there was about how you worked with parents and how you encouraged parents to work with their own children. I also became very political and a feminist, because for the women to join in a lot of them got into terrible trouble. They'd come in with black eyes because they'd had to fight with their partners to be able to come to the meetings. I wasn't experienced enough to realize that you'd got to frame it up in different ways. It's like running classes here, if you want parents who've got literacy problems to come in, you don't call it an Adult Literacy Class because you'd wait 13 years for them to come. You call it a 'How You Help Your Child To Learn' class and then they feel OK to come in. It's finding ways and means to access services for people. I was also managing a very different team, and I was managed by the matron of the hospital. So again health, education and social welfare were all in one package. It certainly influenced the way I think about how little children learn and develop.

After that I came back to England and decided I needed to understand what social work was all about because a lot of what I seemed to have been doing, although it was called education, was social work as well. I also had a young child, and I wanted to spend time with her, so I decided to set up a home visiting service. By this time I guess I wasn't very good at working for people, I wanted to run things. I'd always run things since I left England, so I ran a home-visiting scheme. That was in Milton Keynes, and it was a very good lesson in inter-agency working. I'd never really home visited in this country though I'd home visited all through my time in Brazil and in Papua New Guinea. It was an educational home-visiting scheme and a lot of it I didn't like because I felt it was quite intrusive and prescriptive about parenting styles. But I did learn about other agencies and how our statutory agencies in this country work. I think that heads need to know about that. I don't think we knew enough in the 1970s about families, I don't think a head would have understood how a Social Services department worked. When the Children Act training was offered in our own local authority, very few heads actually saw it as their responsibility to train. I think the fact that I had to work with a social work agency and that I saw how difficult it was, and the kind of pressures social workers work under, was very, very useful.

I only did it for about nine months until I saw two jobs advertised. One was a beautiful little rural primary school in Oxfordshire, which I was being head-hunted for at the time, to be head. I knew I wanted headship, but I didn't see myself as a mainstream school teacher and I knew a lot about early years by now because I'd done a lot of training. In Papua New Guinea I was working with under 8s, because they went into school at about 7 or 8, so I knew that my specialism was there and I'd put a lot into learning about that age range. Often in my first few years in this job at Pen Green, I used to drive past that little school thinking, 'What would it have been like if I'd taken it?' It was very tempting and seductive because a little village school would have probably had a strong sense of community and you could have done a lot. But it was a very well-off area, it was very privileged and it was very small. I didn't know whether I would be too 'big' for it in a sense, having too much bounce and energy and being a bit 'Tiggerish' for a little rural school. And also the challenge for me is about other things. I like the stroppy kids, I like the angry kids, I like the ones who are fighting so the 'leafy' bit didn't appeal in the same way.

Then I saw this job at Pen Green. When I applied for it I thought all the staff were going to be on the same conditions of service. The advert for head-ship said, 'Head, and all the staff will be on the same conditions of service'. I thought that meant the same pay, and I was into feminist co-ops by then. I thought that it would be wonderful to work somewhere where there wasn't a hierarchy but I was a bit naive. The same conditions of service just meant that the social workers, nursery nurses and the teachers had the same holidays not the same pay scales! I came on a wet day to Corby, it was after the steelworks had closed, and was all boarded up and looked awful. The building was horrific, every window had been shattered and boarded up. They showed me this building that had been an old comprehensive school, a whooping cough clinic and a dental clinic and I just thought, 'Oh my God'. It seemed like about 12 people interviewed me. I think a lot of the teachers who'd applied had made the same sort of mistakes about the conditions of service, and hadn't realized they would have to work social service hours. Actually at Pen Green we get better holidays than social services but we don't get teaching holidays. Well, I'd never had those, even at Tunbridge Wells, we never took the holidays. We took kids away half the summer, so I wasn't hooked on balancing my life with a six or eight week summer holiday. So it wasn't a problem for me, I didn't think about it really. It just seemed to me that a seamless, all-year-round service was actually rather sensible, and so I came here, and then had to make all the staff appointments, which was nice to be in at the very beginning, to set it up from an empty derelict building.

Pen Green began operating in 1983 in an old disused secondary school, as a form of combined provision for under 5s and their families. It was jointly funded by local education and social service departments. The centre now has five main strands of work: a community nursery; family work; health work; adult and community education; research, training and development for early years workers and parents.

CP: *Did you feel totally confident about going into that headship? What vision did you have at that point?*

MW: I wanted us all to be on the same conditions of service, having a sense of collegiality and I really wanted this to work. I had no fears about setting up the team. All the appointments were collaborative, and I think that's one thing I had learnt, don't make decisions on your own, get the local support, have the local people in making those decisions, and you'll make better appointments.

CP: Just before we go on to Pen Green and your vision and how you handled headship here, can we just go back a bit and think about your preparation for becoming a head, which was very different to most people's? Given your experience, what's your reflections on preparation for headship within the system?

MW: I would say a really good understanding of how children learn is absolutely essential to being a good teacher, and it must be essential to being a good head. But probably alongside that, believing in yourself as a learner is important. If you're a head who thinks that you've got there, then that would be really tragic. I think my humility comes from the fact that I never feel appropriately qualified for the particular role I've taken on. I've taught right the way through the primary phase, and I'm certainly not an early years specialist, but I want to be. So I think all heads should see themselves as learners and be aware of all the gaps in what they know. I think being a good team member is really helpful but you've also got to enjoy taking a leadership role. You've got to have a sense of your own vision. When I went back through the little notebooks I've kept over the last 25 years, that vision is there. I know that there is a way of working with children, parents and staff that is consistent right the way through these notebooks. I also think for a head it's invaluable to have had the experience of being managed well. If, as a head, you had never been managed well, it would be difficult to do it yourself. A breadth of experience is important. I remember I was invited on the New Heads course in Northants about a year after I was appointed. The inspectors did this role play of interviewing for a headship. They asked me to prepare for it the night before and to use my own CV. The other new heads had to take it in turns to interview me, and they all said, 'Well we wouldn't interview her with that breadth of career, we just wouldn't consider her for a headship.' They thought I'd made up my CV as a joke. Part of me was amused, and part of me thought, 'You really don't know, do you, what living a life can be about.'

All my work with women leaders, who are brilliant heads, was also good preparation. I actually did some work for my PhD over the last two years with some outstanding women heads. They have all had that same broad career pattern, they've not gone in a direct line step by step, they just haven't, and they haven't wanted to. It's not that they've been passed over or neglected, they've been hungry for different kinds of experience, and I think that's much richer.

CP: Can you see how your role as Head of the Centre has changed and evolved over the 14 years that you've been there?

MW: I think the core principles have not changed because I negotiated those with the staff group I appointed, and as we've appointed each member of staff since then, we've ensured those principles have continued. Yet, every time we have an interview for a member of staff we renegotiate the way we work. We've gone through that a number of times. It's interesting; we wrote a curriculum document in 1984, we'd only been open about a year and a half, and the principles we put in that curriculum document are still the principles we have now but we've found very different ways of working. We've also got a lot better at what we do and we're better at evaluating what we do, but I think those core principles are still there.

CP: So what was your vision?

MW: Well the vision was of a flexible and responsive service to children and families, and I actually think that we are a very different kind of set-up to a traditional school, but I would want my school, any school, to be just the same. I think that what we are trying to do is right for any early years setting. Our Centre is very respectful of children's rights and needs, and it also offers support to parents. It recognizes their responsibilities and what they're trying to do, and we try and ensure that there's not a huge dissonance between home and school. We've got to find a way for children to not see school as something that is very separate, very precious. I was reading Andrew Pollard's recent research in which 'Sally' the caretaker's daughter is the child that's most successful in school. It makes so much sense to me because the children who are most successful are those that feel that school is most familiar, where they feel most in control, most powerful, and I think that's what I want this place to be. In one of Christian Schiller's essays he writes about schools being in that place on the street corner where everybody wants to come, and where everybody feels at home. He's talking about primary schools, and I actually think that's what I want this Centre to be. I want it to be a rich, challenging environment, and I want it to be an environment where people are very reflective, and where people are learning all the time so that they're not complacent. I don't ever feel that we've got where we want to get to, we're just on the way.

CP: What kind of leader are you in that context then? How would you describe yourself as a leader?

MW: Ever since we set up the Centre, we did it so there would be a team of managers. That's not me abnegating my responsibilities, I think naturally, I am the sort of person who has a lot of energy, and enjoys being an enabler and a facilitator. I'm not a brilliant finisher or completer, but we've always recruited a management team where we've got people who are good completers and finishers, and people who are charismatic, and people who are good leaders. So I think I have always known that there were things that I'm not so good at, and I've always looked for staff who will complement that. That's not me dumping, if I take on a piece of work I finish it, but I also know that there are people who get a tremendous amount of satisfaction from finishing things, and I'm much more excited about looking at the next step and scanning the horizon, and thinking about what could we do next, and how do we respond to this challenge and that challenge. Yes, I think I am a charismatic leader, whatever that means. When I came back recently after a period on secondment, I'd been away for 18 months, we had a team building event. Some of the staff were saying the things that they had missed about me. One member of staff, who hadn't ever worked with me because she'd been appointed while I was away said, 'When you came into the place it was like somebody had lit the taper of a firework.' Quite a long taper I hope, but there was a lot of energy and there's a lot of enthusiasm. I think I've got both things, but I hope I've got compassion and those other things that I think are desirable in leaders. I think my greatest strength is that I mind about people's learning, I mind about every individual member of staff having a training programme. They have rights and entitlements to develop themselves, because we're a learning organization, and if we're concerned about children's learning then we want to be the richest possible professionals and so we need to go on learning too. In addition we find the parents are hungry for learning. So that's the bits I'm good at. I've always been very fortunate in the people we've recruited who've been committed practitioners with different strengths who've complemented those things.

CP: Do you feel part of your skill is seeing the potential in people, and how they all dovetail and fit together?

MW: Yes. I think parents and staff often say, 'Oh, she put a gun to my head and she made me do this', but I don't think I do. I always see the potential in other people. I get a lot of my energy from seeing people grow and change, and I do love working with adults. I suppose that's a thing I learnt abroad which I never thought I would. I think as a head you've got to enjoy working with adults too. You could get to be a head very easily and not like working with adults very much, or be very shy and withdrawn. I don't think you've got to be an outgoing, bouncy sort of head. My first head wasn't like that, but he did enjoy adults, he could relate to adults. If you couldn't, I don't see how you could do the job well.

CP: The one thing that shines out in what you say is that you see learning and teaching for everyone at the Centre as central. How do you make sure that this is seen as a priority?

MW: Well, first of all, the organization is only as high quality as the weakest link in the chain, isn't it? So if I know there's somebody who isn't committed, for instance philosophically, who holds children in an inappropriate kind of way, or who is didactic or who feels that they have to dictate the content and aren't prepared to follow the child's interest, then I feel that we've got a long way to go with that person. I feel that everybody's got to come on board, the lunchtime assistants, the kitchen staff, everybody. Your school is only as effective as how loving your 'dinner ladies' are with the children and how creative they are with them at lunchtime. If your 'dinner ladies' are making children do things inappropriately or are disrespectful to children or whatever, then the whole enterprise is threatened. The curriculum is all of that, the curriculum is every single experience the child has in that setting, and the way that setting transcends the building and is aware of what's going on at the home and honours the child's context. It is essential for us to understand the child's context. From the very beginning we spend a lot of time discussing issues with staff. I remember a member of staff who wanted 'naughty chairs' because she'd come from a very traditional background and she thought the one way of disciplining children was to put them on a 'naughty chair'! Then you've got other staff who are prepared to go the distance in order to allow a child to push boundaries and to challenge systems. You've got to negotiate within that range of beliefs about how children need to behave and how children learn. So all the time we're negotiating about our belief system about how children learn and how its best to work with them. I'm proud to be a teacher but I'm sometimes scared of the word 'teaching', it's a bit like 'parent education' because it implies that there's a set content that professionals think is appropriate for others to learn in a prescriptive kind of way. I think my understanding of how children learn has grown enormously and I'm much more concerned about how children learn and their attitudes to learning than I am about their acquiring particular bits of knowledge.

The same is true with adult learning, not only the parents but also the staff as well. How do adults learn? How can I convince a member of staff that the way they are working is not an appropriate way of working? I mean a lot of it would be by modelling, some of it would be by introducing them to better practice. So we set up a system at the very beginning where every member of staff has supervision. I think that's probably how the core of our collective belief system about how children learn, and how best to teach them, is transmitted. All senior staff supervise the other staff and every four weeks every member of staff gets supervision. In that supervision session staff look at the way they're working with children, they think about how they're working with individual children and they look at where the challenges are and where they're finding difficulties. They make action plans for children, they look at their observations of children and build on them. We've had that supervision system in place since 1983 and it's got better and much more focused. I think it's through this that we transmit a way of thinking and reflecting on children's learning. Every member of staff gets it, so if a member of staff is off track it's a learning opportunity all the time. We also have staff meetings and we have non-contact time. We've built in non-contact time for nursery staff from the very beginning because traditionally they don't have it, so they've always had about four and a half to five hours non-contact time to negotiate how we work with children. So in a way we've set up forums and structures where discussion can take place because every time you have a new member of staff you've got to find new ways of making it work. My experience is that new staff come in and you can talk to them about the way you work but unless you have that reflective, iterative, ongoing discussion they can have quite the wrong idea. You find out six months later that they've picked up some piece of practice and they've assumed that it was OK, and it's not OK but nobody's discussed it with them.

CP: Let's just shift the focus away to explore the notion of accountability. Who do you feel accountable to and how do you manage that accountability?

MW: Well I've always been accountable to both departments, education and social services, and traditionally been line-managed by both. There was a structure set up that was a little more formal probably than most schools, where we met regularly with the Area Education Officer and Senior Manager from Social Services. That's where I felt there was an external accountability through them, for budgets and things like that. We have a policy group which is a bit like a governing body, it's really our equivalent to a governors' body and I feel very, very accountable to them because on that policy group there are parents, there are county councillors and district councillors, there are officers from all the different agencies that manage us. In a sense they should be driving what the Centre does and those were the same people who were on the original steering group that set up the Centre, so I feel quite accountable to them.

CP: Let's switch to the support bit then because that's another side. Where do you look to for your own professional well-being, and your own support?

MW: I found it fascinating looking at the models in all the different agencies – health, education, social work. I looked at all of them to see which I thought was the most effective model, and the assumption that your line manager can necessarily offer you the professional support you need, or the personal support you need, is an anomaly, because quite often your line manager is somebody who has no experience in your field. Many nursery heads would have Area Education Officers who've got no knowledge or understanding of early years, and that was always the case for me. There can also be a clash between accountability and support because are you going to admit your mistakes? I think I probably drove my line manager mad. I remember throwing a notebook at a manager, I remember bursting into tears at management meetings. I hated myself for doing this but I do think it is important to show that you can cry and be angry and that you can work through your tears. Always being managed by men was very difficult at times. I've been managed by so many different people over 14 years but I've had some very good line managers and we have learnt to work well together, but there have often been gender issues. I don't think as a head you would admit to your AEO that you've got inter-personal problems, and inter-personal issues in a staff group; you're very unlikely to talk to your line manager about things like that.

CP: So where do you go then?

MW: Well, after the first year, I looked at a lot of other new integrated Centres, and the heads were cracking up, literally. In out local authority the 'joke' was that if your contract is issued by social services, then you end up in private psychiatric care. However, if your contract is issued by Education you end up in the local NHS hospital. So I wrote a paper for the Department saying it would be a lot cheaper if they pro-actively bought me in a consultant from a university to take on this support role rather than wait for me to have a very expensive breakdown! So I had a lecturer from Leicester University to supervise me. Actually the lecturer was a social worker because I felt very strong on the educational aspects of the work, and I felt that in terms of team building, a social work model was probably a lot healthier than many educational models. They bought in somebody who could support me, and we did that for a couple of years, and it was paid for. Then they stopped paying for it, probably because they realized I wasn't going to crack up, and I could cope, but we went on doing it, and I actually think it's a wonderful support. I've seen certain Local Authorities where the local inspectors have taken on that role with new heads and it's worked and because then the inspector isn't the heads' direct line manager, they could give development support. Most of the problems for new heads are about inter-personal relationships. Who in education has got the expertise in inter-personal relationships? Very few of us have group work training, counselling training, management training of that sort. I set that up because I knew I needed it. Even now when there are three of us who manage the Centre as a management team, we buy in a consultant so that when the three of us are finding things problematic, we can have support. We don't always do it reactively, we have it about once a year, but also, if we're really finding it difficult to sort something out, we would buy in somebody from outside that we trust. At the moment it's an educational consultant we are using but we've used many different people. We've always had a model of buying in outside expertise to give us the support we needed as heads and managers.

CP: Do you feel headship has got more difficult, and do you still enjoy it? Is it still something you can still get satisfaction out of?

MW: I love it! When I came to be a head in the early 1980s, I think heads had a pretty closed-door attitude and now they've become competitive. I think the atmosphere among heads is very sad, that they're competing for children, they're competing for budgets, and I think that's so destructive. I hope, in the early years it isn't as bad as it is in primary schools. It is tough being a head in the 1990s. There are far more financial constraints and it would be very easy to lose sight of the children. I think language is very important and the thing I find most disturbing is this business-type language and the attitude that goes with it which says that I don't want that child if I don't get any money attached to them, and they're going to be a lot of hard work. I'm a governor in a primary school, and in a comprehensive school. I think that's been very important for me actually, because it's given me a lot of sense of continuity through the system. It scares me to see children viewed like that, as commodities. Also, the more damaged children are, the harder they are to work with, and you've got to look after your staff, and if you don't protect your staff, then you won't have an effective organization. You've got to look after your staff but still mind passionately about engaging all these children. Sometimes, there's a real tension there, and staff become over stretched, especially if the LEA can't give you the resources, and there have never been less resources, and it's never been harder to get them. Despite the Children Act, the agencies are working less well together, and that's a tragedy.

CP: So let's turn that round, and say how you would like to see primary schools and Centres like yours changing and developing for the future.

MW: I would like us to see education as about lifelong learning, and school buildings as the community's buildings. I would like to see teaching as a respected profession again, and children's rights respected, and children being listened to, all those things. I think you could have a package where you've got a community building which is accessible for adult education, community education and young children's learning, where there is continuity through the system. I would certainly like to see early years services being for children from 0 to 6 years, and I would like to see the agencies working together, without those rigid divisions between education and care, and support for youth, and support for families.

CP: Do you think the school system's capable of that?

MW: Oh yes, it could do it tomorrow with the right attitude. You can do it under a tree in Brazil, or in a tin shack with the rain pouring on your head in Papua New Guinea, working in three different languages. Of course you can do it in England, it's about attitude and it's about valuing children and families.

CP: That's the hardest thing actually, isn't it? Talking of the language of possibilities, do you think that it's possible?

MW: I think one of the answers is in our model of training. If we had integrated training we could do it. I have to believe that we'll come to our senses eventually and that in the future there will be a BA Early Years or whatever and that everybody, from whatever agency, whether you go to work in social work, health or education, will have a core training. Then you'll move on, and you will then see how your job relates to somebody else's, and you will see children and families as a whole unit and education and care as a seamless service. I do believe in that. I think that will happen ... because people must see that it would be cost-effective, and it would be high quality, and it's what families and children want. As a professional that's how I love to work, you're missing so much if you don't work in that way.

CP: Given that this Centre is well on its way, what are the particular challenges for you working here?

MW: I think that there is a need for practitioner research. It should have been done before the Centre opened if we were to demonstrate the Centre's effectiveness. I said it when I came in 1983. If only the data had been collected before we started it would have been so useful to monitor for change and evaluate progress. I did collect a lot of data, the first five months I spent walking the streets, but the data I was collecting were how can we make this service relevant to this community, what hours do parents want the Centre to be open, what rooms do they want, what services do they want? But the data we didn't have were the kind of data that would help us to show that this is a very valuable service, the kind of service that makes a difference to children. We've collected it, incidentally, on the way, so in a sense what we're doing is saying 'Right, we know that what we're doing is very purposeful, we know we work in a very reflective way', now we've got to show that that's the most effective way of working, and we've got to show it in a way that's rigorous, that will be accepted by other professionals, and which can help our colleagues. We need to find out how we can work more effectively with parents and children. So it's a bit like everything at this Centre, we built outside play equipment, and then we had to dig it all up the year after in order to put the soft surface down because we couldn't afford it in the first year. I hate to do things that way round, but in a way part of me feels that you can spend a long time thinking about doing things before doing them. You do learn a lot just by doing it. There's a Brazilian phrase meaning that you can always 'find a way' if you want to. I think it's important to set out on things and find ways to challenge boundaries and make things work for people. We want to document our work and research it so that we can make sure it's replicated because I think it's very easy for people to dismiss it, unless it's well researched. Also we make a lot of mistakes, and we learn a lot if we evaluate and review everything that we do in a purposeful, rigorous way. I think that way of working has been part of our culture but I think documenting it has become much more important.

CP: So you are looking to develop a research-centred focus?

MW: Well, I believe all early years centres need to be grounded in that kind of research and development work. Training's always been a core but we've been frightened of the word 'research'. We've used words like review and evaluation, but I think it's time for us to own that word and get on with it, and make it our own.

CHAPTER 11

Developing a radical agenda

DAVID WINKLEY WITH CHRISTINE PASCAL

David Winkley is Head of Grove Primary School in Handsworth, Birmingham. He was born and educated in Birmingham, where he taught in various secondary and primary schools before taking a degree in English at Cambridge University. He was a founder member of the Centre for Contemporary Cultural Studies at the University of Birmingham with Richard Hoggart and Stuart Hall. His professional and academic activity throughout his career has been wide ranging and extensive. He has combined a successful teaching career with an academic life: writing, lecturing, and researching widely on primary and urban education, management, special needs, English and philosophy. He is also founder and National Director of the National Primary Centre and Trust. He is married to a consultant psychiatrist and has two children. He continues to write fiction and practise his musicianship, while maintaining an active and campaigning profile in the development of primary education policy and practice.

CP: First of all, could you explore with me your earliest memories to the end of your full-time education? How influenced have you been by those around you? How did they shape your values and the kind of person you've become?

DW: I was born in Birmingham, in Erdington, to an interesting family. My father was public school educated and came from a very wealthy background but the family fell upon hard times. My mother was working class, from a large Birmingham family. Her father was a bricklayer, so it's an interesting background and I'm not sure where it places me in a class definition, I don't fit a box. I was educated in my primary years at local state schools. I started off at Moor End Infants School, which is no longer in existence, and I remember trudging all the way up to school when I was little. When I was early junior age we moved to Sutton Coldfield, and I went to Boldmere Primary. Those were the days when there was a certain element of accelerated learning on the German model going on, which perhaps we might be going back to. From my own point of view it was undesirable. It meant that I missed my final year of primary school and went into secondary school a year early, so that right the way through secondary school I was a year younger than most of my peers. I went on from Boldmere to King Edward's School, which was in those days was a grant-maintained school but is now an independent school.

CP: Was going through school a year earlier than you should have done a positive experience for you?

DW: My own reflections on this are that it was entirely negative and it's something that I would wish to discourage because emotionally and socially I was not as developed as I was academically. In my view, in the long run this catches up with you and I think it had a negative effect because it meant I went to university a year early too, which itself is very undesirable. I was always the youngest, which caused emotional and social problems for me, particularly emotional problems, because you feel that you're never quite growing up in the way your peers are.

So carrying on that story, I went from KES and got a scholarship to Cambridge and did three years at Cambridge. Looking around for careers, I had no thoughts whatever of teaching. I intended to go into journalism as I did quite a lot of writing. I used to write for the *Granta* as the short story writer, following David Frost incidentally, who also had the same role. I intended to be a writer and journalist and was offered a job at the *Guardian*, which I decided in the end not to pursue. I came into teaching on a part-time basis for a very short time. In those days they were very short of teachers and they would tend to take anybody who could string together some articulate sentences. Even during the university vacations I used to teach in different Birmingham schools, mostly secondary but some primary. I really went round a lot of schools and I taught in about 26 different schools altogether. They used to pay me a reasonable rate, it was really quite a good deal, and it was very interesting because I had an enormous range of experiences prior to making a decision to come into teaching. So, I sort of edged my way into teaching, almost by default, starting with secondary and finding primary very much more interesting at that time. I thought the most radical opportunities and the most exciting learning were, and in my view still are, going on there.

CP: So what were the critical experiences and who were the people that shaped you during that time?

DW: Well, I was academically quite a high flyer, so I had always thought of different options, people would try and poach me to join their department. I was originally intending to be a musician. I did A-level music with Willis Grant, who went on to be professor of music at Bristol, and he was very keen to get me to Bristol to do music. He was also a very charismatic and influential teacher. But in the end I decided to opt for English, partly because I was with a generation of children, musicians of that generation, who were quite unbelievably talented. One of my peers in the same form as me, David Munrow, subsequently became world famous, almost discovering mediaeval music. He established The Munrow Consort but tragically died in his mid-thirties. He was one talent, and there were others who are now very distinguished musicians. I felt I simply could not compete in this kind of world, and decided that it really was an exclusive hotbed of talent. I was particularly interested in composing, I used to compose music for school orchestras and so on, but decided, through the influence of Tony Trott, who was the head of the English department at KES, to do English. I suppose there are always significant individuals who act almost like mentors, and of those the most important was Tony Trott, who really had a very significant effect. He identified me as being someone he wanted in his English department, and he was the one who pressed me to go to Cambridge to begin with.

CP: You said you edged into teaching, what was the thing that decided you?

DW: Well the thing that convinced me was the opportunity I had to find out what teaching was like during vacation periods. I found I rather enjoyed it and got on well with children and felt it was a job with an awful lot of opportunity. People forget what life was like in those days. It was very different from what it is now. There were some brilliant teachers but there were also a lot of very limited talent. Often teachers had been emergency trained and had come into the job almost accidentally. But I could see how you could very quickly pick up the opportunities that were there. So I started in teaching but I didn't do it for very long. I went back into academia and was the first person appointed to the Centre for Contemporary Cultural Studies at Birmingham University. Richard Hoggart created it, Stuart Hall was appointed as director and there was me and five others appointed. We started it off and this was quite an exciting period. The Centre set in motion the whole academic mass media enterprise and became internationally famous. I worked there for a couple of years and remained connected with the Centre for some while. There was a heady mixture of sociologists and English specialists, which created an interesting balance at a time when we were creating almost a new analytical discourse. Subsequently, it became very dominated by a sociological perspective but that's not how it started. Richard Hoggart was, of course, Professor of English and there was a very interesting balance and intellectual tension between Richard Hoggart and Stuart Hall. So that was quite an exciting time. However, I ran out of money and decided not to be a full-time academic, although the opportunities were there. I decided to go back into teaching and then actually hit upon a school that I found exciting and I was head-hunted by an enterprising head.

CP: Was that a primary school?

DW: Yes. I'd decided by then that primary education was more interesting than secondary. I felt that that was where the most exciting things were happening and the real thinking was going on about the nature of learning. You also had far more freedom. The secondary schools struck me as too determined by organizational constraints of various kinds, including timetabling. On the other hand, I worked for a time at Hodge Hill Secondary in the remedial department, with fourth year remedial children (I think they were called 4C2) and that was a particularly interesting and lively department.

CP: What sort of period are we talking about?

DW: That would have been 1965, but then I kind of fixed myself into Perry Common Primary and stayed up to about 1970. I haven't ever really had a career pattern, it's all been very *ad hoc*. I had no intention of continuing in teaching. I also had quite a lot of years out of teaching and I'm probably unusual in that respect. I continued teaching through to 1970, then got a deputy headship of a brilliant school (almost everyone on the staff is now a head), with a very inspirational head. During that period it was an outstanding school, it was an exciting period and I enjoyed it enormously. There were experiments in drama and we ran a club for 300 children every Friday. It was a very good school though now it might look old fashioned in lots of ways. I started as head of the English department and then became deputy.

CP: You said the head was inspirational, can you tell me why?

DW: I think he was extremely talented and I valued him enormously. He kept me in the job and I think without him I would not be teaching now because he gave me an idea of what you could do. He's retired now, a great man in many respects. It was a very difficult working-class community in that area, many of them were catholic children with a lot of problems. The children were mostly white and from a council house intake. The school began from very inauspicious beginnings. It was seen as a problem school, and he went there and appointed me very soon after he arrived, so the two of us, in a sense, created that place. I learnt an enormous amount from him, I was obviously very green. He was charismatic, very much a leader, very strong. We tightened up on the discipline, we sorted it out so the kids were well behaved and he was absolutely brilliant with parents. He knew exactly how to manage that community, he was confident, strong and determined, he made it clear he wouldn't mess about, but he was warm too, a hugely warm sort of guy, who would go up to parents and cuddle them, unpretentious, but absolutely clear. He always got his own way if he felt it was the right thing to do, and it made people feel safe and confident. I try and model myself as far as I can on some of those qualities. The community thought the world of him, and when he left it was really a tremendous loss. The other thing was, he had an amazing antenna for finding quality staff. There are at least six heads in the city I can think of, and a number of others outside the city as far apart as Wales, Manchester and Oxfordshire, who came from the school at that time.

CP: Was he preparing you for headship at that time?

DW: Oh yes, he took the view that I take, which is that I'm looking for talent and that I want to allow it to run its length. He was expecting people from his school to go on to do greater things and he prepared you in many ways.

To some extent you modelled yourself on him but he also insisted on giving you a tremendous amount of freedom. He said, 'I want you to do this. Do it, but you do it your way.' Relationships were excellent, he knew how to manage people, it was very relaxed in terms of the staff relationships but hugely creative and full of ideas, bubbling with ideas. The place developed very rapidly and I had a lot of freedom. I need freedom to move, I can't work in a constrained environment. So it was ideal for me, I wouldn't have stayed otherwise, but he knew exactly how to manage me and we did achieve quite a lot. So it was really quite an exciting period but I wasn't there all that long. I had this pull back to academia and went to Oxford and did a DPhil in philosophy.

CP: And that was full time, so you left teaching?

DW: Yes, for three years. I could have stayed as an academic and the opportunity did arise. My wife is a psychiatrist, she was a GP originally, and she changed to do psychiatry. She went to Oxford, partly because she could get on a married women's training scheme in psychiatry, and she worked with the professor there. This is really quite important because to some extent our careers have had to dovetail. Following this we made a decision to go back to Birmingham (though we could both have got jobs in Oxford), largely on the grounds that the real world was in Birmingham. Oxford was a much more secure and cloistered life, of the kind that I wasn't ready for at that age. I was still very young, under 30, so we decided to come back. Lindy wanted to work in Birmingham as well and we had a house back in Birmingham. She went back into psychiatry and we have stayed in Birmingham, partly to keep both our careers in the same place.

CP: When you came back to Birmingham, did you look for schools again?

DW: Yes, I did. I went onto supply and was on supply for 18 months. Again I recommend that experience for anyone. It means you see a wide range of schools. I think one of the problems teachers have is that they think that all schools are like the one they're in. Certainly people here often think that, whereas in fact, the world is so different when you're out there and schools are so incredibly different from each other. You never really know that until you work inside them. Looking at them from the outside, so much of the teaching process looks the same in a superficial way, but there are striking differences in the cultures, in the way schools are run and organized and so on. So I worked in schools in every part of the city, and every conceivable age range from reception to sixth form. I also supervised university postgraduates, so I probably have an unusual background. I went to a variety of schools and then the Grove job came up, and nobody really wanted it and I believe that is largely why I got it. It was a difficult school with serious behaviour difficulties and a history of community problems. Handsworth was the very first place to take large numbers of, what were then, genuine immigrants (of the 1950s and 1960s). My predecessor had a heart attack after 18 months and said, 'Don't stay too long here my boy.' So there were very few applicants for the job and they gave it me. I think I was the very first person who was appointed from a part-time, supply post to a headship.

CP: Can you tell me about the actual process of your appointment?

DW: In those days there was a consortium governing body chaired by a member of the Local Authority Education Committee. The Education Committee and, what were then, the Inspectorate had much more say and control over appointments than they do now. This group would cover the consortium of schools, so I obviously put an application into them. I remember them asking would I stay two years? I said yes, I would commit myself for at least two years and nobody, I think, ever thought I'd stay longer than two years! Again, I was still very young, so I ended up as head of this school in my very early thirties, the youngest head appointed at that time, in a school with very considerable problems.

CP: You didn't feel the selection process was discriminating then?

DW: Well there weren't many applicants, I don't think they had any others to be honest. I think there were a couple of people interviewed, that's all, as I recall. So in a sense I felt I got the job by default, largely because no one else wanted it, and then there was the question of what I could do once I'd got it.

CP: How did you feel once you'd got the job?

DW: Well, it was a bit like going into the First World War on the front line and I do feel there's a real analogy with war. You are on the front line and it's indisputably stressful. I had quite a lot of difficulties, children were very aggressive, staff tended to be stressed and aggressive to the children and consequently, there were a lot of behaviour management problems.

CP: What do you remember from those first, early days? Did you come in feeling confident in your skills to cope?

DW: Well yes, I've never felt that self-doubt really. I've always felt I can manage these sort of situations but once you're in there you realize there's a lot to learn, and I don't think anyone could teach it to you. I'm currently on the TTA Advisory Committee for the training of heads, and I'm somewhat sceptical as to whether or not you can train heads. Almost every single thing I've learnt of any use at all, I've learnt from being on the job, or watching other people on the job. I've learnt remarkably little from any course. So it was very much about learning how to construct something creative out of disarray. I faced a lot of difficulties, I don't want to over exaggerate, there were teachers here who were managing and had the right idea, I thought, but there was a tremendous amount of stress and some alarming things were happening, such as children climbing out the windows and running up the road and so on.

CP: You have described your pathway to headship. If you were looking at people coming into headships now, what would you do to improve things?

DW: That's a really difficult question. I think the central problem is one of people being locked into worlds that are necessarily limited. People tend to be brought up, as it were, in cultures. If you've been at a school that's not terribly enterprising, or isn't incredibly exciting, or even is just a good school of its kind, inevitably the pattern of experience limits your understanding of what schools can be. The stroke of luck I had was to be at a school which, bit by bit, created a culture and imaginative environment that opened up possibilities, made you think much more widely than you might otherwise have done. I think the problem for people coming into headships or deputy headships is they simply haven't experienced wide enough possibilities, and you tend to think everything is like the school that you're at, whereas in fact schools are hugely different. I've frequently had experiences of people coming to Grove from other schools and it's a tremendous culture shock because it is so different. Some of the things we are trying to do here are so different from some of the experiences they've had, and one almost has to re-educate, even with these intelligent, able people.

CP: So how do you prepare people then and what do you feel about current developments in headship training?

DW: The TTA are currently looking at the kind of training programme that covers every conceivable possibility, like a course with lots of components in it. The real problem I have with it is that it is possible, it seems to me, to go through this kind of process, and still not be terribly good as a head. That sounds ridiculous, but it seems to do with the fact that there are certain things that are absolutely crucial and critical to the enterprise, and other things that you can learn very quickly. For example, there's a great deal made of the management of finance and administration. But both things you can actually learn quickly and are relatively unimportant to the creation of an ideas-creating school. There are other things which I would identify as more important. For example, creating an ambience and a culture within the school, within the people in the school, within the children, a kind of deeper sense of what you're trying to do as an organization. What is it? What is a learning environment? These are really deep, philosophical questions that are both intellectually demanding, but also require you to think about yourself as a person. These are the critical issues. It doesn't matter how many courses you've been on, and how much you actually know intellectually about the process of being a head, unless you can get to grips in depth with those two areas of philosophy and your own emotional understanding, in a sense of how to get from A to B, you will never … make a good head. It is a skill and competency – in fact, it's the ultimate skill and competency – without which none of the others matter, in a sense. That's an exaggeration, of course, but they're certainly much less important. The danger is of creating the conception of school leadership as a managerial enterprise, as a tick list – 'You do all these things and then you're going to be a very competent head' – and that just does not follow. That creates all manner of difficulties when it comes to thinking about appropriate training procedures. To answer your initial question about where would I start with training, I think I would like to see a much more structured network of relationships between schools, of the kind that allowed far more interplay, particularly between senior staff, so that they could actually experience a much wider variety of circumstances than their own school. I think that could be done with a bit of imagination and some central resources and organization. But it is really about networking, I think one of the key weaknesses in the teaching profession has been its failure to network or be networked.

CP: Going back to your first day as a head, how has the job and your particular way of doing it, grown and developed over the years?

DW: The first thing to say is that although this has been my only headship, I've had a number of years off, so I haven't been here all these years. I've been fortunate in this respect, being able to pursue a pattern whereby I've appointed an outstanding deputy, and then I've gone off and left the deputy to run the school. I've done that three times now and each time it's been successful, very good for the deputy, who promptly got a headship. I've also had an accommodating governing body who have always managed to have me back. In those years I've been involved in academia, largely in Oxford, I was a Fellow at Nuffield College.

CP: So you've managed to mix the two careers quite successfully?

DW: Yes I have, and it's fairly unusual for people to do this. Yet I have constantly, as it were, bounced back to Grove School, although various opportunities have arisen. I didn't have to stay at Grove. It's been a choice, and I suppose the choice has been strengthened by an increasing view that running a school is the engine room of the entire education system. The moment you cease running a school, you move to some degree into the periphery. If you really want to try and change the system and demonstrate that something can be done, you're in a much more powerful position as head of a school, simply because you can decide things that rapidly impact on children. I believe there is a strong case for people staying in a school for long periods of time but I'd make that conditional, because I know there's research to show that heads who have been in a school for a long time can become very stale, routinized and rather dull, at which point things will start to die. The truth of the matter is, there is no such thing as the status quo, a school is either getting worse or it's getting better. In order for it to remain even as good as it is now, requires an enormous amount of dynamic effort because if you do nothing it will decline. It's like a gyroscope, it always requires a generating of energy in order to keep it going. But, if you're going to stay in a school a long time, you have got to recreate yourself all the time. You need time out to rethink, to readjust, to reflect and the school does gain because you come back with much more energy, a wider perspective on ideas and so on. The gain for the school in a community like this with someone being in a place for a long time, is that you do give an important stability to the community (all the parents know who you are and learn to trust you), and Handsworth is an area that has had great conflicts and upheavals in the past. Historically it's a very significant area nationally, because of the riots and so on. So there are gains there, and I think I would say that I've really run three schools not one, each with a major turn-over of staff. The periods are of roughly five-year durations and they've each led to a recreation of the school, with a new deputy, new young staff and a constant rethinking and developing of ideas. I think that's what's driven the place forward. It's very different now from what it was.

CP: Can we talk a bit more about your three different visions, the three phases, and how you've created significant differences? What was your vision in the first phase and how has that changed over time?

DW: The curious thing is that the vision hasn't, in essence, changed. I think the basic components, the nuts and bolts, of what we're trying to do now were there at the beginning. The first component was to create a culture that was a positive environment in which adults and pupils respected each other, in which learning took place not because it was enforced, but because people wanted to come and wanted to learn, and liked being at school. It's about building a culture in which people were very positive about each other. I've got an obsession with being positive, I won't accept negative thinking at all and I tend to be very ruthless if people are negative, either about themselves or about each other. So you are steadily creating a sort of feeling in which people actually say to themselves, 'Yeah, I am good, I can do things, I can achieve things' and one of the most rewarding things is when pupils come back and say, 'Yeah, I remember what it was like and I feel positive about myself.' That actually does impact. I am convinced that if you give people sufficient self-belief they actually will make it in the end, even those who have got some way to go in terms of academic expectations. I can find a lot of young people who've been through this school who were not especially distinguished academically at the time, but have gone on to do remarkable things. They are the high achievers, and if you follow them back, that would be interesting. There are a lot of them I keep coming across. It's because they've got self-belief, they actually believed learning mattered and that they could harvest it. I think that long-term, self-belief is much more important than this moment to moment academic achievement. The converse of that is when you put somebody down, if they feel they can't achieve, or they feel inferior to others, that will confirm a negative self-belief and that will slow down things that they will do in the future. So as a head you have a long-term responsibility to create an attitude of mind where children are positive about themselves. Now I reckon that's been the big achievement here, because I think there's a very strong sense of positive thinking, and it's built into a reward system which is multiple and continuous and often very simple, but it does confirm our philosophy ... 'Yeah, I'm good, I'm going to make it, I'm something special.'

So that was something that I believed very strongly right from the beginning, but I can quite honestly say that I never wanted to patronize these children. I always felt that these kids could achieve, they've got all the ability in the world to do whatever anybody else can do. I can give you lots of very interesting stories of kids. An ex-pupil, a girl, who's going to Oxford now, who would never have thought of becoming a lawyer and going to Oxford. I worked with the family (a relatively unauspicious local family) and now she is there. Once the community sees one child round the corner who's got to Oxford, they say, 'So I can do it!' The children realize they can do these things. We've recently had five ex-pupils at Oxford and Cambridge. I'm not setting that up as a kind of elite, just to demonstrate that it's possible for our kids to achieve very high levels. We've got children at lots of universities doing degrees up to PhD from what is a very deprived socioeconomic area.

So, going back to your question of the three schools and the changes. I think the general philosophy has not changed unduly. A school is like a family, in a sense, and I think good schools adopt the circumstances of good parenting. I'm interested in the John Cleese/Robin Skynner book about families and parenting, I'd use it as a seminal book for educators because it is both pragmatic and sensitive, convincingly analysing actual problems. I think it is probably the outstanding book of our time on parenting, a very brilliant book, almost encapsulating what I think teaching also ought to be about. As a teacher you're not the parent, but you're using good enough parenting techniques in relating to children, you're listening, caring about them, you're bothered about them, you go one step further for them, you value them enormously as individuals. You create an environment in which they seem to have a place, so they are part of this sort of family. You create a world in which they are not just coming to an institution, but are actually contributing in some way. I believe that all people are managers, and the stuff about there being in-school managers and non-managers is nonsense, everybody's a manager, even to the tiniest child. You then create a sense of participation in the school. You cannot create a dynamic yourself, the heads can't do it all themselves, it's other people that do things. Everyone has to work together as a team to achieve something. It's like a football team with everyone having to be a part of the game. So you have an interesting role as a head, as a coach, as one of the players, as just one bit of the apparatus that makes the school work.

Now as for the differences between the three schools, these to some extent relate to some of the problems that arose at the time. When we began we had a lot of discipline problems, serious emotional problems amongst the children. This area of Handsworth is very insecure. It's always had a life and energy but it is also volatile and things could blow up at any time. Relations were often tense and there were race problems. At that period there were many insecure children and a lot of immigrant children were not adapting rapidly to the tremendous cultural change that they experienced when they came over here. That required a certain kind of teaching approach and certain sort of patience and strength of character.

CP: And did that require something different of you as a manager?

DW: Yes, I was much more involved in discipline and the whole business of the pastoral side. It was tough. I would never pretend for a moment that it was not extremely tough, and it was very exhausting. I had to be very firm, there was no messing about, and there was a lot of aggression that I had to deal with. I've always been quite good with difficult children and bit by bit you get on top of the problems. There were two really big steps forward. One was the development of home–school liaison. We were one of the first schools in the city to have a home–school liaison teacher, and I fought to get that. The second was to set up a specialist unit for counselling and supporting children with serious emotional problems. That was a significant step forward too. I have to say that everything has been a battle with the local authority. I think Birmingham had some great strengths as a local authority at that period. It was very patrician, very paternal in its support of teachers. It always cared a lot about its teachers, and if you were in personal trouble, no authority could have treated you better, *but* it was also patrician in a negative sense in that it was hard to make decisions, to drive things forward. There were constant problems in trying to do anything here, there was never any proper funding and it was hard to break through. I had immense battles trying to get the unit, but I got it in the end. It was hard work, and unnecessarily exhausting in my view.

I know there are endless complaints about some of the difficulties we've had recently through the plethora of centralized initiatives, but I don't think we should be excessively nostalgic. The decision to devolve funding, for example, was probably the single most important and positive educational decision since the war, a transformatory decision. I'm not the least bit sentimental about local authorities as they were in the 1960s and 1970s. So that first phase was very much about simple containment, I think. I take the view that children can't do anything, not even learn, unless they feel safe. The same applies to the staff, staff reactions are very similar. So if the staff felt I would take quite a lot of the strain, then that made it easier for them and, bit by bit, I got staff in who'd got similar views. That's the way you have to move forward, to bring in people who are dynamic, with similar views of life, well balanced, committed. I gathered a group of very strong staff, many of whom are now heads and deputies.

So we then moved from that first five years into the second five years, which I think I would describe as a kind of developmental phase when we were not simply reactive and containing, but we were actually starting to move forward. So in the second phase I think we were addressing more significant things about curriculum, and I think we were ahead of the field because we, in a sense, pre-empted the National Curriculum. I did a number of presentations nationally about curriculum issues at that time – the late 1970s – and we did construct a curriculum that resembled in some respects the curriculum that we've ended up with, post-Dearing. It was about addressing, in a creative, intelligent way, something that both organized learning and yet also brought the children into the enterprise. We were looking very much at developing independent learning, as well as setting a rationale for curriculum delivery. I think that although some of the areas tended to be a bit crude, the rationale was strong and still remains strong. It also meant that we were not thrown offstream by the National Curriculum because I simply refused, in a sense, to be distracted. I took the view with the staff that the most important thing is that you feel confident about what you're doing. I will not be thrown by central initiatives of this kind, as long as we can justify what we're doing in an intelligent way. So we didn't spend hundreds of hours, like some schools, scratching around trying to respond to the National Curriculum, we just simply carried on developing our own, which miraculously has turned out to be similar to what we've ended up with. That's slightly exaggerating but not altogether. We went through a very exciting developmental phase in which we constructed a curriculum. You could genuinely see signs of progress, and quite dramatic progress in some areas, particularly striking in maths, art and drama, where standards were really beginning to rise.

CP: What was your role at this time?

DW: I don't wish to say that discipline problems disappeared, it got easier, but it was still not an easy school. It was clearly getting better and we had a strong staff, and my role was very much to throw ideas in. I'm an ideas creator, I often drive people mad with ideas, but I'm actually interested in getting ideas that work, trying to build in some kind of pilot, some sort of rationale and some sort of continuing critical appraisal of what's happening. I'm probably hypercritical of things, never satisfied, ever, by anything – this is a weakness I think. But that phase started to show the school developing fairly quickly on the curricular front and being noticed. Some things were beginning to show real signs of success.

And the third phase, which is the phase we are almost at the end of now, accumulates the sense of success. The school has been nationally noticed and extensively evaluated by senior people in OFSTED, we've been coming out in DFEE papers, and so on. There's a strong feeling of moving forwards. We're onto a fast track (using the jargon which I think may be our invention!). We've got lots of ideas but still, you never get it right. You've got to take a view of schools that you will never get them right, they're not about getting something right. Schools are like laboratories. I always get slightly worried about schools that are too tidy and too quiet, because they have the feeling (like middle-class lounges) that their thinking has become comfortable. Lively schools are not like that. Like families, schools are in this constant state of dynamic process and change, so they're like journeys really, education is like a journey. You're not going to get to the end of it but what you do is create a lot of excitement on the way and each bit of excitement is that much more planned, that much more 'ideas-generating', that much more effective than the previous bit, so thus you move forwards.

CP: Has your last role been about promoting the school with the outside world?

DW: To some extent yes, because of the other bit of my life that I build in, which in a way runs concurrently with the school, but has moved into this third phase more, and this has been the National Primary Centre. The idea of that, I suppose, has been to create the kind of environment nationally whereby teachers can relate to each other as they would in a quality school. In a school, one of the things you must do is look where things are good, identify the good things happening and then try to generalize them. So, for example, where somebody is brilliant at art, instead of just leaving it with them, everybody's got to know about it and we've got to find ways of sharing it, creating what I call an entitlement, so every kid, in the end, gets some of it. The same principle applies nationally, we are desperately bad at identifying quality, there is no organized procedure for finding out where the outstanding teaching is, nobody's done that. What we need to do professionally is find out where exciting things are happening, identify, celebrate and network, and publish them, and that's what the National Primary Centre is set up to do, and it has had some successes. In that sense this school's been a useful exemplar, I've learnt a lot from being here and of course I can speak with a fair bit of confidence to other people, because no one can say I haven't done it, or been through it and I'm still here! I'm fairly unusual, I think, in actually staying in one school, most people move, usually to other jobs and usually out of teaching.

CP: You've just been describing this last phase as being more promoting and networking. In a sense that's the kind of climate everyone is into now, having to be more outward looking than inward looking. Would you agree with this?

DW: I think that's what they need to do, I'm not sure that schools yet fully understand what this means, because there is also a kind of counter-culture that is self-protective, competitive, drives you in on yourself. OFSTED by and large, on balance, seems to me to be a misfortune that has really confirmed the counter-cultural mentality. It has failed to create what it could have done, which is precisely the sort of thing I'm talking about, the network of quality. OFSTED will turn around and say, with some indignation, that that is not so, and they will point to the various research data that they've produced and various papers describing quality practice (in which we've actually been described). But the problem with that is, that it confirms a culture of centralism that doesn't really touch individual schools in the way that's most effective, because what it doesn't do is generate the debate from teachers themselves. The initiative comes from outside teaching, is imposed on teachers, most of whom incidentally are women, while most of the people outside are men. There is a sense in which, I think, teachers feel disenfranchised. There are people who I talk to in the management culture who feel that I'm being nostalgic and sentimental but I simply don't believe that because I'm a fairly tough character, and I'm not the least bit sentimental. I'm purely pragmatic as a manager and I actually think that it doesn't require much discussion and debate to demonstrate that the schools that are really successful are those where people work corporately to similar goals, where they have a lot of intellectual independence, self-confidence, self-belief, whereby they have imagination, take risks, demonstrating results against a range of parameters. You simply do not get anywhere by turning around and feeding on the negatives and I'm afraid OFSTED has created a culture of negativism, at very considerable public expense.

CP: Given this context, can you share with me your vision of primary educa-tion and how you see yourself as a head realizing it?

DW: What I'm trying to do is develop and grow along the lines of a prospec-tive twenty-first century school, in a practical way given the kind of constraints that primary education is under. Primary education has still not entered significantly enough into the national debate; it's still a seriously neglected area, an area of public life that is fundamentally undernourished. It's under-resourced and I think you'll find it's not focused on for sponsor-ship either. Some 95 per cent of industrial sponsorship goes to secondary schools. Part of the mission of the National Primary Centre Trust is to campaign to reverse that. If we could get primary education right we'd transform the learning opportunities for all our children. That has got to be on the agenda for major public debate over the next 10 to 20 years and we will get there, but we're not there yet. The quality of the debate has to become a lot more sophisticated and tougher minded. There's still a lot of sloppy thinking in primary education. Tougher mindedness leads directly into the business of what a quality school ought to be and what the compo-nents of it are. There are different ways of coming into this question. I'd start off by reinforcing the point I've already made that you've got to create the right managerial culture. This means attracting the best minds avail-able and giving them the opportunity to run with the ball, so that instead of setting self-defined constraints on the system, we actually say what we could do if we really got ourselves together. My view is that we haven't yet begun to tap into the potential of what pupils can do, that we underachieve on a fairly considerable scale, and there's an enormous way to go. We're simply going the wrong way about getting to where we want to get. I would want to begin therefore by saying that firstly we've got to create an envi-ronment in which serious learning is seen as a participative enterprise between the teacher, the learner and the family, and at the heart of it is the learner. Children who fail to learn do so because their learning strategies are flawed and inefficient. We need to address learning strategies so that we think about teaching as not just teaching, but as teaching and learning. At the moment the emphasis seems to be almost exclusively on teaching. Yet there is plenty of evidence that transforming the teaching process will not, in itself, make that much difference to the long-term outcomes. Unless we address children, and the way their minds work, we will not make progress.

The second point is about what teachers do. I feel this too needs much sharper thinking. I do agree with OFSTED that the planning process is probably at the heart of the teaching enterprise, bearing in mind that it's only one bit of the story. I'd like to see what I call an entitlement curricu-lum, because it seems to me that if you take the national scene in primary education, it's probably true for secondary as well, what one notices is an unacceptable unevenness. Some children get an amazingly good deal and others much less, even within the same school. Daily life for the pupil is like a mountain range, in which there are peaks and valleys dependent upon two things. The first is how well the work was planned by the teacher, and the second is how skilled the teacher is in delivering that particular plan. Those two things are the key: it's no good having the plan without the teacher, it's no good having the teacher without the plan. The problem is that first of all, the teachers never have the time to plan properly and there's no national planning process. I know what I'm saying seems to be sounding like some kind of extension of the National Curriculum, and it is, in a sort of way. I think that we do need to address in a rational way, how we can best create plans and learning experiences of the highest possible quality, so that the child doesn't have to put up with *ad hoc* arrangements. We should aim at generalizing quality experience to every child as an entitlement. What I'm asking for is an entitlement curriculum, and by curriculum I don't mean a syllabus, I mean the actuality that happens in a classroom.

We should begin with the entitlement and then ask the questions about how we deliver it. Now that's the reverse of what we've currently got. What children currently get is what the teachers manage to provide. I want something very different. When we've identified a set of experiences of high quality, we then need to ask how best to deliver them. Now if you cannot find anybody in the school to do it, you then ask other questions – do we buy people in from outside, or create much more targeted in-service training so somebody in the school will be trained up to do it? You've got to be insistent that children have the appropriate entitlement.

If we begin from that position it seems to me that we're no longer driven by whether teachers can do things or not, but by some kind of determination that children will experience the very best available. The current failure in primary education seems to be its ad-hocery, its unpredictability, its dependence upon the variation of teaching skills and ability. In a primary school the truth of the matter is that teachers cannot teach to the level of quality required across the whole curriculum. Somebody should say that. It is not possible without a radical reassessment of the planning and delivery process.

This conception of what a school is about does have considerable organizational implications. It means, for example, that we may need to be thinking about bringing in people from outside, who may not even be teachers. We may need to make greater use of classroom assistants and to make greater use of community expertise. Certainly, we will need to make much greater use of information technology. This leads to all sorts of questions about what schools are as organizations. The teacher is increasingly going to be a kind of insurance, a kind of overlord to ensure that the children are getting what I call a good deal. What we need is to offer a new deal to children, and that isn't just an academic process, it has to be contained in the context of the school as family, the school as the motivator. The teaching role is to build the relationship between the learner and the curriculum, to identify what the learner needs at any given moment and then to do a lot of

readjusting and fine-tuning of the teaching process. At Grove we've initiated
an element of 'fast track' work, but we also provide support for children with
special needs. We've got a place called Rocket, which is a specialist place of
intensive support for kids with particular learning difficulties, and equally
we're trying to provide learning support for kids with particularly striking
talents. You're then into a far more flexible and diverse set of arrangements
whereby the school organization is driven by the needs of the pupil, not the
other way round.

*CP: Potentially that means a lot more diversification and local determina-
tion.*

DW: Yes, it means being much more flexible about how you organize things
in schools, and refocusing the roles of different personnel. It means being
less hierarchical, more team orientated, more flexible, more rapidly adap-
tive to need.

CP: How will your role in this kind of school change?

DW: I don't see my role fundamentally changing because there will still be
a clear role for the school as a holding family, creating a corporate bonding
between people. You will still be heading up a team, even more so in times
of discontinuity. There's a paradox here, because in a way we're looking for
diversification of the teaching process, a more radical view of planning,
more use of a range of different people in the enterprise. Yet, on the other
hand, you have exactly the opposite, this will only work if there is a strong
sense of a corporate feel which is based upon the view that (a) we're going
for the best that it's possible to produce and (b) everybody's got to be positive about what we're going to achieve. It's very much, in that respect, like
running a successful football team, you're determined you're going to score
the goals (not just going to play) as well as keep the audience enthused.
There's a sort of theatre about this and we're about quality performance.
The more you think about it, this sort of rationale does have quite radical
implications for schooling, but I'm convinced this is the way forward, and
the way we are developing. We've got a long way to go yet, of course, and
who knows when we'll get there?

*CP: If you set that vision against the changes you've seen in primary educa-
tion in the last few years, what is your assessment?*

DW: I was involved to some extent at the national level in discussions in the
early days of the National Curriculum and expressed some scepticism and
some support. Let's not be too dismissive about the National Curriculum, its
does in a sense satisfy one of my criteria, by taking the first step towards an
entitlement curriculum. The problem with the National Curriculum is that
it's not a curriculum at all, it's a syllabus. It has been messed up by the fact
that it was over centralized, it was arrogantly and expensively managed
and constructed, so it turned out in practice to be unworkable. So it's had a
poor track record and a bad press, but the principle behind what it tried to
do is right. I could never understand why the government didn't turn to the

Scottish National Curriculum in the 1970s and early 1980s. It was already in place and looks remarkably like the post-Dearing English version, and would have saved £750 million in the process, but there was a great deal of governmental arrogance, and discourtesy as well, to people who could have been very helpful. My own view is that if it hadn't been introduced in the way that it had, if it had been developed in a more evolutionary way, if the focus had been on the exciting schools piloting in a much more research-orientated way, giving some funding to networking and to celebrating what schools were already achieving, it would have been far more successful.

To some extent what I'm asking for, in part, is a bottom-up model that isn't going to just happen, paradoxically, it needs to be centrally facilitated. The old Schools' Council (the SCDC) was starting to move, I thought, in the right direction. It ran one or two remarkable projects which really seriously impacted. It's very interesting that OFSTED is now coming up with the view that one of the weakest aspects of current primary practice is in writing. Everyone seems to have forgotten that the SCDC implemented a major writing project, The National Writing Project, which had more impact, in my view, on the quality of children's writing in the schools than anything since. It has all been forgotten, there is no building on excellencies of the past, and no continuity of discourse. We have failed to appreciate that to develop highly sophisticated practice requires huge amounts of skills, in-service training, understanding, modelling, clear-mindedness, brilliant planning and so on. We're miles and miles away from getting that because nobody is providing the inspiration. We need to reconstruct the National Writing Project. We've had so much stop and go, no wonder people are demoralized. I suspect we're going to run into serious trouble over the next few years, not least on recruitment. I'm worried, I talk to young people and they're not coming into teaching. Even the children of teachers are being lost and that's very interesting because historically many children of teachers have become teachers. There's no doubt that teachers are actively trying to prevent, to discourage, their children from going into teaching. I too would want to question the wiseness of entering the profession that I've devoted my life to. In teaching you need people of sharp intelligence who are creative and well-balanced, very special sorts of people are needed to come into teaching and they are not easily attracted. On the other hand, the standard of teaching and teachers has risen over the last two decades because training's improved. I think quite a few people have come in during the recession and we've managed to recruit some high flyers, but I think there are problems ahead, and we've got to find new ways to make the job intellectually exciting.

CP: Are you saying that you see primary education at this point in a worse state than it was earlier?

DW: It's very hard to generalize. My own view is that overall probably not, simply because, as I say, I think we've got more good teachers than we had. I know there is still a serious variability of quality, but there are more good things going on now than I think there were in the 1960s and 1970s, though I don't think government-led changes have contributed very much. In my own experience, certainly at my own school, except in respect of LMS, I don't think the reforms over the last decade have offered much at all. I think improvement, where it came about, was to do with the quality of thinking that we've managed to generate in the profession itself.

CP: What about the heads? What qualities do they need?

DW: The qualities of a good leader are not just distinctive of schools, they underpin all kinds of successful businesses. It's interesting how our thinking about the theory of management is coming together in all kinds of ways. Industrialists are now talking about a new radical model, focused on low hierarchical, non-authoritative teamwork, team cultures in which different people take on different roles in the culture. Businesses are looking for risk-takers, people with personal balance who've got the ability to drive things forward and it's exactly the same kind of culture we're asking for in schools, with the same sort of people to lead the team.

CP: Can we just focus now on you, in acting that kind of role, where are your support mechanisms, where do you look for support?

DW: There have been periods in my life as a head when I have seriously thought of giving up. The first thing I want to say is that it is a hugely stressful job, there's no getting away from it. My biggest problem has been exhaustion, and sometimes the fear that I'm in a trench with a hat on, waiting for the next shell to drop on my head. Everything seems to have been a battle, everything. It's extraordinary how little has been facilitated. I feel quite strongly about it because a lot of the initiatives which I managed to get here, have now been taken up but I've had to put enormous personal effort in and I've had very little outside support. I've been very critical of the Local Authority over the years, because it's very rare that people have come and said, 'how can we help you with this?' and then seriously done something to help. Now I have to say that things have changed enormously recently, and the last couple of years have been completely different. We have a much more vigorous, supportive and energizing LEA culture, and I feel personally now that there's a different kind of support there. It's very interesting that recently the government has shown positive interest in Grove, and so has OFSTED. But it's taken an awful lot of years for them to get round to looking constructively at what we're trying to do.

Over the years I think the main support has been the school itself. I think it's been the community, it's been the parents, it's been the governors. I've had a very supportive governing body. The role of the governors is interesting. Governors in the last generation have been increasingly important. We've got a governing body that represents the whole community of all different races. They are very exciting, they can work together as a team, they think, they can deliver, they're sharp, independently minded, they're intelligent, thoughtful, interested. We have meetings late into the evening discussing deep, philosophical questions about what schools ought to be and where we ought to be going. I think it's very unusual for a school's governing body to be able to do that. We're not just talking about administrative matters, we're talking about what a school is, what we want to do for our children. This is all exciting, it's created a really tough, independently minded governing body and I've found it immensely supportive and that has been very important. I've had support too from the staff, they have been creative and loyal, and successive teams over the years have given me a lot of personal support.

Otherwise I think it's having a wife who'll put up with me. My wife is also a psychiatrist which helps! But I think it is much tougher than people think from the outside. The problem with being a head is that you are expected to be in control, psychologically speaking. There is an expectation of control over everything, which can lead to kinds of madness. You go around picking up crisp papers all day long, or withdraw into your room because you are simply terrified of the task you are faced with. I think that the current centralist culture has created a sort of mode of headship, where heads feel they must be in control of everything, because they're almost excessively accountable to so many sources. This is wholly the wrong model for the development of the kind of risk-taking, creative, laboratory-orientated, learning culture which great schools feed on. You have got to take risks, accept that things will go wrong, they're going to go wrong sometimes, and you've got to be prepared for that to happen. The OFSTED psychology, the pressure towards centralist delivery and control is very damaging. I have to say that in my view Chris Woodhead is principally responsible for creating this negative, fearful culture. The way the professionals see the current Chief Inspector is as a damaging agent in the educational enterprise. He's simply got it wrong, maybe for the right reasons, because I don't dispute his analysis in a lot of ways. What I do dispute is the tone of the debate and the mechanisms for resolving the kind of issues identified, because I think they're crude, theoretically orientated and fail to understand the texture, the nature of practice and the sorts of worlds in which we have to exist. It's an expensive and serious failing.

CP: I think it's fascinating that when I asked you where you go to for support, you talked about your governors, your parents, your staff, the Local Authority, all those people that you're accountable to. You seem to have turned the issue of accountability on its head and said that these groups are supporting you primarily. So where does accountability come into it?

DW: Accountability is like appraisal and like curriculum, buzz words that require analysis. What is accountability? If you're a parent you're accountable for your children but no one actually says you're accountable. They don't use that word but of course you know you are deeply accountable for the life of your children. It is a deep, personal responsibility. If as a head you are required to be made accountable for something, then you shouldn't be a head. That is not the sort of person you should be, because quite clearly in a job like this, you have got extraordinary and extensive responsibility and if you don't realize it you shouldn't be in the job. The notion of accountability has never impinged on me, it doesn't mean anything, it is not the psychology of what I am trying to do in a school. Of course you feel deeply responsible for what goes on and desperately concerned that what you do is of very high quality. It requires a personal commitment that is not just doing a job. You're not just coming and going through the motions in a way that you might be accountable for, ticking things off on a list as it were, that's not what this job's about. You will sink or swim according to the amount of emotional commitment you make to the job.

There are many damaging initiatives this government has made, in my view, though I also think education academics carry a measure of responsibility. I am quite sceptical and critical of the more quisling aspects of the academic establishment. But the government is the principal agency of control and I can think of a number of instances of what seem to me to be self-evidently damaging initiatives. A good example was the 1265 Hour Initiative. That, together with the teachers' strike action, caused immense damage. I think it knocked us back in our development by at least two years. I would have nothing to do with it from the word go, I know there were many schools that started to set up rotas and registers and all the rest of it. I survived that episode by informing the staff that I would have absolutely nothing to do with it. I am not interested in how many hours people work, it's absolute nonsense. It was a political construction to somehow deal with the problems perceived to be created by NASWT. But this isn't the sort of job in which you can count hours, you can come to this school at 6.00 pm any day and you'll find teachers all over the place. This is a school where people will take kids camping, we built a hostel ourselves, we take kids out in the country, they stay overnight. They do hundreds more hours than they need to do, not only just hours, but emotionally committed hours, because people want to do it. If the teachers pulled the plug on all that and said 'I'm only going to do 1265 hours', at this school I would have given up some time ago, because I don't believe that it's possible to do the job in that way. Any government that actually thought that it is possible was simply so deluded, so failing to understand what schools are, it was quite astonishing. I have to say that even in the early days in the 1960s, teachers were putting in many more hours than they were required to. Every Saturday morning throughout the year we'd run football matches. Even now much of that has gone because of the 1265 hours. There are still individual teachers who run football and clubs after school, but lots of things went. And that was the kind of crass initiative that sets you back.

The truth of the matter is that to create the kind of exciting school that you want, just as you would in a family, you've got to commit yourself to the children, way beyond the call of duty. If you don't, then you're always going to feel you've never got there, in some way you're selling them short. I want to have a staff that thinks in that sort of way, you can't force people to, you can't say, 'You will do this, you've got to stay until 6 o'clock', it's not possible.

You don't do that. You create an environment where people say, 'I think we need to do this, I want to.'

CP: Do you think primary headship is still an attractive proposition? Would you say you enjoyed it less or more than you used to?

DW: I don't know. In a sort of way I must enjoy it, or I wouldn't do it. I think it's a job of enormous potential importance because first of all, I think young children are so important that this gives the job a special status for me. But also because you are in a unique position (rather, I suppose, like a vicar might have been in the nineteenth century), at the centre and the heart of the community, you need powers to deliver and actually get things done. So as a job I'd rate it in that respect very rewarding. In the future, I'm sure, we're going to have a revolution which turns around some of the problems we're facing at the moment. I think it will be seen as an exciting, creative job. But it's got to be valued by society, it's got to be seen to be what it is, it's got to be recognized as really very important. So many people have said to me in the past, 'Oh, you're only a primary school head, why don't you do something else?' I have to say it's almost always men saying this, because I do think, deep down, one of the subliminal themes that runs through the whole debate is that it's about men who are managers, or academics, on the outside, looking in on a society of women. There is a powerful gender dimension in teaching.

Going back to the question, whether I'd come back to do it again, I'm not sure. At the moment I think the stresses involved are enormous and you've got to have so many skills, it's so difficult to do that it frightens me sometimes. You wake up in the night, the school is in brilliant shape, the kids are an absolute joy, I don't know what happened to them, they are totally and completely different from what they used to be, so well behaved, they love school, they talk to you, smiling all the time, and so positive, I mean it couldn't really be better, and I still wake up! I wake up and wonder what's happened, one can't account for why, but you hope that you've been one of the components in making those sorts of improvements. So there is no question about its 'worthwhileness', but I think it's a terribly difficult job to do and we need to have much more of a plan for headteachers. I think the job that I compare it with, apart from a nineteenth-century vicar, might be a hospital consultant. Hospital consultants are very similar in some important respects. First of all it's a job with very great responsibility, serious responsibility for people's lives. Secondly, it's extremely stressful. Thirdly, the interesting thing about hospital consultants is that they do not move about. I mean consultants, by and large, don't go from one job to another to another. If you're a hospital consultant you tend to stay for the rest of your life. That's an interesting thing and I am increasingly of the view that the head should take on the school and the community for as long as it's possible too, in a creative way. There will always be a time when you feel that you must go. But stay four years and you are just putting up pictures on the walls and getting things started. You are not burying yourself deeply into the needs of that community. In that respect, the nineteenth-century vicar and the hospital consultant are both analogues for what the primary head of the future ought to be, which is deeply committed to that school.

I have to say that I think committed heads are still deeply respected in the community. I'm less confident of the national perspective because there is currently a debate going on about how terrible schools are, how second-rate teachers are, and there is a feeling amongst some business people, academics and politicians which is openly cynical about teachers. Teachers are seen as a lot of air-heads who came into the job because they can't do anything else. But that's never really bothered me too much, I've got suffi-cient kind of street cred to be able to fight that one off. But, in a way, you need more people who will actually stand up and try and surface into that very difficult arena and say the kind of things I'm saying, openly. Fighting back is what it's all about.

CP: What would you like to see for heads in the future?

DW: I think people from outside do need to understand that headteachers need a career track, increasingly so, in view of the demise of the advisory services, which used to be their escape route. We need to have patterns of support, clear secondments, with headteachers quite frequently having a day a week to do something else. There also needs to be many more planned relationships between academia and heads, so that heads contribute to the academic debate, they are involved more in research and they feel that they can have periods of time off. I demonstrated at least one thing in my career pattern, that I don't think the school suffers from mavericks like me and that there is a considerable potential gain for individuals, especially as secondment now is virtually impossible. I just think that we need to create a much more flexible set of circumstances in which heads (and not just heads, but deputies and senior teachers too) are much more drawn into the frontline debate, into publishing, writing, debating, developing, working together, into team work, into taking initiatives corporately. That would actually help the networking process and would lead in the long run to more effective primary schools.

Index